THE FEMALE DRAMA

The Philosophical Feminine in the Soul of Plato's *Republic*

MERCER UNIVERSITY

MERCER UNIVERSITY PRESS

Endowed by

TOM WATSON BROWN
and
THE WATSON-BROWN FOUNDATION, INC.

THE FEMALE DRAMA

The Philosophical Feminine in the Soul of Plato's *Republic*

Charlotte C. S. Thomas

MERCER UNIVERSITY PRESS
Macon, Georgia

MUP/ H987

Published by Mercer University Press
1501 Mercer University Drive
Macon, Georgia 31207

9 8 7 6 5 4 3 2 1

Books published by Mercer University Press are printed on acid-free paper that meets the requirements of the American National Standard for Information Sciences—Permanence of Paper for Printed Library Materials.

Printed and bound in the United States.

This book is set in Adobe Caslon Pro

Cover/jacket design by Burt&Burt

ISBN 978-0-88146-743-7
Cataloging-in-Publication Data is available from the Library of Congress

For My Students

Contents

Introduction

Genesis, Trophe, Paideia, and the Philosophical Feminine

At the beginning of Book V of Plato's *Republic* something strange happens—and everyone who reads it knows it. The argument is interrupted. It changes course and character. Despite Socrates' warning that the conversation would take a dangerous turn, his interlocutors push him toward a new set of images and concerns. Adeimantus and Polemarchus insist that Socrates return to an account of the role of women and children in the city they are constructing in speech (449c), a topic they accused him of glossing over when it came up earlier (423e). Socrates does not deny the truth of their claim. Reluctantly, and only after prostrating himself to Adrasteia,[1] goddess of punishment for *hubris* (451a), Socrates admits that there is, indeed, much more to say about women and children in the city in speech. He will do as they ask. He will stage the female (*gynaikeion*[2]) drama in the Attic form: three plays, perhaps tragedies, that stand on their own but ultimately come together to form a whole.

Another, subtler shift occurs in the same passage at the beginning of Book V, and it is often taken for granted or asserted, but rarely questioned. The dialogue seems temporarily to leave psychology behind and to focus almost exclusively on politics. From the moment in Book II when Socrates introduces the city as a device designed to serve their inquiry into the idea of justice in a human soul (369d), the dialectic of the *Republic* follows two parallel paths: Socrates and his interlocutors construct and analyze the structure of the city in speech in order to investi-

---

[1] Adrasteia, like Nemesis or perhaps equivalent to her, was a goddess devoted to the punishment of *hubris*. She is also known to have been the nursemaid to the infant Zeus while he hid on Crete (with Ida) until he grew to be strong enough to overthrow Cronos. Literally, her name means "inescapable." She appears, among other places in Herodotus i. 35 and Aeschylus' *Prometheus Bound.*

[2] γυναικεῖον.

gate justice within an individual and within a city simultaneously. However often Glaucon and the other interlocutors become fixated on the political questions raised by the city in speech, Socrates consistently and clearly brings the conversation back to the individual. But with the inception of the Female Drama that starts in Book V and continues through Book VII, Socrates cashes out the psychological teachings of the city in speech much less often[3]. His interlocutors, meanwhile, who have from the beginning been apt to neglect the path of their argument concerned with the soul and focus on the political content of their conversation, are (more or less) left to do just that, with readers of the *Republic* often following right along.

My argument, in a nutshell, is that the Male Drama of Books II–IV is an account of the being and actualities of the just soul, while the Female Drama is an account of the becoming and potencies of the just soul (an inquiry that opens into a consideration of the activity of the most just soul, philosophy). By the end of Book IV, one knows what all of the parts of the soul need to look like in order for a soul to be just. What one begins to consider in Book V is what needs to be true of each part of the soul in order for it to become what Book IV tells us it needs to be. As the Female Drama illuminates the Male Drama dialectically, the Male Drama itself will require revision. That is, the account of the *telos* of the just soul prompted the inquiry into the origin (*genesis*), nurture (*trophe*), and education (*paideia*) required to approach that *telos*. But when the *genesis*, *trophe*, and *paideia* of the just soul come into focus, they illuminate things

[3] At 462d there is an explicit reminder that the city in speech has been constructed for the sake of understanding the soul, but such passages are rare. Even when the soul is explicitly at issue in Books V–VII, it is often difficult to follow lines of clear allegorical meaning like those drawn in Books II–IV between elements of the city in speech and activities of the soul. The allegory of the Cave is particularly interesting in this regard, and I will consider it at length and from several different perspectives in Chapters 7–10. In the allegory, our focus is on an individual human being, but we are not directly shown his interiority. So, even though the Cave concerns an individual while the other models of the city in speech use multiple individuals to represent different psychological parts or dynamics, we still only have access to the psychological teachings of the Cave by analogy.

about the *telos* of justice that were not clear before. By following this dialectical path, the inquiry in Plato's *Republic* into the nature of justice becomes an inquiry into the nature of philosophy.

Leo Strauss and many Plato scholars who have followed his lead have interpreted the shift from Books II–IV to Books V–VII as a transition from an inquiry of the being of justice to the becoming of justice. They have seen this also as signaling the beginning of an inquiry into the philosophical life.[4] About this point I think Strauss was right, and I am sympathetic to many of the studies that have sought to follow this insight toward deeper interpretations of the *Republic*. Strauss's argument, however, like most studies that pursue the questions he raised, rests in a political mode rather that a psychological one. As far as I know—the scholarship on the *Republic* being impossibly vast—no one has attempted a systematic interpretation of the psychology of Books V–VII, or examined the central books of the *Republic* for their teaching of psychological, rather than political, possibility. That is this study's central aim.

Some of the most careful and insightful scholars of Plato say that the city/soul analogy drops out in Book V and does not emerge again until Book VII.[5] It isn't so. True, in Books V–VII Socrates seldom brings the conversation back to psychology. Occasionally, however (462d, for example), he makes clear that psychology has been with them all along. This raises several new questions. Why would Socrates obscure the psychological meaning of the city/soul in the central books of the *Republic* if the model is still developing? What might women and children represent on the psychological level of the city/soul? Why is Socrates so *coy?* Are women and children analogous to some new parts or functions of the soul? Or, since except for their natural weakness and capacity to bear children they are said to be functionally equivalent to men, do they represent individuals composed of the same parts but in a different arrangement? If women and children do not correspond to parts (or dynamics,

---

4 Leo Strauss, *City and Man* (Chicago: University of Chicago Press, 1978), 116–118.

5 Bernard Williams, "The Analogy of City and Soul in Plato's *Republic*" from *Exegesis and Argument* (*Phronesis* supplement volume 1, 1973): 196–206; and G. R. F Ferrari, *City and Soul in Plato's* Republic (Chicago: University of Chicago Press, 2005).

etc.) of the soul, why insert them into an account of a city in speech constructed for the sake of understanding the order of the soul? Why is Socrates so *cryptic?* Must the feminine be difficult and elusive?

The answers to these questions are, I believe, encapsulated in the idea that organizes this book: the idea of the philosophical feminine. In ancient reproductive biology, femininity is associated with potentiality. All of a soul's activity—in Aristotelian terms, its form—is masculine.[6] A woman is a vessel, a passive condition necessary for the becoming of a new human being.[7] That is the first footing for my argument. The second footing is that books V–VII are thematically concerned with possibility. It is common to interpret the shift that occurs in *Republic* Book V as signaling the beginning of an inquiry into the possibility of the just city in speech that appeared to have been completed in Book IV, so this is not a controversial place to begin.[8] The central argument of this book is that, taken together, these two fairly uncontroversial ideas (1. that femininity evokes potentiality, and 2. the central books of the *Republic* take up questions related to the possibility of justice in the city in speech that is supposed to model justice in the soul) illuminate a psychological theory of Books V–VII that may be corroborated in a dozen different ways both by the arguments and the images of the *Republic*. In its briefest form, my thesis is this: that in the *Republic* women and children represent psychological potencies and developmental processes, and since

---

[6] This is a claim about the role of women in reproductive biology, not about their place in society or of their natural intelligence, strength, or capacity for development. It is a narrow, technical claim.

[7] Although Aristotle, as usual, is the first to offer a systematic account (*Generation of Animals* 716a), evidence of this sense of the feminine is hinted at throughout Greek mythology, for example in Hesiod's account of creation following from the union of Uranus and Ge (*Theogony* lns. 43–46). And, as Michael Dink pointed out to me, at 49a and 59a–d of Plato's *Timaeus*, in passages explicitly linked to the argument of the *Republic*, Socrates points to the existence of a necessary but elusive condition for the generation of the cosmos, the *chora*, which a the negative or potential element required for Being to generate Creation. The *chora* is always described as a female element in the creation of the cosmos, sometimes as a nurse.

[8] Strauss, *City and Man*, 115.

these are among the necessary conditions for the best possible human life (the philosophical life, as it turns out), the introduction of women and children in the dialectic also signals an introduction to the inquiry into the nature of philosophy.

It is also common in Plato scholarship to recognize that the concerns of the central books of the *Republic* are some of the deepest and most important in the dialogue.[9] Within their narrative frame, thanks to Socrates' response to Polemarchus' interruption, philosophy becomes a topic of conversation. The Good, which is higher than justice, becomes the oblique and mediated subject of the inquiry, its nature existing beyond our capacities to apprehend it directly. And since the character and duties of philosophers are shown to be best suited for the guardians of the best possible city, they too become central to the inquiry. A consideration of necessary conditions leads to speculation about what the most complete actualization of those conditions might look like. And so from an inquiry into the "possible," an inquiry into the "best" emerges.

In questioning the conditions for the possibility of something to be actualized, by implication one has already included some notion of the "conditioned" thing in one's thinking. Conditions imply the ideas, however inchoate, of the things they condition. And insofar as those conditions are necessary for something to come into being, then the essential or necessary elements of the conditioned thing are, at least by implication, likewise at issue. Meditating on the possibility of any particular thing implies an idea of the actualization of that particular thing; it implies a teleological approach to one's attempt to understand it. So the introduction of the feminine, the Female Drama of the possibility of the just city, implies the idea of the actualization of the just city.[10]

---

[9] For a few examples, see: Bloom 1991, 401; Brann 2004, 116; Burnyeat 2006, 8; Craig 1996, 214; Roochnik 2003, 63.

[10] Leo Strauss highlights possibility and philosophy as two themes introduced into the dialogue at this moment, but my account of the relationship between them is substantially different from his. Strauss writes, "By answering the question of how the good city is possible, Socrates introduces philosophy as a theme of the *Republic*. This means that in the *Republic* philosophy is not introduced as the end of man but as a means for realizing justice and therefore the just city...." Instead, I think these two themes emerge together because when

So, the argument of the middle books of the *Republic* proceeds with Socrates cornered into a consideration of the conditions that would make the just city in speech possible, and his response leads the dialogue into a consideration of the most complete actualization of those possibilities. The hunt for justice leads to a recognition that the Good is higher than justice, and the question of whether or not the just life is better than an unjust life gives way to the recognition that the philosophical life is the best life of all.

Convention also recognizes that the model of the soul that devolves in Books VIII and IX is not the one that ended (apparently) in Book IV.[11] One striking feature that is often mentioned in the secondary literature is that, though nothing of the sort was mentioned or constructed in the early books, in the later books each part of the soul (*epithumia*, *thumos*, and *logismos*) has its own appetites. Where were these appetites added to the psychological model? The pattern within the dialogue is clear—each part of the city/soul is generated by a principle and then added deliberately to the model.[12] Why should a careful reader think that the capacity of each part of the city/soul to have its own appetites would emerge without comment and only in the context of the unraveling of the city/soul in the taxonomy of injustice? As I see it, one should not, and need not. There is an expansion of the city/soul in the central books of the *Republic* that follows the pattern established earlier in the dialogue: it is prompted by the interjection of a new principle, and it includes the capacity for the parts of the city/soul to have specific appetites (among other things). The psychological staging of the Female Drama is the expansion of the city/soul to include several different forms of possibility (including appetite). At each level of the soul, certain necessary conditions for the possibility of individual justice also point to the possibility of the most complete realization of justice. The philosophical feminine is,

---

the conversation turns to the conditions for the possibility of justice, it triggers teleological thinking about what the complete fulfilment of those conditions would look like. Leo Strauss, *The City and Man* (Chicago: University of Chicago, 1964), 122.

[11] For example, Cooper 2001, 345 and Moss, 2006, 523.

[12] I will explore this pattern of city/soul construction and how it appears consistently throughout Books II–IV in Chapter One.

indeed, shorthand for the conditions for the possibility of becoming just in the light of the Good—for becoming philosophical. Not only does the soul continue to be Socrates' central concern in Books V–VII, the particular sort of soul now at issue in the central books of the *Republic* is the philosophical soul, the best soul.

I will argue that the model of the soul that emerges in Book V is compatible with the model of the soul completed in Book IV, but more elaborate.[13] The most substantial change to the soul is its inclusion of *nous*, giving it the capacity to see beyond itself. There is, Socrates tells us, something higher than justice, and it is the Good (504d). The soul of Book IV lacks the capacity to apprehend the Good or anything else outside of itself. For the soul of Book VII, apprehending the Good is the pinnacle of one's educational journey; it is that toward which every step of life is oriented. One must ask, when did such a journey become possible? At the end of Book IV, the soul's orientation is entirely inward. Between the end of Book IV and the beginning of Book VII, when and how did the soul develop the capacity to see beyond itself as required by the image of education presented in the allegory of the Cave?

My purpose in this book is to present the philosophical feminine as a framework for addressing these questions and for contributing to an interpretation of the *Republic* as a whole. As with any attempt to make sense of Plato's most magisterial dialogue, my first caveat is that by no means is this meant to be an exhaustive account of the *Republic,* or a reductive one.[14] I will, by necessity, leave much uninvestigated, and there

[13] It works nicely with ring or temple pediment theories of the structure of the *Republic* to see each subsequent constitution as an elaboration on the earlier ones rather than a substitute that rejects earlier iterations. In such theories Books V–VII are the center of a ring or the pediment of a temple. Books I–IV work in to or up to Books V–VII, and Books VIII–X work back out or down in parallel to Books IV–I. For an excellent illustration of a temple pediment theory of the *Republic* and a review of several other theories see Debra Nails, "Plato's *Republic* in its Athenian Context," *History of Political Thought* 33, no. 1 (Spring 2012): 3.

[14] For a study that acknowledges the possibility of an analogical interpretation of women and children in the *Republic* but that makes a strong case for taking them to be meaningful for real human women and children, see Mary Townsend, *The Woman Question in Plato's* Republic (New York: Lexington

are many other ways of reading the *Republic* that will both be compatible with my interpretation and better at explaining other important aspects of Plato's philosophy. This book is my attempt to present a coherent and systematic way of looking at the central books that I trust will illuminate some important things about the *Republic* that I have not seen written about elsewhere—and some that I have. Still, it makes no pretensions to being complete, let alone exhaustive.[15] I have attempted to read all of Books V–VII with this psychological framework in mind, which means I have dealt briefly with many things, many of which warrant a much deeper and more nuanced treatment. Perhaps, if there is world enough and time I will return to some of these issues in the future, but it was important to me to attempt to display in this book the whole arc of the psychological argument in Books V–VII, so I had to keep moving even though it meant neglecting many things. Really, though, one can no more hope to present a complete account of the *Republic* than one can hope to know completely the city of Rome. The *Republic* is the eternal

Books, 2017). In this wonderfully interesting book, Townsend provides an account of the *nomoi* concerning women in classical Athens that reframes Socrates' dialectical presentation of them in the *Republic*. If my argument regarding the symbolic meaning of women and children in the central books does not appear to leave room for Townsend's argument regarding real women and children, then I will not have made myself clear.

[15] Danielle Allen helped me believe that it might not be preposterous to think that one could see something new in Plato even after some of the brightest lights of more than two millennia have done their best. "So how can it happen that a person might have a new idea about a subject as long-lived as Plato's philosophy? Reactivating older bodies of knowledge for present use often seems to also spur discovery. Why is that? Human knowledge is inevitably partial, by which I mean both incomplete and situated: the combined total of human knowledge emanates from hundreds of billions of individuals each situated in a specific place and time and with individualized curiosities, preoccupations, and desires. As we ourselves learn what our predecessors have known, we discover not only their successes—ideas worthy of being relit-but also their limits—conceptual points where corrections, revisions, subtractions, or additions are necessary. Our own views will have similar blemishes; we should never pretend otherwise." *Why Plato Wrote* (Malden MA: Blackwell, 2013) 2.

dialogue. This book offers one map of one part of the *Poleteia*. Other maps of other parts will lead you to other things.

I will argue that throughout the *Republic* the soul is Socrates' central concern, that his focus never shifts to politics per se, but only to an increasingly complicated political model (i.e. city in speech) that ventures into topics dangerous to both politicians and philosophers. Though the *Republic* offers deep political teaching, I strongly resist the idea that Socrates makes any policy recommendations in the *Republic*.[16] Furthermore, I argue that Socrates substantially revises and augments the model of the soul in Books V–VII, and the new schema that emerges, derived from the principle of the philosophical feminine, is invulnerable to many critiques of Plato's psychology that have been levied throughout the centu-

[16] It is clear to me that there is political philosophy in the *Republic*, but I do not believe it presents any policy recommendations. My resistance to this particular form of political reading of the *Republic* stops short, however, of the line in the sand Julia Annas draws in *Platonic Ethics Old and New* (Ithaca: Cornell UP, 1999). There, Annas argues that "we have no evidence for situating the *Republic* in the context of Plato's supposed attitude to politics..." (77). This goes too far. My view, in short, is that we clearly have in the *Republic* a dialogue populated with historical figures associated with the Peloponnesian War, set in the home of an arms dealer shortly before the war. There are real Athenian issues framing the *Republic* and real political conclusions to be drawn, as well as philosophical ones. My contention is strictly that we are never presented in the *Republic* with a political model that Plato (or his Socrates) would recommend that any Athenian politician attempt to enact. Debra Nails also argues against seeing within the *Republic* a set of policy recommendations to be implemented, but she does so with the understanding that the dialogue was deeply and definitively embedded in the Athenian political contexts, especially the aftermath of the Peloponnesian War. For Nails, the political reading is made up of extreme counterweights to actually existing political practices in Classical Athens. They attempt to right things by bending the reed too far in the opposite direction. I am not entirely convinced by this argument either, at least at its margins. Nails's repositioning of the myth of metals in light of the existing demographic distribution in Athens and her contextualization of the proposals for the equality of women in light of Athens' unusual restrictions on women in the Classical Hellenic world are very helpful, as well as many of her other points. But, when she proposes that the rule of philosopher is a way of highlighting the problems with dissolving and reconstituting the Athenian Assembly so often, I find myself less persuaded.

ries. I will also make the case that the political model presented in Books V–VII looks very different when considered in parallel to its psychological analog, and argue that many of the traditional critiques of Platonic politics are not really responsive to Plato's text. Socrates could not possibly be more different from the image Karl Popper famously presented of him in *The Open Society and its Enemies*.[17] To say that Socrates was a lover of liberty in the modern sense would be an exaggeration. But an intolerant fascist committed to censorship and totalitarian control? Not even close.

The general framework of the philosophical feminine follows from what I see as lacking in the model of the soul that Socrates completes in Book IV, as well as how those deficiencies are addressed in the revision of the model in Books V–VII. In brief, the soul as modeled in Book IV lacks two essential elements: (1) a capacity for motion or development, and (2) a capacity to apprehend anything outside of itself.[18] So a new question defining the development of the expanding model of the city/soul to include the philosophical feminine emerges: how, assuming it is possible, can one become just? Another defining question guiding the Socratic dialectic: what, if anything, beyond the city/soul is necessary for becoming just, and if it can be apprehended, how does one apprehend it?

One objection to framing the structure of the *Republic* this way might be that Socrates has already presented a story of the development of the city/soul in Books II–IV. I will argue that although the construction of the city in speech that Socrates claims to complete in Book IV

---

[17] Karl R. Popper, *The Open Society and Its Enemies vol. 1: The Spell of Plato* (London: Routledge, 1945).

[18] It is tempting to make an anachronistic appeal to Aristotle's *De Anima* in reference to this part of my argument, since these are two definitive features of soul presented in Aristotle's account there. One could argue that what is called "soul" in the Books II–IV of the *Republic*, insofar as it lacks these capacities, is not soul at all in the Aristotelian sense. If one is sympathetic to reading Aristotle back into Plato in this way, one might further conclude that the soul of Books II–IV was yet another statue—an inert object that looks sort of human, but isn't really human at all because it is not alive. My thanks to Norman Fischer for thinking this through with me.

appears to be a sort of genetic account, it is not.[19] When, as he builds toward Book IV, Socrates gives an account of where each part of the city/soul came from, he tells the story of the function of each part of the soul— of how and why it does what it does. Nowhere in Books II–IV does he explain how one might come to have a soul analogous to the just city. Nor does Socrates offer a description of the dispositions, habits, or education required for becoming just. What he provides is a beautiful, powerful framework for understanding the value of internal harmony and the costs of internal faction, but it does not include an account of the conditions for the possibility of its coming into existence. For that we will need the Female Drama.

The model of the soul completed in Book IV also lacks any capacity to see beyond itself. The virtues, including justice, enumerated in Book IV all refer to the internal arrangement of the parts (or functions) of soul described in Books II through IV. Wisdom is the excellence of the calculating part of the soul in its activity of coordinating all of the functions of soul (442c). Courage is the excellence of the spirited part of soul in maintaining and protecting the order ordained by the calculating part (442c). Moderation is each part of the soul recognizing its place in relation to all the other parts (442c). Justice is each part doing its work (443c). In this model, all of the virtues are internally oriented and self-referential, even wisdom. One might argue that the calculating part of the soul cannot truly be called wise unless it effects the internal ordering of the soul according to the apprehension of the Good. I would agree. That is not a part of the model as it is presented here, though. The capacity of *nous* to look outward does not come into play until Book VI. In fact, *nous* does not exist in the model completed in Book IV. The highest rational capacity of soul is *logismos*, calculation. Beginning in Book VI, the rational soul has two aspects (*nous* and *logismos*) and three functions: external apprehension, internal apprehension, and internal ordering.[20] But this

[19] See Brann, *Music of the Republic*, 165.

[20] As Eva Brann argues in *The Music of the Republic*, 166, "Division (*diaresis*) is here not a very formal method, as can be gathered from the numerous names given to these parts: kinds, sorts, parts, affects (*eide*, *gene*, *mere*, *pathe*, 435bc, 439e, 441c, 443d, 442bc, 612a5)." What we have in Book IV, despite the claim that it is "complete," is a working model meant to serve a particular func-

complex account of rationality is a part of the model of soul that emerges in the central books; it has no presence in Books II through IV. The highest, purest form of the philosophical feminine is *nous*, the rational capacity to apprehend (some reflection of) the Good.[21] It has no place in the Male Drama. Without it philosophy, not to mention good government, is impossible.

Despite knowing well the arguments for the insufficiency of the model of the soul presented in Book IV by scholars of Plato who have most influenced my own understanding of the *Republic*,[22] I believe that the model of the soul completed in Book IV is sufficient for the question it was designed to answer: which is better in itself, justice or injustice?

---

tion, but not in itself precise. As we move into the central books of the *Republic*, the model is both amended to address what has been neglected in Book IV and rendered more precise by the more consistent account of what the "parts" of the soul are, what they do, and how they do it.

[21] When one says things such as "the rational capacity to apprehend the Good," one is on very shaky ground. The Good is beyond being, so one could very sensibly argue that it is beyond reason. But the Good is relevant to one's attempt to live a good life, and it certainly plays a role in philosophical inquiry. In *Republic* Book VII, Socrates deals with this problem in various ways, generally involving analogies. He cannot give an account of the Good, he says, but he can talk about the Sun, which is "a child of the Good." And he can show that the Good is a condition of things that we can see and know, so that if we understand those things, we can come to understand something about the Good. I do not mean to simplify the problems that attend our attempts to apprehend the Good by claiming that *nous* is the faculty capable of such apprehension. I do mean to say that whatever complexities and frustrations attend our attempt to approach the Good, they attend our *noetic* capacities, our *nous*.

[22] See, for example: Seth Benardete, *Socrates' Second Sailing: On Plato's* Republic (Chicago: University of Chicago Press, 1989); and Ronna Burger, "The Thumotic and Erotic Soul: Seth Benardete on Platonic Psychology," *Interpretation* 32 (2004). My view in brief, which I will elaborate on in the body of this book, is that Benardete, Burger, et al, are correct about the inaccuracy of the model of the soul that is presented in *Republic* IV. My argument, which is at least largely, if not entirely, compatible with theirs, is that: (1) the structure of the should presented in Book IV is sufficient for the dialectical matter at hand and (2) it is meant as an unfinished model that will be completed in Books V–VII.

The Female Drama is necessary for an inquiry into the best life, but not for an inquiry into a just life in its most minimal instantiation. The main way Socrates makes the case for the superiority of justice is by showing that internal harmony is better than internal faction. That argument is sufficient to show the superiority of justice to injustice. The shortcomings of the model do not undermine its power to serve its purpose. When Polemarchus and Adeimantus demand that Socrates give more time to the roles of women and children in the city in speech, Socrates is not being asked to do something helpful in relation to their agreed upon goals. But, rather than point out that they have lost the thread of the argument (as Socrates knew well how to do), he takes up the challenge. Why? Because in doing so, he turns the dialogue toward four of the most important teachings of the *Republic*: the shape of the philosophical soul, the inherent tension between *nomoi* and philosophy, the dangers of philosophical education, and the beauty and power of the philosophical life. He wishes to impart these lessons to the young, powerful men with whom he speaks so that they might live better lives.[23] These hyper-thumotic souls need, if possible, to cultivate their *noetic* capacities. They need an education in the philosophical feminine.

For the conversation to be more meaningful for the interlocutors' moral education, Socrates must acquiesce—not only to describe the look of the just soul, but to attempt to account for how one might become just. Because these interlocutors are potentially powerful people in Athenian society, there will likely be public and political consequences to their private decisions. Socrates' introduction of the question of the possibility of justice, his staging of the Female Drama, leads directly to the need to question the authority of conventional norms (*nomoi*), putting Socrates, his interlocutors, and the city of Athens in a precarious position. Unless Glaucon, Adeimantus, and the others go on to see that there are higher (and more demanding) authorities to which one should demur, Socrates will have both shown them the best ways of managing unruliness in men and cities, and he will have untethered them from the conventional ways

[23] By showing his interlocuters the superiority of the philosophical life to a political life, Socrates may not turn them toward philosophy, but if he moderates their attachment to politics at all he will have improved their situation.

that people and cities protect themselves from tyranny. In freeing his spirited interlocutors from *nomoi,* Socrates creates a terribly dangerous situation. If and until they bind themselves to the Good, his adherents will be capable of anything and beholden to nothing. Socrates risks nothing less than creating moral and political monsters.[24]

How does Socrates present his case in the central books of the *Republic* for the possibility of goodness in the soul that has the maximum potential for it? I argue that in the central books of the *Republic* three modes of the philosophical feminine are systematically explored, three sets of conditions for becoming just (implying three complete satisfactions for each condition): the dispositions of a potentially just soul (its *genesis*), the formation/habituation of a potentially just soul that will make it educable (its *trophe*), and the education of a potentially just soul that will convert those dispositions and good habits into actual justice (its *paideia*). With some overlap, these three sets of conditions are explored in each of the three central books of the *Republic. Genesis* is a dominant theme in Book V, *trophe* in Book VI, and *paideia* in Book VII. Within each book, those conditions are explored in relation to each of the parts of the soul, so the account of *genesis* in Book V takes up the dispositions

---

[24] This part of Plato's argument has perennial political significance. Socrates realizes that the best, most powerful political leaders must see that conventions are contingent; they must be able to evaluate what we would now call social norms in light of higher standards and values. Anyone without this capacity will simply be moving political furniture around, but not engaging in political work that could improve the lives of people under their authority (except insofar as better arranged institutions that enshrine accepted norms might be marginally more pleasant for some). But there is always a risk associated with the recognition that there is no necessity to the norms one has previously taken as necessary: one may perceive oneself to be existentially free. One cannot be a political leader without recognizing the contingency of norms, but if one does not join that recognition with another one—the recognition that there is something higher than the *nomoi* to be beholden to—then one is positioned perfectly to use one's political power for exploitation and self-aggrandizement. In order to become the best kind of politician, one must become capable of being the worst kind. Socrates offers us no way to avoid this risk.

of soul necessary for philosophy in terms of *epithumia*,[25] *thumos*, and *logismos*, in turn. The pattern continues in Book VI with a consideration of the *trophe* necessary for *epithumia, thumos, logismos, and nous*.[26] In Book VII the inquiry concerns the *paideia* required for *epithumia*, *thumos*, *logismos*, and *nous*.[27] Together, the central books of the *Republic* look something like an Attic cycle of tragedies, each "play" having its own interests but all three coming together to form a whole.

In addition to the frames of (1) *genesis*, *trophe*, and *paideia* and (2) *epithumia*, *thumos*, *logismos*, and *nous*, a third centrally important distinction supports my account, an obvious one: potentiality and actuality. As I've already indicated, when Socrates agrees to Polemarchus and Adiemantus' argumentative detour at the beginning of Book V, Socrates makes clear that they have completed the Male Drama (in Book IV), but he goes on to say that he will now acquiesce to considering the "female drama" (451c). As I have already said, it is my sense that the distinction, both in the city in speech and in the individual soul, comes down to that between actuality and potentiality. When Socrates completes the model of the soul in Book IV, he has given a somewhat schematic account of the actuality of a generic soul.[28] What he turns to in Books V–VII is an

[25] It is provocative that *epithumia* is the only function of soul described with a feminine word. There are good linguistic reasons for Plato to use the term, but it also fits nicely with my interpretation of the philosophical feminine that the one wholly passive part/function of the soul is described with a femine term; while all the other parts, all of which, have active modes, have are described with male terms.

[26] In Book VI, the inquiry into the conditions for the possibility of justice illuminates the insufficiency of the model that includes *logismos* as its only mode of rationality. *Nous* is introduced as an expansion of the psychological model that makes it possible for an individual to perceive ideas that exist outside oneself. *Nous* is essentially feminine, in the sense used in the title of this book, in that it is receptive. It had no place in the Male Drama, but without it, the human soul is only self-referential.

[27] Strictly speaking, this is not quite right, since *epithumia* cannot be habituated or educated and *thumos* cannot be educated. But explaining why the framework is still meaningful is a story that requires detail and care. It will be presented in Chapter Six.

[28] See, for example: Leo Strauss, *The City and Man*, 118–119.

account of the potencies that serve as necessary conditions for those actualities. As one follows the specific accounts of *genesis*, *trophe*, and *paideia* as they apply to *epithumia*, *thumos*, *logismos*, and *nous*, one must also keep the more generic dynamic between *potentiality* and *actuality* in focus. In the central books of the *Republic* the theme of procreation looms large, especially in Book V. I will argue that the central books describe a union of the male and female, one that engenders a child. But if one focuses only on the parts at the expense of the whole, that drama will be invisible to us.

Part One

The Frame

1

Constructing the City/Soul in Books II–IV

Books V–VII of the *Republic* are the focus of this book, but in order to introduce my account of the Female Drama, I need to say a bit about the Male Drama for context. This chapter focuses on Books II–IV, where I will sketch how the city/soul is introduced and evolves up to the interruption at the beginning of Book V that signals the detour into the Female Drama. In the next chapter, I will consider the structure of this same city/soul that is generated by the Male Drama—the one that Socrates says is sufficient to support their inquiry into the nature of justice and to answer the explicit question that spurs the central argument of the *Republic*: whether it is better to live a just or an unjust life. In order to ask how the Female Drama fits in the *Republic*, how it functions, what makes it female, and why it is given such pride of place in the central books of the dialogue, one needs to consider the the Male Drama—the frame within which it is presented. Chapters Two and Three are my attempt to sketch that frame. Readers who are familiar with the Male Drama might consider jumping to Chapter Four, where the original work of this book begins in earnest.

Book II, line 368e is where the city in speech makes its entrance into the conversation of the *Republic*. It remains Socrates' central concern until a few pages before the end of the final book of the lengthy dialogue (612c-e). Socrates' image of the city is so compelling that it is difficult to see beyond it. Maybe that's the point. It could be that Plato constructed his most magisterial dialogue so that his readers would find politics overwhelmingly compelling. Perhaps it is important for it to be difficult to see past the political arguments of the *Republic*, even if we are told that it is more important to look beyond them—that our lives might depend on it (621c).

Richard Patterson argues that the images of the *Republic* (and the images of *agon*, in particular) are "reflections of, and an entirely fitting and proper stimulus and encouragement to, the intellectual desire, discipline, and stout-heartedness essential to the life of philosophy . . . ."[1] While looking for the psychological arguments in the central books of the dialogue in this study, one will see over and over again that the images support the arguments. At different moments, some of the interlocutors will be more attached to the image at hand than the argument, or vice versa, and they will get off track. However, Socrates' images and arguments always agree, even when they do not appear to, and he uses them alternately to bring his interlocutors back on track. Here in Book II, Socrates introduces the most expansive image of the *Republic*, the city in speech, and it appears that Glaucon is is immediately thrown off track by it, but Socrates will bring him back around by Book IX, if not before.

The first sign that Socrates' main interlocutors in the dialogue, Glaucon and Adeimantus, are hypnotized by politics is that they do not question the precise function or even the usefulness of introducing the city into their conversation. Glaucon and Adeimantus' challenge to Socrates in Book II is to show that individual justice is, in itself and independent of its consequences, better (more choice worthy) than injustice. Political justice was only tangentially relevant to the prelude to their challenge in Book I. (Thrasymachus brought tyrants into the conversation, but not tyranny per se.) Their discussion concerned what sort of life an individual should live and whether there was an undefined standard called "justice" that should apply to one's choices.

None of Socrates' main interlocutors introduces political justice into the dialogue. Socrates does, and he brings it in for very strange reasons. Socrates says that because the soul is so small, inquiring into the nature of individual justice requires a cleverer mind and sharper eyes than he has. Because the city is bigger, understanding it will require less mental acuity and less perfect vision (368d). This is just odd. In what sense is the soul "small?" What does its size, even if we could fix it, have to do with

---

[1] Richard Patterson, "Philosophos Agonistes: Imagery and Moral Psychology in Plato's *Republic*," *Journal of the History of Philosophy* 35, no. 3 (July 1997): 327–354.

their inquiry? They are not actually using their eyes to investigate justice. That is simply a metaphor. Furthermore, leaving size aside, why would it require less cleverness to make sense of a city than to make sense of a soul? That may be true, but it is not obvious, and it is not substantiated with any evidence or argument. These undoubtedly clever and sharp interlocutors do not seem to mind, though. If Socrates wants to talk about politics, they will not divert him.

Plato's other interlocutors in the *Republic* do not question Socrates' motivation for focusing on the city in speech instead of the soul, either. Neither do they ask for an account of exactly how Socrates imagines the city and soul to be conceptually related to one another, and Socrates does not volunteer much. He says, "If you are willing, let's first inquire into what justice is in cities, and then examine it in individuals. Afterwards, we will examine the likeness of the bigger idea to the smaller."[2]

Socrates does not say here that justice in the city in speech and justice in the soul will be perfectly analogous. There is only the vague claim that it will somehow be helpful to investigate political justice, then to consider whether it is "similar in form" to individual justice. Of course, it will not be possible to make that comparison if one has not yet apprehended the form of individual justice, so the need to compare political justice to individual justice in order to check the accuracy of the model appears to imply a logical circle. We will investigate political justice in order to understand individual justice better, but, one will not know in what ways political and individual justice are comparable until one considers them together. We will try to get to an understanding of individual justice through an inquiry into political justice, but one will not know in what way our inquiry into political justice is helpful until one has acquired an understanding of individual justice. Chicken. Egg. Chicken.[3]

---

[2]βούλεσθε, πρῶτον ἐν ταῖςπόλεσι ζητήσωμεν ποῖόν τί ἐστιν: ἔπειτα οὕτως ἐπισκεψώμεθα καὶ ἐν ἑνὶἑκάστῳ, τὴν τοῦ μείζονος ὁμοιότητα ἐν τῇ τοῦ ἐλάττονος ἰδέᾳ ἐπισκοποῦντες (368e–369a). All Greek citations of the *Republic* are from *Platonis Republicam*, ed. S. R. Slings (Oxford: Oxford University Press, 2003). All English translations are my own.

[3] This implied pattern calls to mind the similar apparent paradox that is at issue in the *Meno*, i.e., how can one know that one has found what one is looking for unless one already knows what it is; but if one already knows what one is looking for,

We are reminded of the vagueness of the relationship between individual and political justice when, in Book IV, the interlocutors have put the final touches on the city in speech (they think) and turn to the challenge of interpreting its teaching for individual justice. Socrates says, "Now, let's complete the consideration in which we supposed that if we found justice in a larger things and examined it there, it would be easier to discern what it is like in one human being," so it is explicit that one part of their inquiry is coming to a close and another is opening. He goes on with his attempt to be perfectly clear about the premises that their initial inquiry was based on, the goals they had for their inquiry, and what has already been accomplished. "We shared the opinion that the larger thing was a city, so we founded the best city we could, confident that justice would be present in a good city." Then, Socrates turns toward the part of the project that he has been promising from the start, the application of the results of the inquiry into political justice to the question of the nature of individual justice. Just when Socrates seems to be at his clearest and easiest to follow, he adds an odd twist. "Let's apply what came to light there [in our inquiry into the city] to a single human being. If the two agree, all will be well, but if something different shows up in the individual, we will go back to the city to test it. Perhaps by examining the two side by side and rubbing them together like sticks, justice will spark like fire and, once it has come to light, we will be able to see it for ourselves" (434d-435a).[4]

---

why would one need to seek it? The answer in *Meno* seems to be that we can know something about a thing (or idea), but not have it put together in our mind in a clear or coherent way, and that the process of education is at least as much about rearranging ideas that we already have as it is about acquiring new ideas. The structure of the *Republic* implies something similar, i.e., that by looking systematically at things we already know about cities and individuals, we will be able to organize our thoughts about both more clearly.

[4] νῦν δ᾽ ἐκτελέσωμεν τὴν σκέψιν ἣν ᾠήθημεν, εἰ ἐν μείζονί τινι τῶν ἐχόντων δικαιοσύνην πρότερον ἢ ἐκεῖ ἐπιχειρήσαιμεν θεάσασθαι, ῥᾷον ἂν ἐν ἑνὶ ἀνθρώπῳ κατιδεῖν οἷόν ἐστιν. καὶ ἔδοξε δὴ ἡμῖν τοῦτο εἶναι πόλις, καὶ οὕτω ᾠκίζομεν ὡς ἐδυνάμεθα ἀρίστην, εὖ εἰδότες ὅτι ἔν γε τῇ ἀγαθῇ ἂν εἴη. ὃ οὖν ἡμῖν ἐκεῖ ἐφάνη, ἐπαναφέρωμεν εἰς τὸν ἕνα, κἂν μὲν ὁμολογῆται, καλῶς ἕξει: ἐὰν δέ τι ἄλλο ἐν τῷ ἑνὶ ἐμφαίνηται, πάλιν ἐπανιόντες ἐπὶ τὴν πόλιν βασανιοῦμεν, καὶ τάχ᾽ ἂν παρ᾽

Socrates does not say, "let us unpack the analogy of the city to the soul," or whatever the fourth century BC version of that might have been. He says, let's use political justice and individual justice like fire sticks (*pureion*[5]) to see if we can make justice "spark like fire" or "blaze forth" or "shine" (*eklampo*[6]). This is beautiful and evocative, but it is not remotely clear. At the very least, it should signal to us that neither side of the city/soul analogy seems to be entirely authoritative regarding the other.[7] Political justice will help us understand individual justice and vice versa, but we need to be ready to (1) consider revising one in light of what we learn about the other, (2) recognize that they may not be perfectly analogous to each other in form, and (3) examine (or rub?) both together in order for justice to come to light.[8]

These passages delineate important boundaries for any inquiry into the city/soul analogy in the *Republic*. They mitigate against any simply mechanical reading of the relationship between the two forms of justice, and they forfend any attempt to refute the teaching by locating loop holes or inconsistencies between the two. Like any good heuristic for an overwhelmingly complicated dynamic, the city/soul analogy is straightforward enough for us to feel oriented as we begin our inquiry and flexible enough for us to continue to appeal to it as we delve into the inquiry's

---

ἄλληλα σκοποῦντες καὶ τρίβοντες, ὥσπερ ἐκ πυρείων ἐκλάμψαι ποιήσαιμεν τὴν δικαιοσύνην: καὶ φανερὰν γενομένην βεβαιωσόμεθα αὐτὴν παρ' ἡμῖν αὐτοῖς.

[5] πυρεῖον.

[6] ἐκλάμπω.

[7] As G. R. F. Ferrari points out, unlike other images in the *Republic*, such as the Cave and the Ship of State, the city is never called an εἰκόνες (icon, image, simile). Something different is going on with this image in particular. Ferrari, *City and Soul*, 60.

[8] "Socrates does not assert unequivocally that the city is the soul writ large. He says first that if someone were to direct us to larger letters that were "perhaps" (*pou*) the same as the smaller, this would facilitate our task (365d5). A few lines later, he predicates the utility of the larger letters "if they should happen to be the same" as the smaller ones (368d7). This is not to overlook the fact that he argues henceforward as though the two sets of letters, that is, justice in the soul and in the city, were the same. But no proof is ever given of this isomorphism, which is instead a basic assumption that governs the entire discussion of the founding of the just city." Rosen, *Plato's* Republic*: A Study*, 2005, 70.

vicissitudes.[9] Socrates does not offer us a simple analog, but that does not mean that the argument is specious or lacks a foundation. What we have instead is a complex and dynamic set of possible analogs that are mutually illuminating—we have a dialectic.[10]

Although neither the account of the city nor that of the soul is fixed at the outset, they also are not presented as having exactly the same status in the inquiry. Socrates begins his construction of the city in speech with the soul in mind. He does not turn to an actual city, but instead to a principle and then to the playing out of that principle's logical consequences. Like the contract theorists who would follow his lead more than two thousand years later, Socrates conjured a state of nature from which he imagined political society emerging. And, also like those contract theorists, he constructed his presumptions about nature with an agenda in mind. For Hobbes, pre-political life is solitary, poor, nasty, brutish, and short.[11] For Locke, the state of nature is ruled by the law of nature, which is reason.[12] For Hume, human beings in the state of nature are the most pathetic creatures on the planet, wholly incapable of sustaining them-

---

[9] Giovanni Ferrari's understanding of the city-soul analogy is that it operates as a proportional metaphor of the sort Aristotle describes in Book 3 of the *Rhetoric*. There, the defining characteristic of a proportional metaphor is that it is reciprocal (*Rhet.* 3.4.4). Ferrari cites as an example Aristotle's use of a proportional metaphor attributed to Pericles: "the city's youth who perished in the war disappeared from the state as if someone had removed the springtime from the year" (*Rhet.* 3.10.7). Although this is not precisely my view of how the city/soul functions, it is a compelling way to make sense of the mutually illuminating but (almost) wholly separate accounts of cities and souls in the *Republic*. G. R. F. Ferrari, *City and Soul in Plato's* Republic (Chicago: University of Chicago Press, 2005), 61.

[10] Leo Strauss argues that the city could not be perfectly analogous to the soul because cities, including the one Socrates founds with Glaucon and Adeimantus "do not come into being like natural being[s]." The city in speech of the *Republic*, however, "in contradistinction to all other known cities…will be according to nature." That is, the city in speech in the *Republic* will, at least in this respect look more like a soul than a city. But, in principle, they can not be brought into perfect alignment without abandoning fidelity to one or the other. Strauss, *City and Man*, 92

[11] *Leviathan* I.9.

[12] *Second Treatise* II.6.

selves independently, but human imagination is capable of inventing society in order to overcome natural human frailty.[13] None of these philosophers based their arguments on empirical evidence. They could not. And all of them admitted that no such state of nature really existed in the sense of a pre-political global state of affairs in human pre-history.

Hobbes was trying to make a case for a strong authoritative monarch, Locke for constitutional monarchy and the preservation of property as the primary end of government, Hume for an acknowledgement in politics of human frailty; and, in all three cases, their states of nature set up their arguments. The case of Socrates is, of course, different from Hobbes, Locke, and Hume in dozens of important ways, but not in this one. Socrates starts where he does because he knows where he wants to end up. And, he begins with insufficiency, our inability to provide ourselves with what we need. "A city comes into being," Socrates says, "because none of us is individually self-sufficient, and we lack many things we need" (369b).[14] Although a careful reader should know better, in this first moment of the inquiry into the city and soul, the analogy seems perfect. In the city, it is clear and uncontroversial—human beings come together into civil and political society because they see in collaboration a promise for a better life than each could hope to achieve independently. Presumably, we will find a similar dynamic within an individual.

For one who has looked ahead to the model of the soul, one can also see the aptness of insufficiency as the internal organizing principle of an individual life. No part of the soul is self-sufficient. Neither appetite (*epithumia)*, nor spirit (*thumos*), nor mind (*logismos/nous)* is independent in an individual life. Many, if not all, of the psychological pathologies (i.e., injustices) that Socrates will later elaborate stem from a misunderstanding of the dependencies of these different parts on each other.

The original city in speech is constructed from the principle of insufficiency. What this principle engenders is the minimal city,[15] which

---

[13] *Treatise of Human Nature* Book III, Part II, Section II.

[14] γίγνεται τοίνυν, ἦν δ' ἐγώ, πόλις, ὡς ἐγᾦμαι, ἐπειδὴ τυγχάνει ἡμῶν ἕκαστος οὐκ αὐτάρκης, ἀλλὰ πολλῶν ὢν ἐνδεής.

[15] η γε αναγκαιοτατη πολισ.

has also been called "a city with the barest necessities"[16] and "the city of utmost necessity,"[17] among other things. I prefer the translation "the minimal city," because it sets the baseline for what follows as the interlocutors continue to construct more elaborate cities in speech.

The first of our needs that Socrates enumerates is food, the second is housing, and the third is clothing (and such things). The fourth need is leatherworking, apparently for shoemaking. The fifth is the vaguest of all: "some other person who cares for bodily things."[18] The minimal city, Socrates tells us, is constituted by "four or five men," each of whom responds to one of these four or five basic human needs Socrates presents and to which the other interlocutors acquiesce. So, the four or five members of the minimal city are: the farmer, house builder, weaver, shoemaker, and "some other person who cares for bodily things."

It is odd that the number of people required for the minimal city is indeterminate. Especially since Socrates seems to be setting a baseline for the minimally necessary conditions for a group of human beings to call themselves a city, why not just say that the minimal city consisted of four members and leave that possible fifth member to the next expansion of the model? Setting "four or five" into the minimal conditions for the city and the soul builds in an indeterminacy that makes the model more frustrating, but also more accurate. If we consider the model in purely political terms, the inclusion of "some other person who cares for bodily things" implies that each of the members of the city has to be understood as having their own needs and not just as instrumental to the needs of others. The fifth member of the minimal city cares in a general way for the bodies of all the other members, while the other four provide for spe-

---

[16] Plato, *Republic*, trans. C. D. C. Reeve, (Indianapolis: Hackett, 2004), 47.

[17] Plato, *The Republic of Plato*, trans. Allan Bloom, (New York: Basic Books 1968), 46.

[18] ἀλλὰ μὴν πρώτη γε καὶ μεγίστη τῶν χρειῶν ἡ τῆς τροφῆς παρασκευὴ τοῦ εἶναί τε καὶ ζῆν ἕνεκα...δευτέρα δὴ οἰκήσεως, τρίτη δὲ ἐσθῆτος καὶ τῶν τοιούτων... φέρε δή, ἦν δ' ἐγώ, πῶς ἡ πόλις ἀρκέσει ἐπὶ τοσαύτην παρασκευήν; ἄλλο τι γεωργὸς μὲν εἷς, ὁ δὲ οἰκοδόμος, ἄλλος δέ τις ὑφάντης; ἢ καὶ σκυτοτόμον αὐτόσε προσθήσομεν ἤ τιν' ἄλλον τῶν περὶ τὸ σῶμα θεραπευτήν;...εἴη δ' ἂν ἥ γε ἀναγκαιοτάτη πόλις ἐκ τεττάρων ἢ πέντε ἀνδρῶν (369d).

cific external necessities. The indeterminacy of whether or not this person is necessary to the minimal city suggests the possibility that food, shelter, clothing, and shoes might be sufficient to keep a city alive, but might not. Contingency is built in to the city at its deepest footings.[19]

When we look at the same indeterminacy and inquire into its role in the model of the individual soul, a new set of questions emerge. If the minimal city is akin to the minimal soul, then our guiding question should be what are the minimally necessary conditions for calling a soul human? That is, at the most minimal level, what are the distinctively human ways that human beings are animated? Clearly, we need nutrition and protection from the elements. Although separating out clothing and footwear (both in the city and the soul) seems a bit odd, it makes sense that the city formed to respond to basic human needs would line up nicely with the basic needs any individual human would need to subsist.

It is important to notice that Socrates sets up these minimal conditions as clearly human needs rather than beginning with the necessities we share with other animals. Food, of course, is an animal need, but Socrates specifies farming, not hunting or foraging, which are modes of food acquisition that humans share with animals. All animals need some sort of shelter, but Socrates specifies "houses" and "house building," which is a specifically human variation on the satisfaction of that need, as opposed to seeking shelter in trees or caves, for example. Clothes and shoes most clearly respond to human needs, since they have no real analog in animal life. These appeals to distinctively human needs already may imply the need to acknowledge the very sort of concerns Glaucon will say are neglected in the healthy city. If, for example, one wears clothing to avoid a shame of nakedness that animals do not experience, is vanity and the desire for attractive clothing a qualitative leap, or just an incremental step away? Such luxuries belong to a later elaboration on the city, but the desire for them may already be latent in the earliest, most minimal of cities in speech.

In the context of looking at the minimal city as a heuristic for inquiry into individual human need (rather than political necessity), the

---

[19] For a deeper look at the oddness and possible significance of this fifth member of the minimal city, see: Carl Page "The Unnamed Fifth: *Republic* 369d" *Interpretation: A Journal of Political Philosophy* 21, no. 1, (Fall 1993): 3–14.

"other person who cares for bodily things," continues to be a bit of an enigma, but perhaps a bit less of one. As philosophical anthropologists from Ancient Greece (and India and China, for that matter) forward have observed, human beings have a natural tendency to want to keep living. The Latin term that emerged as canonical for this idea is "conatus,"[20] and its contemporary instantiation in evolutionary biology is the instinct for self-preservation. We need not get lost in scholastic inquiry or contemporary science to understand the dynamic, however. One of the minimal conditions of the humanity of the farmer is that he not only wants to continue to exist as a farmer, but as a human being. Likewise, the house builder, the weaver, and the shoe maker.

If this natural desire for self-preservation is so obvious, though, why does Socrates offer such a fuzzy account for its satisfaction? The reason is, I believe, that Socrates is reflecting a real diversity of perspectives on the fundamental nature of the human being and, thus, on the necessary conditions for its possibility. In a sense, we will need the whole rest of the dialogue to genuinely address this issue, but here are a couple of preliminary examples of what I mean.

Although Socrates is careful not to name the fifth citizen of the minimal city, it seems reasonable to think of one who "cares for bodily things" as a physician of sorts.[21] In Book III of the *Republic*, Socrates elaborates on a fundamental disagreement between physicians about the proper end of the medical art. The relevant aspect of the controversy hinges on whether medicine should be used to prolong life on the premise that life is valuable in itself, or whether medicine should be used only for those who are likely to make future contributions to society.[22] If one is sick but has reasonable chances of recovering to the point of making a significant contribution to society, physicians on both sides of this debate would understand themselves to be warranted to provide treatment. But,

[20] The Stoic notion of *horme* (ὁρμή), or impluse, may be the locus classicus of this idea.

[21] cf. Page, "The Unnamed Fifth: *Republic* 369d," 1993.

[22] Other key aspects of the debate in Book III are hypochondria, dissipation, and gymnastic, but they are less relevant to the situation of the minimal city/soul.

if a patient has no reasonable hope of recovering to the point of making a contribution, the two camps split. Herodicus seeks to prolong any life for any reason, and thus would attempt to heal whomever he could heal regardless of how his patient became ill or what he might or might not do with his life. Asclepius and his sons, on the other hand, only use medicine for those who are likely to recover and be productive (405c–408c).

This debate over the proper end of the physician's art might clarify a bit of the fuzziness of the "four or five" provision in the minimal city because it suggests a possible divergence between the model of the city and the model of the soul. If one held to the Herodican position that the end of the medical art was the health of the individual, then the "some other person who cares for bodily things" would fit nicely into both models. For the individual, the fifth need is to preserve oneself as a human being, and the response to that need is a minimally necessary part of what it means to be human. In the minimal city, it would be much the same. If the minimal city responds to basic human needs, and if self-preservation is one of those needs, then it is incumbent on the minimal city to include someone who can do this work. But, if one follows Asclepius in understanding the health of the city as the end of the medical art, then one might not include the fifth member in the city, or might only include him insofar as he could keep the other four members productive. In that case, the model of the soul and of the city might fall out of alignment.

The far more complicated, and perhaps important, possible explanation for the fuzziness of the minimal city having "four or five" members is that the minimal conditions for being human are controversial. This follows in a sense from the debate over the end of the medical art, but it also pushes toward the conflict between philosophy and politics that interested Plato so deeply. What it means to desire to preserve oneself as a human being depends entirely on what one understands a human being to be. For one who understands one's individual ends to be entirely aligned or perhaps subordinated to one's political ends, there is no conflict between "the care for the body" that serves the city and "the care for the body" that serves the individual, but for one who does not see these ends as necessarily aligned, there may indeed be conflict. And, in the rare case where one sees one's identity defined by a resistance to being subordinated to anything but the Good, that conflict is not just a possibility; it is a necessity.

Even the minimal city, the simplest model of the city/soul that Socrates presents, is subtle and nuanced. It must be, since the minimal conditions for the possibility of a city/soul are subtle and nuanced. If the model is going to help us understand what justice is, and if it is going to help us see why justice is, in itself, preferable to injustice (both in the city and soul), then the model must be carefully constructed, especially at this foundational level. For even though the model becomes huge and detailed, it never leaves this basic structure behind. Minimal needs are a part of the human condition, and meeting those needs continues to be an essential part of what it means to be a functioning city and to have a flourishing human life. The revisions to the model not just through Book IV, but also all the way through Book VII, are elaborations, not changes.[23]

In one sense, the city in speech that Plato's interlocutors complete in Book VII is the same one that they begin in Book II, but in another important sense, they consider several distinct cities in speech along the way. Socrates says they are finished constructing the city in speech three times (371e, 427b, and 543c), so there are at least three models that Socrates explicitly marks as sufficient to support their inquiry into whether or not justice is better than injustice. This is especially clear in Book II where Socrates introduces two organizing principles in turn and, for each of them, plays out their implications for city/soul model.

As we have already seen, the first principle Socrates introduces is insufficiency (369b), and the city engendered by that principle is the minimal city (369d). The first significant emendation to the model of the city/soul comes from the introduction of a new principle which, for the moment, we will call *efficiency* (370c). Socrates calls the city engendered by the principle of efficiency "healthy," so I will follow his lead. But it is

---

[23]For an example of a contemporary commentator who agrees that the later models of soul are revisions, and not repudiations, of earlier models of soul, see Elana Duverges Blair, *Plato's Dialectic on Woman* (London: Routledge, 2012). For an argument that later models of the soul repudiate earlier ones in the *Republic* see Townsend 2017. The explicit aspect of their disagreement that Townsend focuses on (in fn. 17 on p. 21) concerns the status of the first two waves relative to the previously constructed city/soul.

important to note at the outset that Glaucon offers a different opinion; he says that Socrates' healthy city is a city fit for pigs, not men.

The principle that I am calling efficiency develops from 369e to 370c where Socrates argues that if we diversify the work of citizens into specialties, the result will be more plentiful goods that are also more beautiful and of higher quality.[24] The idea that engenders the healthy city is that although the minimal city is functional, it is inefficient. The farmer, if he is to farm well, would benefit from not also having to produce all of the things he needs in order to do his work, as would the weaver, the shoemaker, and all the other citizens of the minimal city. The principle of insufficiency that engendered the minimal city (i.e. that human beings are insufficient in themselves to provide for their basic needs) is still in place. The question that has emerged is no longer what are the minimal conditions for addressing these needs, but instead what are the most efficient conditions for satisfying them. And, the interlocutors' preliminary answer is that the most efficient way of meeting these basic needs is to establish a division of labor in the city such that each citizen may focus on what he does best by nature and may be liberated from other tasks that might inhibit his capacity to do what his art requires at the optimal time.

Efficiency, then, immediately breaks down to two implicit principles: (1) each citizen should do what he is naturally best at doing and (2) each citizen should be free to do what his art requires at precisely the time his art requires it. With these guiding principles in place, the city grows first by the addition of carpenters, smiths, and craftsmen. Then, cowherds, shepherds, and other herdsmen join the city on the same principle.

The next phase of expansion introduces a third subdivision of the principle of efficiency, which is also an extension of the principle of insufficiency. Socrates says that it would be nearly impossible to find a place where a city of this size could provide for all its needs without having to import some goods from other cities (370e). So, (3) a collective, rather than individualistic, conception of insufficiency is presented as a

---

[24] ἐκ δὴ τούτων πλείω τε ἕκαστα γίγνεται καὶ κάλλιον καὶ ῥᾷον, ὅταν εἷς ἓν κατὰ φύσιν καὶ ἐν καιρῷ, σχολὴν τῶν ἄλλων ἄγων, πράττῃ (370c).

subdivision of efficiency, and this turns out to be the final expansion needed to complete this version of the city in speech. In the same way that the insufficiency of individuals to provide for all of their own needs led to the founding of the minimal city, the insufficiency of an efficient city to provide for all of its own needs leads to the founding of the healthy city.

Trade is the institution that is implied by collective insufficiency (to operate efficiently). First, the quantities of goods produced must increase to create a surplus for export. This means that the city will need more people engaged in the arts which produce goods for foreign trade. It also means the city will need people whose art is trade, itself: merchants, exporters, and importers. It will need a market and currency. Finally, Socrates adds wage laborers to the city. Then, he calls it complete (371e).

A pattern of interlocking and embedded ideas is first instantiated here with the principles of insufficiency and efficiency, and persists throughout all of the elaborations on the city in speech that continue through Book VII. Socrates introduces ideas that appear to function independently and that can be understood individually, but as the city in speech becomes more elaborate, these principles become more intertwined. Such is this case here where the principle of efficiency is presented as a higher ambition for the organization of the city in speech than sufficiency, but also implies a new form of insufficiency (vis a vis other cities) which requires a new application of the apparently more basic principle of insufficiency. Put concretely, the principle of insufficiency generates the minimal city, the principle of efficiency expands the city to include specialization, and specialization implies a new sort of insufficiency which expands the city to include specialists in all aspects of trade. Only when all all of these principles have generated institutions is the healthy city called complete.

At this moment of the dialogue (371e), Socrates makes his first attempt to move from the activity of constructing the city in speech and into the work of locating justice and injustice within it. Although the interlocutors never make that transition, Socrates points to where one should begin one's search for justice. One should consider, he says, the sort of life that one might lead in such a city (372a). And, then Socrates becomes rhapsodic. There is something of the Garden of Eden in Socrates' description of life in the healthy city. Everyone has what they need.

Life is natural, responsive to the seasons, in touch with nature. They have families and feasts, sex and religion, moderate drinking, good health, long lives, and apparently no discontent.

Glaucon, however, is not impressed. Before Socrates can move from his description of life within the healthy city to a consideration of what such a life could reveal about justice and injustice in the city/soul, Glaucon interrupts to say that the life Socrates describes is not fully human. And, of course, he is right.[25] But, the task they embarked upon together was to create a city in speech within which they could find justice and injustice, then to see what they could learn about individual justice and injustice, and finally to determine whether justice or injustice was more choice worthy for an individual. The model of the healthy city was, according to Socrates, sufficient for that task. Had Glaucon not interrupted, Socrates would have been able to come to a definition of justice very quickly. In fact, he was right there. But, like Odysseus, Socrates gets blown far, far off course at 372c, and it will be a very long time before he will glimpse the destination of their inquiry again.[26]

We know from Book IV that in the *Republic*, Socrates will define justice as "regarding things concerning ruling and being ruled, each part within [a person] minding its own business."[27] This definition of justice emerges, along with definitions of wisdom, courage, and moderation, after a long and arduous construction of a much more complicated model

---

[25] As Walter Newell points out, Platonic *eros* is necessarily interpersonal or social, if not political, so Glaucon is not wrong to think that a good city should make room for what he finds missing. "As interpreted by Plato, *eros* is the longing for union with the beautiful, for which the Greek word means the same as the noble (*to kalon*). *Eros* is therefore at once the strongest of passions in the individual and so structured as to involve us necessarily with others—friends, family, lovers, and fellow citizens—for its satisfaction." Newell, *Ruling Passions*, 2.

[26] As Rosen puts it, "The peaceful life of the true, austere and healthy city (372c1, d2) is about to be lost by another kind of neediness or necessity, namely, the necessity of desire, of which the deepest and most pervasive form is *eros*." Rosen, *Plato's* Republic, 76.

[27] αὐτοῦ τῶν ἐν αὐτῷ ἕκαστον τὰ αὐτοῦ πράττειαρχῆς τε πέρι καὶ τοῦ ἄρχεσθαι (443b).

of the city that Glaucon's interjection at 372c engenders. And at 441d, the interlocutors agree that the definition holds both for the city in speech and the individual soul. But one can see how the model healthy city would have been sufficient to get to this same definition. For the healthy city/soul to be just, each part of the healthy city/soul must "have and do" what belongs to it.

It is counterfactual and thoroughly speculative, of course, but it is not hard to see how Socrates might have led the conversation toward a consideration of injustice in the healthy city, compared justice and injustice, and made much the same core argument for the superiority of justice over injustice that he presents most fully in Book IX, but alludes to throughout the dialogue: harmony is better, more powerful, and more pleasant than faction (disharmony). As Eva Brann puts it, "This city is . . . the most literal model for a reading of the definition of justice that runs through the *Republic*."[28] But, once again, that argument is delayed by the demand that Socrates revise and expand the city in speech, regardless of the fact that the city he has constructed seems to have been perfectly well suited to support their inquiry.

If the explicit goal of the conversation is not served by Glaucon's interruption, why does Socrates not shut him down? What ends are served by developing the model in light of Glaucon's concerns in Book II? It does not seem that the more elaborate model will make the hunt for justice any easier or the comparison between justice and injustice any clearer. It also does not provide any straightforward assistance to anyone interested in implementing public policy. It will, however, offer a more accurate and illuminating image of the human soul.[29] Here in his choice to yield to Glaucon's pressure to revise the model, as in many other plac-

---

[28] Brann, *Music of the Republic*, 122.

[29] For Stanley Rosen, Glaucon's apparently misguided intervention signals the beginning of the truly central topic of the dialogue. "I would therefore modify the Straussian view that the main purpose of the *Republic* is to show the dangers entailed by an excessive pursuit of justice. This is a subsidiary purpose. The main purpose is to show the impossibility of the full satisfaction of philosophical *eros*." Rosen, *Plato's* Republic, 82.

es, Socrates' primary commitment to an inquiry into the individual soul is evident.[30]

Glaucon wants relishes in his city, but they are just the by-products of what he really finds lacking in Socrates' description of life in the healthy city—ambition, honor, a venue for his huge and beautiful spirit. Socrates is not at all surprised, it appears, by Glaucon's interest in luxury, and he makes almost no fuss about changing course. So, the principle that Socrates will employ for the next expansion of the city/soul appears to be clear: it is luxury. But, really, the principle that he appeals to lies behind those luxuries, and Socrates seems to go to quite a bit of effort not to name it. What Socrates says explicitly is that it is a fine idea to expand the city/soul because (1) we will still be able to find justice within the expanded model and (2) not everyone will be satisfied with the way of life in the healthy city, which is governed by insufficiency and efficiency.[31]

Socrates repeats several times the idea of not being satisfied with necessities, and says that what follows from such dissatisfaction is the production of adornments. What Socrates seems to be appealing to here is desire, *eros*.[32] Given Glaucon's huge spirit, it might seem more likely to appeal to *thumos*,[33] but outlets for *thumos* already exist in the healthy city. Glaucon is not attracted to the options that would be available to him, but opportunities to distinguish oneself exist at just about every level of Socrates' description of the way of life in the healthy city. One could seek

[30] "[T]he city is for Plato an artificial construction that is required in order to overcome, or better, to control, the natural divisions within the human soul. This is of course in no way to deny that for Plato, human beings are better off in the city than in the state of nature. One has only to mention that philosophy arises exclusively in the city. But it makes no sense to speak of politics as the natural fulfilment of human nature if that fulfilment in turn depends upon compulsion. It may seem anachronistic to some to say that the city is for Plato an artifactual reconstitution of the radically defective work of nature. I myself regard it as the obvious teaching of the two most important political dialogues, the *Republic* and the *Statesman*, to mention only these." Stanley Rosen, *Platonic Productions* (South Bend: St. Augustine Press, 2014) 92.

[31] ταῦτα γὰρ δή τισιν, ὡς δοκεῖ, οὐκ ἐξαρκέσει, οὐδὲ αὕτη ἡ δίαιτα (372e).

[32] ἔρος.

[33] θημός.

and find recognition for one's art (cooking, winemaking, etc.), for one's physical fitness, for one's feasts, one's songs, one's family, etc. It is not the quantity of opportunities for *thumotic* satisfaction that Glaucon finds lacking in the city, it is their quality. These are mundane, domestic modes of recognition. They are small and local. They would die with the person who achieved them or, at best, survive a generation or two in the memories of those to whom one was close. This is simply not good enough for Glaucon. He wants much more.

The principle that guides the expansion of city/soul that begins at 372e is desire unhinged from necessity, i.e., *eros*.[34] The treatment of *eros* in the *Republic* is extremely tricky and deeply important. For now, I will limit myself to an orienting comment or two. The parts of the soul that frame Socrates' account of the city/soul in the Books II–IV are *epithumia*, *thumos*, and *logismos*. And, when the model is expanded and revised in Books V–VII, these continue to be the parts of the soul that frame the model, but *nous* is added to the mix. The activities of these modes of soul change, in some cases, but not their natures. The fact that *eros* appears to be left out of the account is a big problem given the importance of *eros* throughout the Platonic corpus.

Nevertheless, *eros* is all over the *Republic*, explicitly and implicitly. Explicitly, it is centrally important to the treatment of women and children in Book V and the account of tyrants in Book IX. It plays key roles in Books VI and VII, as well. Implicitly, it serves as a sort of boundary condition for the proper activity of each of the other parts of the soul throughout the dialogue. Appetite in the *Republic* is *epithumia*, but when one believes one's appetites should govern one's soul, one has made an erotic mistake, not an epithumetic one. *Eros* is being drawn toward what one thinks/feels will complete oneself, but it is often misleading, mistaken. Believing that satisfying one's appetites is the path toward living a

---

[34] According to Jessica Moss, being "unhinged," is a definitive feature of *eros*, as it is presented in the *Republic*. "I hold that the *Republic* distinguishes desires for pleasures qua pleasure from other sorts of desires—desires for truth and honor, for example, which when gratified yielded their own particular pleasures, but are not properly construed as desires for pleasures—and assigns these desires to appetite (το επιθυμητικον)." Moss, "Pleasure and Illusion in Plato," 522.

flourishing life is a mistake. *Epithumia* (appetite) wants what it wants. It cannot direct itself. When one mistakenly believes that the object of an appetite can satisfy a deep need, the mistake is not *epithumetic*. It is an erotic mistake because it is displays a misunderstanding of what one is, ideally, and what one should do or have in order to more fully approximate that ideal.

Glaucon thus makes an erotic mistake at 372e. He believes that what he lacks—what he should pursue in order more fully to approximate the best possible version of himself—is recognition for great deeds. *Thumos* is central to his point of view because his erotic mistake concerns the proper role of *thumos* in a healthy soul, but it is an erotic mistake nonetheless. And the principle that Socrates derives from Glaucon's mistake, which he says is a mistake that other people are likely to make, is to disengage the objects of each of the parts/activities of soul from necessity. So, in the healthy city, we needed shoes and clothes and food. In the luxurious city, we need fancy shoes, embroidered clothes, and elaborate dining rooms.

As Socrates almost immediately points out, the luxurious city is really better called the feverish city (372e). It does not instantiate a bigger, more beautiful version of health. Instead, it undermines health. It has to be legislated, doctored and, eventually, purged. This is the work of the rest of Book II, all of Book III, and the first third of Book IV. At 427d, the city engendered by *eros* is constructed and purged of its fever so that the hunt for justice can begin. Because my concern in this chapter is to trace the development of the city/soul through Books II through IV, I will not comment on much of what transpires in this section of the *Republic*. Most of this part of the dialogue concerns the nature and training of the guardians and auxiliaries in the city in speech, which does not change the structure of the model, so I will largely skip over it in my account.

The feverish city is not structurally identical to the healthy city, though, and we must have a look at the changes to the city/soul engendered by the erotic principle Glaucon interjects. The city first is enlarged to include the producers of luxuries. Hunters are listed first and then imitators of all different sorts: poets, rhapsodes, actors, choral dancers, theatrical producers. Next come the craftsmen needed to support those producers of luxuries. Socrates specifically mentions producers of adornments for women. The third phase of enlargement is the addition of servants to the city Socrates includes in his list of servants: tutors, wet nurses, nannies, beauticians, barbers, and relish cooks (perhaps with a wink to Glaucon). Finally, in this list, which plays out the expansion of the city directly traceable to the desire for luxury, Socrates adds pig farmers. The healthy city had farmers, but not pig farmers. The luxurious city will need them because, presumably, pork is delicious and people are going to want it even though it is not good for them.[35]

Socrates seems also to think that pork is unhealthy. That must be why the healthy city did not have pig farmers. But, the unhealthiness of pork seems to be the reason that Socrates jumps straight from the fevered city's need for pig farmers to its need for doctors. So, Socrates generates the next short list of citizens who will belong to the fevered city that did not belong in the healthy city by a different principle: those who serve needs created by the feverish city. We may or may not have needed some sort of doctor in the minimal city, and since the healthy city is an elaboration on the minimal city, it may or may not be implied that there are physicians there, too. But, there is no question about whether or not citizens of the luxurious/fevered city will need medical care. If the citizens of the healthy city eat and drink and live according to their desires instead of according to their needs, then they are going to make themselves unhealthy, and they are going to need doctors. The city engendered by *eros* has no natural boundaries.

The healthy city grew to its complete size when it had provided for all of its needs through production and trade. Since those needs were finite and intelligible, so was the city engendered by those needs. However, *eros* has no such finite reference point—so no such logical conclusion. In fact, following *eros* often has the consequence of increasing rather than satisfying one's desires. This plays out in the city in speech at 373d with Socrates' recognition that the fevered city will not be satisfied with the borders drawn between it and its neighbors. The fevered city will want more land, and it will seize it. This, says Socrates, is the origin of war (373e), and war demands an army.

---

[35] For a delightful contemporary account of deliciousness and luxury that is deeply influenced by Platonic philosophy, see Leon Kass and Amy Kass, *The Hungry Soul* (Chicago: University of Chicago Press, 1999).

Socrates adds two sets of citizens to the fevered city to respond to needs that it creates for itself. The first is the need for doctors created by the unhealthy way of life organized by desire rather than by need. The second is the need for soldiers created by the fact that desire, as an organizing principle, has no natural boundaries. And, since the earlier principles that guided the city in speech are still operative, each of these new types of citizen will be better at what they do and more effective for the city if they are specialists. This seems to be an uncontroversial point in regards to doctors, but one that needs some elaboration in the case of soldiers, i.e., guardians.

As every student of the *Republic* knows, once Socrates begins his inquiry into the work of the guardians and the nature, training, and education required of them, we have taken the first step on a long, treacherous, circuitous path. And that path does not lead to where this inquiry wants to go, so we will pause right here. But, as we pause, let us consider the guardians for just a moment.

The guardians are introduced into the fevered city as professional soldiers, members of an army needed to fight wars caused by border disputes or, more accurately, the fevered city's disregard for the borders it shares with its neighbors. However, as Socrates makes the case that the fevered city needs citizens who specialize in defending the city from external and internal threats, the nature of the guardian's role in the city shifts quickly and dramatically. By 414b, the original category of guardian has been expanded and subdivided so that there is a sub category understood as "complete" guardians[36] of the city and thus its proper rulers. And there is another sub category, conventionally called "auxiliaries," who are the helpers and aids to the "complete guardians."[37] Both the expansion of the work of the guardians from military duty to political leadership and their subdivision into complete guardians and auxiliaries are centrally important to the structure of the city/soul that Socrates will unpack in Book IV and the definitions of justice, wisdom, courage, and moderation he will derive from it.

---

[36] φύλακας παντελεῖς.

[37] ἐπικούρους τε καὶ βοηθοὺς.

The final point I would like to make about the large and important part of the *Republic* that my account is largely passing over (roughly 374d–427c) is to highlight the transformation that the "fevered" city undergoes during this part of the argument: its purge or purification.[38] As I recounted above, the fevered city is engendered by an erotic principle, but it continues also to be guided by the principles that engendered the earlier cities: insufficiency (the minimal city) and efficiency (the healthy city). And, furthermore, as the city engendered by *eros* develops, it develops new insufficiencies that need to be addressed efficiently. The fevered city creates unhealthy lives that need to be tended to by physicians, and it creates unstable borders that have to be tended to by guardians. But, as physicians and (much more prominently) guardians tend to the fevered city, it becomes less feverish. It is purged.

It is telling that Socrates does not say that the fevered city is healed. The implication seems to be that although the city can be brought back to some approximation of health, it can never be returned to the balance that existed in the healthy city before *eros* was unleashed from necessity. It can be treated, though, and it can be brought into a state of functional health. This is important because although the structure of the fevered city does not change in the process of its purification, strictly speaking, it is in the purged city and not in the fevered city that the interlocutors will search for and find the virtues, including justice.

---

[38] διακαθαίρω.

2

The Psychology of the City in Book IV

At 427d, a third of the way into Book IV, Socrates says that they have completed the city that was inspired by Glaucon's objections to the healthy city. In order to respond to Glaucon's dissatisfaction of what he called "the city of pigs,"[1] the interlocutors infected it with *eros*, constructed the institutions *eros* engendered, and then purged it of its erotic fever by way of a long and difficult dialectic, which mainly concerned the character and duties of the guardians.[2] This is the second time in the *Republic* that Socrates has claimed to have completed a city in speech,[3] but it is the first time his interlocutors have been willing to use such a model polity to seek answers to their questions about justice. For the moment, Glaucon is happy to begin the work of interrogating the purged city in speech to learn what it might teach them about individual justice, so they begin.

At this moment in the dialogue, there is no pause or interlude or mediating discussion to break up the connection between the city in speech and its explicit purpose in the dialectic. The purged city "seems to

---

[1] ὑῶν πόλιν.

[2] Debra Nails argues that Plato here suggests an alternative theory for the cause of the Peloponnesian War against Thucydides' claim that fear was at its root. For Nails, Glaucon's *pleonexia*, his greed, creates the conditions for war in the city in speech and is an image of the Athenian *pleonexia* that caused the Peloponnesian War. This seems right to me, but perhaps slightly over-drawn as a contrast. Thucydides argued that Spartan fear of Athenian expansion made the war inevitable (I:22). If that expansion is seen to be driven by *pleonexia*, which it may or may not be, then Nails theory would already be a part of Thucydides'. Debra Nails, "Plato's *Republic* in its Athenian Context," *History of Political Thought* 33, no. 1 (Spring 2012): 9.

[3] The first time Socrates claims the city in speech is complete is at 371e and the third time is at 543c.

have been founded," Socrates says. He then immediately invites Glaucon to "look around," and "invite your brother and Polemarchus and the others" to join in to try to see "where justice and injustice exist in it and... which of the two a person would need to possess in order to be happy."[4] Glaucon resists taking primary responsibility for the search, and he immediately puts that work back into Socrates' hands, but he does not balk at the project itself. The city in speech was created to facilitate the inquiry into the nature and choice-worthiness of justice, and 427d marks the moment where the interlocutors begin to put it to work doing what it was designed to do.[5]

We will pass over for now a provocative part of Socrates' instructions to Glaucon because the interlocutors ignore it. Before he tells Glaucon to look around for justice and injustice, Socrates tells him to "provide a light from somewhere"[6] presumably to make justice visible. Much later in the dialogue, Socrates walks the interlocutors through the need for such a light, its function, and the importance recognizing the capacity to apprehend such light as an essential part of the work of a human soul. But, it is already here, undeveloped and uncommented upon. The description of the soul in Book IV already implies the developments to the model that will not emerge explicitly until Books VI and VII.

---

[4] Ἀρίστωνος, ἡ πόλις: τὸ δὲ δὴ μετὰ τοῦτο σκόπει ἐν αὐτῇ, φῶς ποθὲν πορισάμενος ἱκανόν, αὐτός τε καὶ τὸν ἀδελφὸν παρακάλει καὶ Πολέμαρχον καὶ τοὺς ἄλλους, ἐάν πως ἴδωμεν ποῦ ποτ' ἂν εἴη ἡ δικαιοσύνη καὶ ποῦ ἡ ἀδικία, καὶ τί ἀλλήλοιν διαφέρετον, καὶ πότερον δεῖ κεκτῆσθαι τὸν μέλλοντα εὐδαίμονα εἶναι, ἐάντε λανθάνῃ ἐάντε μὴ πάντας θεούς τε καὶ ἀνθρώπους.

[5] As Ferrari points out, the city/soul analogy is presented differently from the other images in the *Republic*, and not just because of its scale. The Ship of State and Cave, for example, are not introduced so that ships and Caves might be better understood, but the city is. The city, unlike the similes in the *Republic*, is itself an object of inquiry—an essential element in the dialectic, not an instrumental image. But, this does not mean that Socrates is equally interested in or focused on the city and the soul in the *Republic*. Plato may be equally interested in cities and souls. That is a matter for speculation. But, while Socrates is interested in both halves of the city/soul dialectic, the text clearly and repeatedly indicates that he is ultimately most interested in individuals. G. R. F. Ferrari, *City and Soul in Plato's* Republic, 60.

[6] φῶς ποθὲν πορισάμενος ἱκανόν.

Even without trying to make sense of his unexplained comment on of the need to find a source of light to illuminate their inquiry, Socrates' strategy for seeking justice in the city in speech is odd. In fact, it is apparently incoherent, but his interlocutors don't seem at all to mind. At 428e Socrates says that if the city in speech has been well founded, then it will be completely good (*teleos agathen*[7]). First of all, if they were talking about an actual city and literal political policy, this would be absurd. No real city is or could be completely good. We can leave that absurdity aside, though, since it is clear for other reasons that this particular city exists in speech. Even for a city in speech, though, it is difficult to understand what it might mean to say that being a "completely good" city follows necessarily from being well-founded.

The issue of whether or not the city in speech can be what, following Eva Brann,[8] I will call a "city in deed" looms large over much of the central books of the *Republic* (generally because Adiemantus repeatedly brings the question up), but the nature of the relationship between the city in speech and the "real world" is an issue from the beginning. As Danielle Allen points out, this is not just an issue for the *Republic*, although it is foregrounded there. The imaginary and the real are always intermingled in the "real world." "Our real worlds," she writes, "are constructed as much out of conceptual orders and symbol systems as out of wood, steel, and concrete."[9]

---

[7] τελέως ἀγαθὴν.

[8] Brann, *The Music of the Republic*, 116.

[9] In the same article, Allen engages this same thought in order to contextualize the utopian character of the *Republic* in a very helpful way: "To write a utopia is to invoke an explicit distinction between 'imagined' worlds and 'real' worlds. Yet commentators on Plato's *Republic* have typically been dragged down—despite the text's many flights of fancy—into questions of *realia* when considering the political institutions proposed in the text. They ask, 'Can these imagined institutions be put into practice?' which is also to ask, 'Can this imagined place become real?' The question of whether the *Republic's* institutions can be realized suggests that the 'imagined institutions' and 'real institutions' somehow exist in completely separate cognitive domains; and that the imaginary has to be translated into the 'real' before the two can be properly compared or the imaginary world assessed. The real, on this account, refers to the material world.

While the frame of the *Republic* emphasizes the involvement of the ideal in our apprehension of the real beyond our typical awareness of it, it also mirrors a dynamic that is always at work in our attempts to engage the intelligibility of the world. We employ our imagination in order to make sense of political realities in the *Republic* and in life. And, perhaps even more strikingly, it is only with the aid of the imagination that we can work to alter political realities. Or, as Allen puts it, "The *Republic* operates on the basis of two assumptions about the imagination: first that it is a fundamental component of the real, and also plastic or malleable, and second that these features make the imagination an instrument for transforming culture." [10] In this sense, the *Republic* may emphasize imagination in a way that appears distant from political philosophy, but actually it engages the imagination in a way shared by everyone who has ever aspired to enact reform in politics or in one's own soul.

Allen's account of the ubiquitous presence of imagination in political theory and political reform points to another way that a focus on the psychology of the *Republic* need not entail a rejection of political interpretations. We may disagree on the priority of the accounts in the text (i.e., whether the political teaching or psychological teaching of the *Republic* is presented as more fundamental) without excluding the profundity of both. I understand the psychological inquiry to drive the construction of the political model to the point that fidelity to the former creates

---

But of course, the 'real' does not consist only of the material stuff of the world around us as embodied in 'things.' Our real worlds are constructed as much out of conceptual orders and symbol systems as out of wood, steel, and concrete. The idea of the 'real' includes the 'normal' or orthodox symbolic systems that members of a community use to organize and make sense of their world. The imaginary, when understood in contrast to the real, includes, among other things, symbolic orders that attempt a certain heterodoxy *vis a vis* the hegemonic conceptual system that defines what is 'real.' A utopian text that sets the imaginary against the real may be asking us to consider not whether a given set of fantastical institutions can be realized but rather whether anything changes in the world that we inhabit if, in our imaginations, we sometimes conceive of 'things' differently than they 'really are.'" Danielle S. Allen, "Envisaging the Body of the Condemned," 113.

[10] Allen, "Envisaging the Body of the Condemned," 134.

distortions in the latter.[11] One could argue that the text works in the opposite direction (i.e. that the commitment to the political inquiry of the *Republic* creates a distorted psychological account). Or one could argue that the city and soul are presented with equal priority. But, it would be absurd to suggest that either the psychological or the political inquiry were not there. Focusing on one of the modes of inquiry in the *Republic*, as long as one's arguments are not reductionist, should serve to illuminate the whole of the text regardless of which way one leans in these debates.

The model of the healthy city (371e) may have been completely good by some as of yet unsupplied definition of the Good, despite Glaucon's dissatisfaction with it. We did not get a chance really to see Socrates' analysis of the healthy city beyond his rhapsodic description of life within it (443c–444a). But, the city in speech under consideration by the interlocutors is the purged city, the one that began fevered and to which a course of remedies has just been painstakingly applied. It is clearly flawed and imperfectly remediated. What could it possibly mean to say that this city is completely good?

One must speculate at this point, since there is no argument or explanation explicitly given in the dialogue, but I think the key is to think of the goodness of the model in terms of the dynamics it was designed to illustrate. The healthy city was an incomplete and unrealistic model of the human soul, and Glaucon was right to be dissatisfied with it even if it would have been sufficient to support a set of answers to the questions he and Adeimantus had asked Socrates about justice. *Eros* was missing in the healthy city in speech, and there is no human soul that exists without *eros*.

---

[11] For example, while Julia Annas pushes harder against political readings of the *Republic* than I do, her account of the primacy of the soul in the analogy seems exactly right: "It is sometimes thought that the structural analogy between the soul of the individual and the organization of the state implies that neither can be properly studied in independence, and thus that either can have interpretive primacy; it is taken to imply a politicized ethics and an ethicized politics. Nothing overtly in the dialogue justifies so strong an interpretation, however. What is actually said is that the state is brought in to illuminate the soul, because justice in the state is supposedly easier to discern (368d-369a)." Julia Annas, *Platonic Ethics Old and New* (Ithaca: Cornell UP, 1999), 80.

The use of the world *teleos* for "complete," in the description of the city as "completely good"[12] at 427e suggests this sense of fulfilment or *telos*. If the city in speech is well-formed,[13] then the model will be *teleos*, complete. It will have within it everything we need it to have. The model of the city may now be said to be completely good[14] because it appears to contain all the essential elements of the soul that it is constructed to reflect, not because it, in itself, reflects perfection. By the same logic, the healthy city may be said to have been perfect, but not completely good. Insofar as human beings are not perfectly balanced and self-contained (leaving aside the question of whether or not we are perfectible), a model of the human that presents them as perfectly balanced and self contained is not a good model. Although it appears to be a paradox, any model of the human that presents perfection is not "completely good."[15]

The unlikely combination of being perfect but not "completely good" also occurs in the account of Eden in Genesis in an analogous way.[16] Now that the fevered city has been purged, we can see that resemblance even more clearly. While Eden might seem to offer a paradisiacal human way of life, only a little bit of thought makes it clear that life in

---

[12] τελέως ἀγαθήν.

[13] ὀρθῶς.

[14] τελέως ἀγαθήν.

[15] Ronna Burger, expanding on an argument introduced by Seth Benardete, argues that the soul presented in Book IV is represented in a "thumotic mode," and that it only includes reason in its prohibitive function. As such, it is an inadequate representation of a human soul. While I think *logismos* plays a more important role in the Leontius and Odysseus stories than Burger and Benardete do, I agree with them completely on the inadequacy of this model of the soul. *Nous* will not be drawn out of the image and developed until Book VI, so it is only there that we will have all the essential functions of the soul explicitly included in the model; only there, in Book VI and following, will it be possible to give a complete account of what a healthy soul looks like. My argument here is that this model, which is inadequate in itself, is adequate to address Glaucon and Adeimantus' original question about whether justice or injustice was a better organizing principle for a human life. In the sense of being an adequate schema to support an inquiry into the answer of that question, I believe that the purged city/soul is "completely good." Burger, "The Thumotic Soul, p. 151–167; Seth Benardete, *Socrates' Second Sailing*, 91–102.

[16] Genesis 1–3.

the garden as it is described in *Genesis* does not really describe the human condition, or perhaps it would be more precise to say it does not present a fully formed model human experience.[17] Consider what it would be like to live without shame, without needs, and with an unmediated connection to a divine creator. What would it mean to be human, but to lack self-awareness? What would a human life without any scarcity, necessity, or desire look like? What would it mean to possess an intelligence capable of apprehending the perfectly good and perfectly powerful ground of our being? These are excellent questions for drawing more clearly the boundaries of the human condition, but they do so by coloring outside the lines. The paradise of Eden is a world in which we do not face the dynamics that make human life the most difficult, but these are also the dynamics that define the human condition, per se. The Garden of Eden may be a paradise, but it is not populated by human beings.

If we focus on the terms used for analysis in the previous paragraph, is not difficult to see the analogy between Eden and the healthy city. Socrates portrays the way of life in the healthy city as a paradise. But precisely what makes it paradisiacal is that it offers an escape from the definitive challenges of being human. The healthy city is perfect, but it does not represent the completeness of a human life. The purged city, on the other hand, is human. The introduction of *eros* into the city creates an illness, but the city has resources to combat its fever and become purged, if not wholly healed.

In the sense that the fever engendered by *eros* is a necessary part of the human condition, the completely good model of the human soul would be one that wholly accounts for, incorporates, and responds to *eros,* not one that ignores it. Likewise, the completely good city in speech, which is designed to illuminate the inner workings of a human

---

[17] There are strains of Jewish and Christian thought that attribute one form of humanity to Adam and Eve in the garden and another form of humanity to those of us who exist in a post-lapsarian world. St. Thomas Aquinas is among them. But, even in these accounts it is clear that no other human beings have participated in this form of humanity, so I believe it is more accurate to argue that the form of life that existed before the fall and the form of life that exists in Socrates' healthy city are a not another form of humanity. They represent a pre-human or non-human mode of existence.

soul, would be one that was well-founded in part by its successful response to the tendencies of *eros* to compromise health and overstep bounds, not one that left *eros* out of its constitution. This is one of the reasons why Socrates will later say that it was good that they took the detour of Books V–VII, even though he was reluctant to go that way.

Whether one accepts this or some other explanation of the claim that a well-founded city will be completely good, Socrates' next bit of strategy remains problematic. Since the city is completely good, Socrates says, "Clearly, it will be wise, courageous, moderate and just" [18] (427e). Let us bracket the question of whether this is a good list of virtues or whether or not more needs to be said about moving straight from complete goodness to the possession of all the virtues, and instead focus on the next step in the argument.[19] At 428d, Socrates says that if we find three of the virtues in the city in speech, then we will have found justice in the remainder.[20] This is very odd.

The interlocutors have just engaged in a very long, very detailed conversation about life in the fevered/purged city that included consideration of dozens of different specialists (teachers, doctors, judges, and lawyers, not to mention swineherds, jewelry makers, etc.) and the complicated and multi-faceted responsibilities of the guardians and auxiliaries. How could Socrates seriously propose that the virtues are the only four things in the city or, even more ridiculously, that by finding three of them the fourth would be obvious? The nature of the city in speech as an architectonic ideal is rarely more evident than in this moment where Socrates claims to be able to locate justice by process of elimination. The virtues, these "four things" Socrates will locate in the city, will be presented as relationships between the parts of the city/soul defined in the conversation that occurs from 435b to 441c. So, when Socrates says that

---

[18] δῆλον δὴ ὅτι σοφή τ' ἐστὶ καὶ ἀνδρεία καὶ σώφρων καὶ δικαία.

[19] Thrasymachus, for example, denied that justice should be understood as a virtue at all.

[20] ὥσπερ τοίνυν ἄλλων τινῶν τεττάρων, εἰ ἕν τι ἐζητοῦμεν αὐτῶν ἐν ὁτῳοῦν, ὁπότε πρῶτον ἐκεῖνο ἔγνωμεν, ἱκανῶς ἂν εἶχεν ἡμῖν, εἰ δὲ τὰ τρία πρότερον ἐγνωρίσαμεν, αὐτῷ ἂν τούτῳ ἐγνώριστο τὸ ζητούμενον: δῆλον γὰρ ὅτι οὐκ ἄλλο ἔτι ἦν ἢ τὸ ὑπολειφθέν.

by locating three of the virtues we will have already found, by process of elimination, the fourth, what this seems to mean is that together the virtues make possible a complete speech about the human soul. Everything in the model should be intelligible according to these three parts understood in terms of these four relationships. If this were not the case, then it would not be possible to find justice by process of elimination.

Because the virtues are presented as relationships among the three parts of the soul, the claim that the virtues collectively offer an exhaustive definition of the excellence of a human soul also implies that these three parts of soul are sufficient elements for a model of the soul that leaves nothing out. We need not appeal to any other elements in order to give a complete definition of the city/soul. We have all we need to tell a complete speech about the purged soul. *Epithumia*, *thumos*, and *logismos* are presented here as sufficient categories of soul. Wisdom, courage, moderation, and justice are presented as sufficient relationships between these elements.

It is difficult not to seem to contradict oneself when talking about the completeness of the Book IV model of the city/soul in a larger account that argues for a substantial expansion of the model in Books V–VII. My contention is that the purged city/soul that is completed in Book IV is sufficient for an inquiry into the nature of justice and its merits relative to injustice, which was the original ambition of the dialogue. The purged city model is insufficient for an inquiry into the highest version of a just life, however, because it has no capacity to orient itself to the Good. So, as a model of the soul intended to support an inquiry into the philosophical life, it is not at all complete. But, for the purposes for which it was explicitly designed at this moment of the dialogue, it is.[21]

[21] I do not mean to suggest that the model of the soul that the interlocutors "complete" at this point of the dialogue is, indeed, complete, so I do not disagree with interpretations such as the one presented by Laurence D. Cooper that argue "What is needed to do justice to Socrates' account, and hence to the dialogue as a whole, is a psychodynamic interpretation, one that recognizes and concentrates on the forces that operate within and among the various parts of the soul—the forces that transcend the tripartite structure—and not just the structure itself." In fact, I will take Cooper's argument one step further: not only are we lacking an account of the dynamic forces of the soul in the model pre-

But if this simple, architectonic model with three elements and four dynamics is "completely good,[22] how should we make sense of the account that runs from the last part of Book II through the first third of Book IV? Socrates and Glaucon may "find" *thumos* in a brief exchange from 439e to 441c, but their quick, productive conversation about the parts of the soul is only possible because of their long, circuitous conversation about the role of the auxiliaries in the city in speech and its implications for the other elements and dynamics in the model. The quick, clear definitions of appetite and reason are, likewise, only possible because of the hard dialectical labor regarding the education of the guardians. The account in Book IV of the parts of the soul and the virtues is complete, but the path to it (at least in the *Republic*) has to run through Books II and III.

If the central aim of 368c–427c is to develop the ideas of each of the parts of the soul and to lay the groundwork for Socrates' eventual account of the proper dynamics of their interrelationships; then, education is not the central concern of that long section of text, although it appears to be. This is a subtle and difficult point. Of course, Socrates and other interlocutors discuss education and, because of that, there are lessons to be learned about education in 368c-427c. But, I do not believe we are given an account of the process of education in this part of the *Republic*. Instead, we are given a story that helps us see the proper ends of education. This is not an account, however, that could or should be emulated in any educational endeavor. It is not a curriculum, it offers no pedagogy, and it is not a template for educational policy. [23]

---

sented in Book IV, we also lack one of the central functions of soul, *noesis*, which will not explicitly be added to the model until Book VI. Laurence D. Cooper, "Beyond the Tripartite Soul: The Dynamic Psychology of the *Republic*," *Review of Politics* 63, no. 2 (Spring 2001): 341–372.

[22] τελέως ἀγαθὴν.

[23] Leon Harold Craig points to the mechanism by which the city in speech grows to highlight its artificiality. There is no growth or reproduction of any kind in the healthy (and then purged) city. There is only addition: "[H]aving established strict occupational specialization as the basic principle of their regime, their own particular city in *logos* initially grows in size—not by natural mechanisms of sexual reproduction but by more specialized craftsmen being

One way of making my point in Platonic shorthand would be to say that in Book III and the sections of text that ramp up and down from it, Socrates discusses the education of the guardians and auxiliaries, not the education of a human being. The latter will be the central topic of Book VII. This is not a fully satisfying answer, even if decoded, because, as Socrates will argue repeatedly in Books V–VII that appetite cannot be educated (or even trained); it has to be contained.[24] The only parts of the soul that are educable are reason (the guardians) and, in a more limited but still important sense, spirit (the auxiliaries). The answer has to be a bit subtler.

One of the most confusing aspects of this understanding of Books II–IV as the specification of a *telos* for justice rather than account of the education of the soul is explaining how the account of the education of the guardians should not be read as an allegorical account of the education of *thumos*. Socrates describes musical and gymnastic training in great detail and explicitly says that both are aimed at the cultivation of the

---

added in speech as a need for them is recognized." *The War Lover: A Study of Plato's* Republic (Toronto: University of Toronto Press, 1996), 213.

[24] One of the clearest accounts in the *Republic* of how *epithumia* can be managed but not educated comes in the form of the chimera-like image of the soul presented at around 588c in Book IX. There, *epithumia* is imagined as a many-headed beast, and there is no suggestion of its being trainable. One manages the beast by feeding the good heads to strengthen them and starving the bad ones to weaken them; Socrates likens the activity to what a farmer does with his livestock. *Epithumia* can be shaped in this way throughout the *Republic*, but it cannot be educated. It is not capable of listening to reason. In the secondary literature, Joshua Wilburn presents a compelling case for this reading by looking at all of the explicit references in the *Republic* to reason and spirit attempting to control appetite and showing that it is always done by force or fear, and never by persuasion. Wilburn also takes on the passage in Book VIII often cited by those who argue that appetite is open to persuasion. He argues that the issue at 554cd, Socrates' criticism of the oligarch, is not that he comports himself to his appetites improperly when he uses force and fear to control them, but that the oligarch has let unnecessary appetites arise and thrive in his soul. Wilburn, Joshua. "Is Appetite Ever 'Persuaded'?: An Alternative Reading of *Republic* 544c–d," *History of Philosophy Quarterly* 31, no. 3 (2014).

souls of the guardians. Why not take this to mean that they are accounts of the education of the part of the soul the guardians represent in the city in speech? My short answer is that the Book II–IV account shows clearly and in detail what *thumos* should be able to do, and that the proper activities of *thumos* described in this section of text (i.e., the Male Drama) continue to constitute a substantial part of the legitimate role of *thumos* for the remainder of the dialogue. But the account of how one should develop those capacities is not presented in Books II–IV. Like so much of what is elaborated in Books V–VII, references to the origins (*genesis*), training (*trophe*), and education (*paideia*) of *thumos* pop up in Books II–IV, but they are undeveloped. The reason internal to the structure of the text that they cannot yet be developed is that *thumos* cannot be educated in abstraction from the rest of the human soul-from the wholeness of a human life. We can talk about *epithumia*, *thumos*, and *logismos* separately if we want to know about their specific roles—what is required of them in order for a soul to be just. But we can not talk about the development of any of them without considering them together as abstracted parts of an organic whole, which is precisely what happens in Books V–VII.

It is necessary for Socrates' account of education to have a *telos*, and this section of the *Republic* provides just that; but the account is not yet fully accessible to the interlocutors in 368c to 427c. They cannot yet see each of the parts of the city/soul clearly enough in themselves or in their proper relationships to support an appreciation of the teleological nature of this part of the dialectic. The second two-thirds of Book IV (427c–445e) begin to provide this perspective by allowing readers and interlocutors alike to step back from model and see it whole. The bulk of Book IV provides a necessary synoptic moment in which each of the terms (both for the city and the soul) are clearly defined and where, in part because of this clarity, it is possible to begin to see how each part should function in relation to the others. This is where we begin to be able to rub justice in the city in speech together with justice in the soul like fire sticks and hope that justice itself sparks into view.

When each of the parts of the soul is clarified in Book IV, each will already have a shape and a character because of the founding of the most necessary city in Book II. Each will be recognizable because of the dialectical work done to construct the city in speech that has led to their definition. Much of what will be at stake in defining the parts of the soul and in inquiring into their interrelationships will already be on the table through their analogs in the city in speech. So although the parts of the soul are emerging explicitly for the first time in the latter part of Book IV, readers of the *Republic* and its interlocutors are well prepared to engage them. This is often how Socratic/Platonic dialectic works.[25]

How exactly does Socrates describe each of these parts of the soul, how do they line up with the parts of the city that have already emerged dialectically, and what are the terms that define their proper interrela-

---

[25] As M. F. Burnyeat notes, a benefit of this approach to justice through the imagery and structure of the city in speech is that one may engage in a robust inquiry into the nature and structure of justice without having first to engage the more difficult and refined concerns that attend an inquiry into the nature of the most just (i.e. philosophical) life. "[Plato] takes great care, when writing the *Republic*, not to make the main moral argument depend on the high metaphysics of the Theory of Forms. That would be on the map of the 'longer route,' but readers find it confirmed in the 'digression' (so called at 543c) of the 'central books' V–VII. The welcome implication is that we do not have to understand or believe the Theory of Forms to be motivated to pursue justice for its own sake, as an intrinsic good." M.F. Burnyeat, "The Presidential Address: The Truth of Tripartition," *Proceedings of the Aristotelian Society* 106 (2006) 8.

Waller Newell makes a similar point from a different angle. Rather than emphasizing the value of arriving at a model for justice that does not depend on the Theory of Forms, he focuses on the value of modeling justice in a city purged of *eros*. "By 'pleasure' I mean here, specifically, the 'feverish' pleasures of spontaneous *eros*—the longing for all varieties of luxury and refinement—that Glaucon introduced in Book 2 when he rebelled against the sobriety of the City of Sows. By agreeing to banish these unreformed pleasures and longings from the class of Auxiliaries, Socrates and Glaucon excluded from the outset the possibility that *eros* could be rehabilitated by the kind of educational and eudaimonistic ascent to virtue that Diotima thought inherent in the nature of *eros* itself. At the same time, however, they have educated the Auxiliaries in such a way as to make them friendly—a friendship mediated by the harmoniousness of the cosmos instilled in their characters through their poetic and gymnastic training. In other words, unlike Diotima, Socrates in the Republic explores, through the elaboration of a civic education, the prospect that citizens can be friends without being lovers of the beautiful and good" Waller R. Newell, *Ruling Passion: The Erotics of Statecraft in Platonic Political Philosophy*, (Lanham, MD: Roman and Littlefield, 2000) 127.

tionships? In particular, what is justice? At 435a, Socrates and Glaucon are in agreement that they have successfully located wisdom, courage, moderation, and, by process of elimination, justice in the city in speech. So, it is at this point they turn to an attempt to locate each of these virtues in the soul. The plan is to find justice in the soul and justice in the city in speech, then to bring them together "like fire sticks" to see if a clear idea of justice will "spark." There is a problem, however—the definition of justice (and the other virtues) in the city in speech are all descriptions of relationships between the parts of the city, and it is not obvious that the soul has parts, much less parts that are analogous to the parts of the city in speech.[26]

Socrates does not, however, look to the city in speech to find the parts of the soul; he looks to human life. As promised, justice in the soul and justice in the city in speech are derived independently. But, the city in speech is not a description of an actual city. It is a construct, and it was put together by Socrates, who knew all along what the purpose of the city in speech was to be. Of course the soul has parts that are sufficiently analogous to the city in speech. The city in speech was built as an image

---

[26] Michael Morris characterizes the challenge facing Socrates and his interlocutors at this juncture of the argument this way: "The passage from 435c to 441b has some claim to being the most fundamental argument in the *Republic*. Although the work is often treated as a work of political philosophy, the official rationale for introducing a discussion of the state at all is merely that it will enable us to see more easily what it is for a single person to be just, because in a city we see the same thing on a larger scale. Justice in the city turns out to be a matter of its three functionally defined classes standing in appropriate relations to each other, so justice in a person requires there to be comparable parts of a person. On Socrates' account, this means that we need to find analogues in the soul for the rulers of the city, for the city's security forces, and for those who supply the city's material needs. It is natural enough to regard reason, spirit, and the appetites as psychological analogues, in some sense of these three classes in the city. But a claim as vague as this is not enough for Socrates: he needs reason, spirit, and appetites to be capable of standing in the same kinds of relations to each other as the classes of the city do, if he is to use justice in the city to shed light on justice in the person. In effect, he needs reason, spirit, and the appetites to be three different political agents within the same person." Michael Morris, "*Akrasia* in the *Protagoras* and the *Republic*," *Phronesis* 5, no. 3, 2006, 205–206

of the soul for the purposes of this argument. So, the work of finding the psychological analogs to the parts of the city in speech is quick and clear, though not simple.

First, at 436b, Socrates presents a principle: "the same thing cannot do or undergo opposite things; not, at any rate, in the same respect, in relation to the same thing, at the same time."[27] Then, after a bit of clarification, he presents the case of one who chooses not to have a drink even though he is thirsty (439c) as an example that violates that principle. The argument is that if a human being is capable of simultaneously wanting and not wanting to drink (i.e., experiencing thirst and choosing not to drink), then the human soul must have at least two parts, the appetitive part experiences thirst and the calculating part does not want to drink.

In order to match the structure of the city in speech, the human soul must have a third part. To illuminate this yet to be named third part of the soul, Socrates turns the interlocutors to the story of Leontius (439e), which begins with much the same dynamic as the case of thirst. A part of Leontius wants to look at the corpses lying outside the city walls of Athens, but another part of him is disgusted by them and does not want to look.[28] The appetitive and calculating parts of the soul (*epithumia* and

---

[27] δῆλον ὅτι ταὐτὸν τἀναντία ποιεῖν ἢ πάσχειν κατὰ ταὐτόν γε καὶ πρὸς ταὐτὸν οὐκ ἐθελήσει ἅμα, ὥστε ἄν που εὑρίσκωμεν ἐν αὐτοῖς ταῦτα γιγνόμενα.

[28] For two brilliant readings of the Leontius episode in the *Republic* see Seth Benardete's *Socrates Second Sailing* and Danielle Allen "Envisaging the Body of the Condemned." Benardete (and Ronna Burger in an essay that expands on this section of Benardete's argument) looks to the story of Odysseus presented alongside the Leontius story to open an interpretation that emphasizes the role of *thumos* in Leontius's soul. They argue that the internal conflict Odysseus experiences in Polyphemus' cave is the basis of the model Socrates presents. Allen contextualizes the Leontius episode within the conventions of criminality and punishment in Classical Athens, indicating that there is a great deal at stake in this episode beyond its fundamental importance to the development of the psychological thread of inquiry that runs through the *Republic*. Here is a brief glimpse of her sense of the meaning of this scene: "An image is worth a thousand explicated ideas, and so was the sight of the corpses beside the walls of Athens. Lying on the side of the road, the corpses were a visible product of the Athenian regime. Their exposed forms bespoke the practices and principles of the political order that had installed them in the city's landscape; they symbol-

logismos) are in conflict, indicating that they are distinct from one another. But, Leontius is not just conflicted, he is also angry. This anger, which occurs simultaneously with the appetitive desire to look at the corpses and the calculating desire not to look, implies a third part of the soul, spirit (*thumos*).[29]

It is worth noting here that there is no activity of soul in the Leontius episode capable of determining whether or not looking at the corpses is good. The part that comes to be known as *logismos* is disgusted by the corpses and would prefer not to look because, presumably, the vision will create internal disharmony. The part that comes to be known as *epithumia* is curious and would prefer to look. And the part that comes to be known as *thumos* is angry about the conflict between *logismos* and *epithumia*. But none of these parts is capable of looking at these choices in light of an external standard or of defending any of those preferences in terms of a principle. There is no argument for why turning away in disgust or indulging in curiosity would be Leontius's proper response, and there is no way for the soul to appeal to an external standard according to which one could adjudicate between these preferences. The soul of Book

---

ized Athenian power. To look at the corpses without being too discomfited was to accept the forms of power, the penal practices, and the ideologies that not only culminated in but also validated their presence in the landscape." Danielle Allen "Envisaging the Body of the Condemned: The Power of Platonic Symbols," 137; Seth Benardete, *Socrates' Second Sailing*; Ronna Burger, "The Thumotic Soul."

[29] My interpretation of the Leontius episode finds the source of Leontius's anger in his *thumos*, not his *epithumia*. This is, in fact, what I take the central point of the story to be. So I disagree with commentators such as Rana Saadi Leibert who take the episode to mean that "the inclination to pity and sympathize with others, as well as to pity and grieve for oneself, emerges as a base, appetitive impulse that jeopardizes our well-being and clouds our moral judgment." Leontius's judgment is, indeed, clouded, and his emotional response has something to do with why that is the case, but the problem is not that he feels pity for those who are now corpses, if he does, but instead that he is not successfully bringing that pity (or curiosity or outrage or fear) into harmony with what he believes he should feel about them. (Rana Saadi Leibert, "Pity and Disgust in Plato's *Republic*: The Case of Leontius," *Classical Philology*, Vol. 108, No. 3 (July 2013), 179–201.)

IV is simply not capable of these activities, but the soul of Book VI will be.

Socrates successfully negotiated the first task he set for himself in preparation for unpacking the teaching of the city in speech for the soul. He located the three parts of soul analogous to the three parts of the city. His next task is to see if there are virtues in the soul analogous to the virtues the interlocutors located in the city. And, of course, there are. One is *just* (*dikaios*[30]) if each of the parts of one's soul does its own work (441d). One is *courageous* (*andreios*[31]) if the spirited part defends against internal and external threats according to the direction of the calculating part (442b). One is *wise* (*sophos*[32]) if the calculating part rules one's soul and has knowledge of what is advantageous for each part and the whole (442c).[33] One is *moderate* (*sophrosyne*[34]) if all of the parts of oneself are in agreement that the calculating part should rule (442d).

At this point (443c) Socrates goes as far as to say that they have fulfilled the "dream"[35] that inspired their inquiry. They have defined justice and sketched how it would operate optimally in a flourishing soul. But, Socrates does not move on to an inquiry into the nature of injustice immediately. He takes a moment to make sure the image of justice they have worked toward together is absolutely clear. And Socrates is almost as rhapsodic about the interior life of one whose soul mirrors the purged city as he was at 372a when he described the way of life in the healthy

---

[30] δίκαιος.

[31] ἀνδρεῖος.

[32] σοφός.

[33] Once again, Socrates account presumes capacities that will only emerge later in the dialogue. The possibility of wisdom is predicated the existence of true knowledge, and it will not be possible to know whether or not we have apprended the truth at least until we have the capacity for *noesis*. Like the need for a source of light that Socrates mentions at 427d, this comment on true knowledge connects the model of soul in Book IV to the more elaborate model that emerges in Books V–VII. They are the same model, and this earlier form implies the existence of elements within it that will not emerge explicitly until later.

[34] σωφροσύνη.

[35] ἐνύπνιον.

city. Socrates says that the just person is concerned with "what is inside" and "what is his own." He "becomes a friend to himself" and harmonizes the three parts within him into a whole "as if he were marking the notes at low end, the middle, and the high end of a musical scale." And he does all things, whether they are concerned with wealth, health, or politics, in a way that will "preserve this harmony" (443c–444a).[36]

The understanding of justice that Socrates describes in this passage is essentially internal to an individual, even though it also plays out externally in all of his endeavors. It is concerned with what is inside a human being. It is self-government and self-friendship. Socrates goes beyond clarifying his definitions, however. In this elaboration on justice, Socrates sets out the central tenet of his argument for justice being superior to injustice. Justice is a harmony or unity (*harmonia*[37] can mean either), which is created by wise application of true knowledge. Injustice is the disharmony that ignorance cannot overcome; it is characterized by conflict, pain, and inefficacy. We are not yet privy to exactly how injustice manifests as disharmony or exactly why a disharmonious life might be unproductive and unpleasant. While Thrasymachus planted those seeds in Book I, they sprout here, and Socrates is ready to begin tending

[36] τὸ δέ γε ἀληθές, τοιοῦτόν τι ἦν, ὡς ἔοικεν, ἡ δικαιοσύνη ἀλλ' οὐ περὶ τὴν ἔξω πρᾶξιν τῶν αύτοῦ, ἀλλὰ περὶ τὴν ἐντός, ὡς ἀληθῶς περὶ ἑαυτὸν καὶ τὰ ἑαυτοῦ, μὴ ἐάσαντα τἀλλότρια πράττειν ἕκαστον ἐν αὑτῷ μηδὲ πολυπραγμονεῖν πρὸς ἄλληλα τὰ ἐν τῇ ψυχῇ γένη, ἀλλὰ τῷ ὄντι τὰ οἰκεῖα εὖ θέμενον καὶ ἄρξαντα αὐτὸν αὑτοῦ καὶ κοσμήσαντα καὶ φίλον γενόμενον ἑαυτῷ καὶ συναρμόσαντα τρία ὄντα, ὥσπερ ὅρους τρεῖς ἁρμονίας ἀτεχνῶς, νεάτης τε καὶ ὑπάτης καὶ μέσης, καὶ εἰ ἄλλα ἄττα μεταξὺ τυγχάνει ὄντα, πάντα ταῦτα συνδήσαντα καὶ παντάπασιν ἕνα γενόμενον ἐκ πολλῶν, σώφρονα καὶ ἡρμοσμένον, οὕτω δὴ πράττειν ἤδη, ἐάν τι πράττῃ ἢ περὶ χρημάτων κτῆσιν ἢ περὶ σώματος θεραπείαν ἢ καὶ πολιτικόν τι ἢ περὶ τὰ ἴδια συμβόλαια, ἐν πᾶσι τούτοις ἡγούμενον καὶ ὀνομάζοντα δικαίαν μὲν καὶ καλὴν πρᾶξιν ἣ ἂν ταύτην τὴν ἕξιν σῴζῃ τε καὶ συναπεργάζηται, σοφίαν δὲ τὴν ἐπιστατοῦσαν ταύτῃ τῇ πράξει ἐπιστήμην, ἄδικον δὲ πρᾶξιν ἣ ἂν ἀεὶ ταύτην λύῃ, ἀμαθίαν δὲ τὴν ταύτῃ αὖ ἐπιστατοῦσαν δόξαν.

[37] ἁρμονία.

to them immediately.[38] We have sketched the *telos* of our argument; what remains is to consider how to approach it, both in our inquiry but also in our own lives. And, as we approach it (in both senses), we will have to revise our understanding of that *telos*. The process of mutual reconsideration and redefinition is at the heart of dialectic, so nothing is fixed in stone.[39] But, we are making very good progress. We have both to reconsider and revise our understandings of the city in speech and the structure of the soul in light of one another, but insofar as both are images of justice, they constitute together the just city/soul which will itself be reconsidered through the dialectical inquiry into its comparison to injustice in the city/soul.

The dialectical structure of the inquiry exists in the most basic elements of the arguments of the *Republic* and in its most elaborate and well-developed implications. On the psychological level, the case of Leontius is a ground zero of sorts. In the mutually illuminating dialectical inquiry into calculation (*logismos*) and appetite (*epithumia*), both activities of soul are better defined, but our consideration of them also generates the need for a third activity of soul (*thumos*). As the inquiry continues, the dialectic will also reveal the insufficiency of *logismos* to account for human rationality and another activity of soul will be added to the model, *nous*. The expansion of the city/soul to include *noetic* activity, makes it possible for the dialectic to reach up and out to higher, more complicated, and more carefully defined aspects

---

[38] It will not be until the last lines of Book IX (592b) that the speech about the superiority of justice over injustice is completed. Practically the whole of the *Republic* is drawn toward the *telos* that is sketched in these lines.

[39] One of the chief criticisms Socrates levies at Glaucon and Adeimantus in Book II when they present to Socrates the challenge of the perfectly just man who appears perfectly unjust and the perfectly unjust man who appears perfectly just is that they are statues—made of stone, not flesh. This seems at least to mean two things: (1) that they are not really images of livable human lives and (2) they are presented as elements in the argument that he is not at liberty to revise. The answer to the latter criticism comes almost at the end of the dialogue, at 612c, when Socrates ask to have returned to him what he had granted them for the sake of argument; and that turns out to be the possibility of those statues actually manifesting as human lives. The response to the former criticism seems to me both immediate and persistant. Helpful models of human lives cannot be made of inert like stone; they must move and live.

of the human condition. The constraints change multiple times throughout the dialogue, and the topics shift, but every advance deeper into conditions and further out into implications of their inquiry is made by a dialectical movement.

Socrates will not get to turn to injustice immediately. One can already see Polemarchus and Adeimantus whispering. They are not enthralled by Socrates' paean to individual justice. They are still thinking about the politics of the city in speech, and they have some big questions. In just a moment, they will interrupt the conversation and throw Socrates into an even longer detour than Glaucon prompted by voicing his dissatisfaction with the healthy city. What do Polemarchus and Adeimantus think is missing in the city/soul as it is portrayed in Book IV? Why does Socrates agree to this great and blasphemous diversion from his charted course, especially when he is so clearly on the right track? That is a long and complicated story that I hope to tell well. The key to it is Socrates' claim at 504d that there is something yet greater than justice and the virtues—the idea of the Good. And, as beautiful as the just life is, it cannot compare to the best life. Polemarchus and Adeimantus may provide the prompt for Socrates to begin this dangerous conversation, and Socrates may be sincerely afraid of the effect this particular dialectic may have on his great souled interlocutors, but this is the dialogue Socrates was made to lead, for it shows the way, the perils, and the promise of the philosophical life.

The detour that begins in Book V and runs through Book VII is the central focus of this book. The analysis of Books II–IV in the last two chapters is here to set the stage to frame the argument. The model of the city in speech is about to change again, and the model of the soul will change with it. But most of the elements are set, as are the basic dynamics that exist among them. Throughout the analysis of Books V-VII, we will continue to attempt to understand the human condition according to the three-part soul of Book IV: *epithumia*, *thumos*, and *logismos*; but we will add *nous* to the model when Socrates does in Book VI. We will continue to inquire into the optimal relations between those elements of soul presented as the virtues of Book IV: wisdom, courage, moderation, and justice. And, we will keep an eye out for *eros,* which is already in the city because of Glaucon's intervention at 372d, but which is rarely mentioned by any of Plato's interlocutors in the *Republic* except implicitly.

One rare and odd appearance of *eros* occurs at 401b, where in the context of inquiring into the proper education of the Guardians, Socrates turns the conversation toward the very personal topic of Glaucon's erotic reaction to a boy that he had loved. The context of that part of the dialogue is too elaborate to neglect and a careful treatment of it is too far off my topic to pursue. But, insofar as Socrates and Glaucon are concerned with *eros* and harmony in that part of Book III, we will turn later to a related conversation when the topic of love reemerges near the end of Book V.

Our understanding of each of the virtues will have to shift as the dialectic pushes us deeper into an understanding of the foundations of the arguments that established them and farther out into their implications for the city/soul. The most substantial revisions will follow from the inclusion of *noetic* activity into the model, which was neglected in the healthy/purged city. The most important implication of the inclusion of *nous* will be the recognition that justice, though choiceworthy, is not the highest or best thing—goodness is. This insight, and the description of what it would look like to live a life defined purely by one's love of the Good, points to the most important conclusions Socrates presents in the *Republic*.[40]

[40] Bradley Lewis argues that not only is it legitimate to understand the *Republic* in terms of its focus on moral psychology, but that doing so solves longstanding controversies in Plato scholarship. For example, conventional impediments to reconciling the political philosophies presented in the *Laws* and the *Republic* dissolve when one focuses on the role of the Good in orienting both accounts. He puts it like this: "The problem to be explored in both the *Republic* and the *Laws* is that of identifying a standard by which to explain the defects of traditional regimes. The two dialogues must be regarded as offering two stages of a single answer. The *Republic* treats the question at the level of the individual, the *Laws* at the level of the city. Before one can design a regime with its arrangement of laws and practices, one must understand human nature, human psychology. The *Republic* is precisely this sort of inquiry. It poses the question: why should I behave with justice even if I know that I could successfully prosecute of life of perfect injustice, that is, of tyranny?...From the very first sentence, the *Laws* approaches these [same] questions from the perspective of the laws and regime: from the perspective of the city, from the common as opposed to the private" (348–349). V. Bradley Lewis. "Politeia kai Nomoi: On the Coherence of Plato's Political Philosophy," *Polity* 31, no. 2 (Winter 1998): 331–349.

Part Two

Philosophical *Genesis*, Book V

3

The Female Drama
(The Genesis of Epithumia)

As Book V of the *Republic* opens, Socrates changes the subject from justice to injustice. The purged city was a fine model, and the analysis of that model yielded a definition of justice suitable to investigate the comparative value of justice and injustice for a human life. So, Socrates says, it is time to consider injustice in the four kinds of deficient cities and souls that their inquiry has generated. If all had gone according to Socrates' plan, the interlocutors would have proceeded to compare the form of justice they found in the proper arrangement of the three parts of the purged city/soul with each form of injustice implied by rearranging those parts into other configurations. After comparing the just soul with each of the four unjust souls, they would have determined which was conducive to happiness in each case. At the end of the comparisons, they would have arrived at an answer to their original question: whether it is better to live a just or an unjust life. But, of course, that is not the way the *Republic* goes.

Instead of leaving the just city in speech behind, Adeimantus and Polemarchus insist that Socrates return to elaborate on a matter that they accuse him of intentionally neglecting—the role of women and children in the city. Glaucon joins with them in arresting (*epilambano*[1]) Socrates and insisting that he continue to develop the constitution of the city in speech.[2] Even Thrasymachus, who has been silent since shortly after Socrates made him blush in Book I, adds his voice to the cause (450a).

---

[1] ἐπιλαμβάνω.

[2] Many scholars have commented on the repetition at the beginning of Book V of the "arrest" scene in Book I and how it sets Books V–VII apart. For example: Laurence Lampert, *How Philosophy Became Socratic,* 279, 306, 311–12; Stanley Rosen, *Plato's* Republic, 167–9; Jacob Howland, *The Republic*, 41; Eva

All four of Socrates' most impressive interlocutors in the *Republic* insist that he explain in more detail the role of women and children in the city in speech. Other than the implicit agreement at the beginning of the dialogue that Socrates should stay and talk to them, this is the only time in the dialogue that Glaucon, Adeimantus, Polemarchus, and Thrasymachus are portrayed as agreeing on something. Furthermore, this is, without qualification, the only thing they explicitly agree about.

Specifically, Adeimantus, asks to be told more about (1) how arrangements with women and children will be a case of friends sharing everything in common, (2) how procreation will be handled, (3) and how young children will be reared before they begin their formal education (449d). Socrates capitulates, of course, but reluctantly. He warns that they will have to start from the beginning (450a), that they will be unleashing a "swarm"(*esmos*[3]) of arguments (450a), that they are asking him to produce arguments about things of which he is uncertain (450e), and that what they are doing is frightening (*phoberos*[4]) and treacherous (*sphaleros*[5]) (451a). Socrates says that he is afraid that if he is unsuccessful, he will not only fail himself but also do harm to his friends (451a). He bows to Adrasteia, also known as Nemesis, the goddess who punishes *hubris*. He asks for forgiveness in advance for what he is about to do (451a).[6]

Brann, *The Music of the Republic*, 150; David Roochnik, *The Beautiful City*, 2–4; Leon Harold Craig, *The War Lover*, 185; Diskin Clay, *Platonic Questions*, 247; Leo Strauss, *The City and Man*, 64, 155; Kurt Hildebrandt, *Platon: Logos Und Mythos*, 393; Eric Voegelin, *Order and History, Volume III*, 46–52; and Mark Blitz, *Plato's Political Philosophy*, 169.

[3] ἐσμός.

[4] φοβερός.

[5] σφαλερός.

[6] Laurence Lampert describes Socrates prostrating himself to Adrasteia as "the most breathtaking image in the whole *Republic*," and calls Socrates' account of it his "most solemn speech in the whole *Republic*." Lampert, who casts Socrates in the *Republic* as a new Odysseus, sets the scene this way: "The solemnity of Socrates' speech derives from the greatness of its occasion: returned Odysseus, having manipulated them into compelling him to do what he alone compels himself to do, now embarks on the introduction of a great novelty into the

As we begin to work through the arguments of Book V and their implications for the further development of the city in speech as a model for the soul, we should face the swarm of questions implied and expressed in the rich dramatic opening to this new section of the dialogue. And, since the focus of this study is the psychology of the *Republic*, chief among those questions for our inquiry are: (1) How do the accounts of women and children in the city in speech illuminate the individual soul? (2) What do "procreation" (*genesis)* and "rearing" (*trophe*) mean in the context of an individual soul? (3) And, since Socrates offers us a heuristic for this narrative shift, we must also inquire into why he names it as he does. That is, what does it mean for an inquiry into the psychology of the *Republic* that the dialectic within which the city in speech is constructed in Books II–IV is called a "Male Drama," and the dialectic that begins after Socrates pays his fearful respects to Adrasteia[7] is called the "Female Drama?"[8]

---

stream of Greek wisdom and he cannot know whether introducing the rule of the philosopher will succeed. He stands over an abyss unable to know for certain whether it is possible and, if possible, if it is for the best. He must ask himself: is it a prayer? Fearing that he will bring his genuine friends, the few wise, down with him in this boldest of projects on behalf of wisdom, he in fact offers a prayer, the most solemn of prayers and the only one becoming a philosopher: "I will prostrate myself before Adrasteia." He prays the prayer of a philosopher compelled to act on the grandest scale not knowing whether he can succeed; he submits himself to Nemesis, the necessity that rules all, knowing the rashness of his deed while judging that necessity itself calls it forth." Laurence Lampert, *How Philosophy Became Socratic*, 310–311. Whether or not one follows Lampert on the identification of Socrates with Odysseus, the account of Socrates' fear of the consequences of his impiety and the necessity of taking the risk for the sake of philosophy seem precisely right.

[7] Jacob Howland notes that the reference to Adresteia may also be an allusion to Aeschylus' *Prometheus*. Jacob Howland, *The* Republic*: The Odyssey of Philosophy* (Philadelphia: Paul Dry Books, 2004) 111.

[8] "Female" is my choice of translation for *gynaikeion*/γυναικεῖον mainly because "the Female Drama" is the conventional translation of what Socrates calls the episode that begins in Book V. But, as Mary Townsend notes, any choice of English words is fraught. "This adjective (γυναικεῖον) has a range of meanings, from 'ladylike,' or 'womanly' in a good sense, to 'womanish' or 'effeminate' in the

The dramatic introduction to Book V offers several provocative clues about how Socrates intends to proceed in the dialectic and why he is intimidated by the work that lies ahead. First, Socrates says that they will have to begin again, which suggests that women and children are not a new part of the city in speech that can be tacked on to the account. They are some version of something that already exists in the city in speech, or a basic condition that will change the model fundamentally, or something that pervades the model. Exactly what women and children are to the city in speech is not obvious, and we will have to look carefully at the dialogue to discern their meaning, but that they are central or fundamental or pervasive seems indisputable given that we have to return to the beginning and retrace our steps in order see where they fit in.[9]

---

bad. Socrates uses the word to decry the practice still in use among Greek male soldiers of stripping the corpses of the fallen after a battle, a practice he paints as a womanish custom unworthy of his male and female guardians (469d); I will note that however the reader would wish to gloss this word here, 'feminine' is hardly the right word for tearing valuables away from the dead in a bloody field." Townsend, *The Woman Question*, 15

[9] Steven Forde provides a helpful survey of interpretations of the role of women and children in the *Republic* ("Gender and Justice in Plato," *American Political Science Review* 92, no. 3 [1997]). Susan Muller Okin argues that Plato should be credited with a pioneering argument for women's political equality ("Philosopher Queens and Private Wives: Plato on Women and the Family," *Philosophy and Public Affairs* 6, no. 4 [Summer 1977]: 345–369), while Arlene Saxonhouse ("The Philosopher and the "Female in the Political Thought of Plato," *Political Theory* 4, no. 2 [May 1976]: 195–212), Julia Annas ("Plato's *Republic* and Feminism," in *Philosophy* 51, no. 197 [July 1976]: 307–321), and Allan Bloom (*The* Republic *of Plato*. New York: Basic Books, 1968) argue that Plato is not a feminist. I do not believe that the account women in Book V creates any meaningful equality for women, and Jean Bethke Elshtain (*Public Man, Private Woman: Women in Social and Political Thought*. Princeton: Princeton University Press, 1981) argues that Plato creates gender equality, but at the expense of both male and female identity. Since the publication of Forde's piece, a few important variations on these interpretations have appeared, including Catherine Gardner's argument that women play an important role in Kallipolis, but that they are mainly understood as instrumental in its eugenics project ("The Remnants of the Family: The Role of Women and Eugenics in *Republic* V," *History of Philosophy Quarterly* 17, no. 3 [July 2000]: 217–35); Catherine McKeen's argument that

Secondly, Socrates tells us that the city in speech that includes a fuller explanation of women and children might appear just to be something to be prayed for (*euxos*[10]), rather than something, to be worked for (*ergon*[11]) (450c). That is, it might seem practically impossible. Socrates asks whether or not their hopes for the best city/soul is like a *euxos* several times in Books V and VI (450a, 456b, 461a, 499c, and 540d), and the conclusion seems to be clear at 540d, that they are not. The best city would be difficult to realize, but not impossible.

The idea that what Socrates will present to them might look like a *euxos* is particularly provocative because he seems to be setting it up on the opposite end of the spectrum as *ergon*. That is, the interlocutors ask over and over again whether or not the city in speech can be a "city in deed," an *ergon*; and Socrates admits at 473a that it cannot be fully instantiated in deed. But, he rejects the conclusion that the unattainability of the fully formed *ergon* of Kallipolis implies that it is just a *euxos*, a lofty dream. Instead, it is a model to be strived for and a thing that is achievable in dialectical conversation among great souled friends—a possibility that seems to sit on the line somewhere between *ergon* and *euxos*, but at least closer to *ergon*.

This particular claim points in several directions. It suggests that Socrates might consider the city in speech constructed in Books II–IV to be plausible (or, at least, more plausible than the version of the city in speech they are about to investigate). This is, on the level of political interpretation, implausible. If, for the sake of argument, we bracket the noble lie and even the stringent requirements for qualifying as a complete guardian, achieving the political order described in the city in speech is still extremely implausible, if not practically impossible. If a suitable guardian were to emerge, which is unlikely, the odds that every citizen would agree to his power and commit wholly to their supporting roles in

women must rule in Kallipolis ("Why Women Must Guard and Rule in Plato's 'Kallipolis.'" *Pacific Philosophical Quarterly* 87, no. 4 [December 2006]: 527–48); and Mary Townsend's recontextualization of the role of women portrayed in Book V in the political and religious culture of Classical Athens (*The Woman Question in Plato's* Republic. New York: Lexington Books, 2017).

[10] εὖχος.

[11] ἔργον.

his regime are extremely long. Other necessary conditions for the well-functioning purged city are just as unlikely.

When Socrates warns that including a fuller account of women and children in the city in speech might make their project seem like a *euxos*, it seems far more likely that he is referring to the city/soul's implications for psychology than politics. Socrates seems to be concerned about whether what they have done and will do to describe the proper arrangement of a human soul will seem to be possible or not. This suggests that Socrates may consider the model of the soul in Books II–IV to be apparently achievable, but that the elaboration on which they are about to embark may not be.[12]

Socrates' concern that he and his interlocutors may be developing their image of justice in an apparently implausible way leads to the third dramatic clue in the narrative frame of Book V. Socrates strongly indicates that adding a fuller account of women and children into the city in speech will be dangerous. The germ of this danger appears to be Socrates' fear that he might make justice appear to be unachievable. If Socrates makes justice seem unattainable, he will, first of all, be doing harm to himself because he will look like a fool for devoting himself so completely to something impossible. He says, though, that the threat of appearing ridiculous doesn't trouble him (451a). Instead, what seems to worry Socrates deeply is the risk of hurting his friends. What would become of these great souled, politically powerful men with whom he is having this conversation if Socrates inadvertently convinces them that it is impossible (or radically implausible) to become just? Glaucon, Adeimantus, and Polemarchus (not to mention Thrasymachus) might feel unleashed to a life of injustice—precisely the opposite of what Socrates hopes this conversation (and perhaps every conversation) will encourage. And, of

[12] Catherine Zuckert, commenting on Leo Strauss's long list of quotations from the *Ecclesiazusae* in the *Republic*, notes that Plato underlines the "imaginary and non-historical character" of the dialogue by quoting a play that was not performed until after Socrates' death. Catherine Zuckert, *Plato's Philosophers: The Coherence of the Dialogues* (Chicago: University of Chicago Press, 2009) 353 fn. 134. Leo Strauss, *The City and Man* (Chicago: University of Chicago Press, 1964) 61.

course, the corruption of Socrates' interlocutors in the *Republic* could also be a terrible political outcome for Athens.[13]

Socrates' first move in his reluctant, apparently hubristic, attempt to account for women and children in the purged city/soul is to return to his discussion of the proper natures (*physeis*[14]) of the guardians from Book II. Socrates says that "for people born and educated the way we have described, there is no way to acquire and employ women and children other than to follow the path we first set them on." The Male Drama was not wrong, it was incomplete. So, Socrates says, "let's proceed by giving them corresponding rules for birth and rearing, and see whether or not they are fitting."[15]

The proper place to have introduced women and children in the city in speech would, apparently, have been the first moment the guardians were mentioned. What Socrates said they achieved in the argument was establishing the guardians as guard dogs of their flocks. What they need now to consider are the rules for the *genesis* and *trophe* of those guard dogs. It appears that the argument for establishing the guardians as guard dogs was what Socrates is now calling the "Male Drama,"[16] and now as we consider where those guard dogs came from, their *genesis* and *trophe*, we are turning to "the female."[17]

As I argued in the previous chapter, although much of Books II–IV appears to be about education, an argument about the proper form of education is not actually presented there. What is presented in Books II through the beginning of Book IV is an argument for the *telos* of *logismos*

---

[13] According to Debra Nails, the people present at Cephalus' house for the conversation of the *Republic* represent every sort of person who lived in Athens just before the war, perhaps suggesting that everyone had a stake in what was to come. Debra Nails, "Plato's *Republic* in its Athenian Context," *History of Political Thought* 33, no. 1 (Spring 2012): 3.

[14] φύσεις.

[15] ἀνθρώποις γὰρ φῦσι καὶ παιδευθεῖσιν ὡς ἡμεῖς διήλθομεν, κατ᾽ ἐμὴν δόξαν οὐκ ἔστ᾽ ἄλλη ὀρθὴ παίδων τε καὶ γυναικῶν κτῆσίς τε καὶ χρεία ἢ κατ᾽ ἐκείνην τὴν ὁρμὴν ἰοῦσιν, ἥνπερ τὸ πρῶτον ὡρμήσαμεν...ἀκολουθῶμεν τοίνυν καὶ τὴν γένεσιν καὶ τροφὴν παραπλησίαν ἀποδιδόντες, καὶ σκοπῶμεν εἰ ἡμῖν πρέπει ἢ οὔ. (451c–d)

[16] ἀνδρεῖον δρᾶμα.

[17] τὸ γυναικεῖον.

in a just soul—the realization of a proper education.[18] The full actualization (*telos*) of the calculating part of the soul (*logismos*) is an important and necessary part of an account of education, but it is far from a sufficient one.[19] Because the *telos* of *logismos* includes authority over the other parts (*thumos* and *epithumia*) of a just soul, understanding it involves also understanding a great deal about the whole soul, but it cannot answer at least one essential question: how does one develop a fully formed soul? Or, in simpler terms, how does one become just? Book II–IV give us a target to shoot for, but no instruction in archery.[20] Socrates' answer to that question comes in Book VII and is a continuation of the accounts of

---

[18] As Strauss puts it, "The question of possibility came to the fore only at the beginning of the fifth book as a consequence of an intervention initiated by Polemarchus. The two earlier comparable interventions—that of Glaucon after the description of the healthy city and that of Adeimantus after the abolition of private property and of privacy altogether—were limited to the question of desirability…." Strauss, *The City and Man*, 122.

[19] Eva Brann gives a remarkably economical summary of what was established about the soul in Book IV. "There are then, to begin with, two parts, the rational part (*logistikon*) 'with which man calculates' (*logizetai*), and the desiring part (*epithymetikon*) which is unreasoning (*alogiston*) an in which desire (*epithymia*) is located (49d). Between these two, the forms (*eide*) that are ordinarily recognized, Socrates inserts a pivotal third, the spirited part (t*hymoeides*)… Finally, these three parts are arranged within us as the "three terms of a musical proportion" (443d6), and *thymos* becomes "the in between power" (479d8), which, while itself obedient to reason, can in turn govern the body (403d, 411e6). Brann, *The Music of the Republic*, 162.

[20] While I will later in this study consider the relationship between *logismos* and *nous* in the *Republic* in detail, it is important to notice that Socrates is careful only to refer to the former in Book IV. Once again, Brann's account is extremely helpful. "Why then does Socrates call it the *logistikon,* connecting it explicitly with *logizesthai*, to reckon or to calculate (439d5), rather than with the *logos* of *dialegesthai* (511b4, 534c)? It is because the *logistikon* is a restricted power, a power of planning, whose specific work later does turn out to be calculation (cf. *Nicomachean Ethics* 1139a13), measuring, and weighing—in short, whatever corresponds only to the lower level of knowing power, to that power of mathematical thinking which Glaucon will discover later on as a mean between opinion and knowledge; it will be called *dianoia*." Brann, *The Music of the Republic*, 163–164.

the *genesis* and *trophe* that begin in Book V. All three of these modes of development (*genesis*, *trophe*, and *paideia*) are a part of what Socrates is here calling the Female Drama. They are what was left out of the city/soul of Book IV.

What we have in Books II and III under the guise of the education of the guardians is really an account of their proper characteristics—the full actualization of all of their characteristic determinate potencies. If we were to carry the image of dogs into the contemporary context of breeding and dog shows, we could think of it as their "conformation." Beagles and Great Danes are held to different conformation standards at dog shows, and breeders need to understand what each aims to be before they can undertake a plan to breed a dog to approach those standards. They need an account of what is desirable before they will be in a position to consider the conditions necessary for making the desirable actual. With apologies for the crass example, Books II–IV does the work of specifying (most of) the standards according to which a guardian should be judged (i.e. what is desirable); but it is not until Book V that Socrates begins to inquire into what would need to happen for such a guardian to come into being, (i.e. the conditions for actualizing what has already been determined desirable). For example, when we learn that the courageousness of the guardians requires that they not be told stories that make them fear death (386a), we are not actually being given a curriculum for the guardians. Instead, Socrates is telling us that a guardian's *logismos* must not fear death or be animated by images that feed such fear.

Because of the elaborate accounts of music and gymnastic in Books II and III, we know what needs to be true of the guardians and auxiliaries if they are to be capable of ruling and protecting the city in speech. And, it is these same arguments in Books II and III that show us in Book IV what needs to be true of *thumos* and *logismos* if they are to be capable of ruling and protecting a just soul. But, neither the arguments of Books II and III nor their alignment with the soul in Book IV show what must be true of *thumos* and *logismos* in order for the soul to become just. That is the business of the Female Drama.

My argument, in the briefest terms, is that the Male Drama is an account of the being and actualities of the just soul, and the Female Drama is an account of the becoming and potencies of the just soul (which opens into a consideration of the activity of the most just soul, philosophy). What we know at the end of Book IV is what all of the parts of the soul need to look like in order for that soul to be just. What we begin to consider in Book V is what needs to be true of each part of the soul in order for it to become what Book IV tells us it needs to be. And, as the Female Drama illuminates the Male Drama dialectically, the Male Drama, itself, will require revision. That is, the account of the *telos* of the just soul prompted the inquiry into the origin (*genesis*), nurture (*trophe*), and education (*paideia*) required to approach that *telos*. But when the *genesis*, *trophe*, and *paideia* of the just soul come into focus, they will illuminate things about the *telos* of justice that were not clear before. Generically, this is how Platonic/Socratic dialectic often operates. Specifically, it is the process by which the inquiry into the nature of justice turns into the inquiry into the nature of philosophy in the *Republic*.

Socrates marks the beginning of the Female Drama by saying that we must return to the beginning of our account of the guardians and consider their *genesis* and *trophe* (451d). I will argue that this is, indeed, exactly what he does in Books V and VI. There are three sorts of possibility or becoming that are systematically presented in Books V–VII: *genesis*, *trophe*, and *paideia*, and these three are, for the most part, taken up in Books V, VI, and VII respectively, the three "plays" of Plato's Attic cycle in the central books of the *Republic*. What this implies for the soul is straightforward in principle, but extremely complicated in practice. Books V–VII will take up the potencies of soul necessary for the possibility of becoming just and the processes of becoming that move those potencies into actuality.

Socrates takes the conversation back to the beginning and turns our attention to what it would look like to introduce women and children into the city in speech. So, we find ourselves considering once again the dog-like disposition appropriate to potential guardians; but now we are prompted to consider the case of female dogs. First, we are asked whether female dogs should be considered capable of becoming guard dogs; the answer is a quick yes, they should. This first point about female dogs is not argued, just affirmed. The first claim to be scrutinized is the second one to be made, and it is an apparent implication of the capacity of female dogs to become guard dogs: i.e., female dogs with such a nature should share everything with similarly disposed males, including their nurture (*trophe*) and education (*paideia*, 451e).

The first principle of this further elaboration on the city/soul is that women and men can do the same work, and the first implication of this principle for the city in speech is that they should. This principle is no more argued than any of the principles that led to the organization of the cities constructed in Books II and III (insufficiency, efficiency, and desire). An immediate implication of the assertion that women can and should do the same work as men is that they should be prepared to do this work, just as men are. They should share the same rearing (*trophe)* and education (*paideia*), regardless of the fact that women are, generically, weaker than men (an idea that will be scrutinized at length).

When Socrates says he must go back to the beginning to account for the role of women and children, he does not go back to the most necessary city or the healthy city or even to the structure of the feverish city. He goes to the first moment of the discussion of the nature of the guardians—the beginning of the construction of the purged city. This is the beginning of the account of women and children. This is where the distinction between male and female first matters.

Not every dog, male or female, will be born with a nature suited to be trained and educated as a guard dog, but some will. So, by implication, maleness and femaleness can not be categories Socrates uses to explain the *genesis* of justice. Whatever maleness and femaleness are to the soul, they are both compatible with the nature (*physis*) of the guardians. We should be prepared to see that the proper *genesis* of the guardians may distinguish guardians from auxiliaries and workers, but it will not distinguish maleness from femaleness. It is too soon to try to unpack the analogy for answers, but the psychological question is clear. Which parts or versions of the calculating[21] part of the soul (analogous to the guardi-

[21] "Calculating" is the conventional translation for λογιστικός, and I will use it consistently. "Planning" or "logical" might be better, except that "calculating" has become so well-known, and only insofar as logic is understood to deal with validity (or internal consistency) and not with soundness. The *logismos* of the mind is what calculates the best set of arrangements, given some set of given conditions or premises. *Nous* is the power of mind to apprehend the truth or well-foundedness of those conditions or premises (and thus the soundness of those arrangements), but the psychology of Book IV does not include *nous*. The soul of Book IV is capable of knowing that its arrangements are valid, but is

ans) are male and which are female, and what does maleness or femaleness mean in relation to *logismos*?

When Socrates said what would have to be done to give a fuller account of women and children in the city in speech, he said that he would have to go back and consider birth and rearing (*genesis* and *trophe*) (451d). Now, he says that female guard dogs (which will immediately change, by analogy, into human female guardians of the city in speech) should share completely in the upbringing and education (*trophe* and *paideia*) of the male guardians (451e). Taken together, these two passages indicate the formal relationship of maleness and femaleness to the three categories of potentiality and becoming that run through Books V–VII: *genesis*, *trophe*, and *paideia*. *Genesis*, which would seem to mean "origin" in terms of procreation or breeding in this context, precedes the maleness and femaleness of the progeny, but the specifications of *genesis* relevant to the potential to become guardians is shared by women and men. When it comes to *trophe* and *paideia*, female guardians should also be treated just like males and included in every way.

In an important sense, the next two sections of argument happen in reverse order. First, Socrates moves to what I take to be the crucial problem of this section—the apparent ridiculousness of the proposal to educate men and women the same and together (452a–d). Secondly, the dialogue returns to defend the original organizing principle of this elaboration on the city/soul, i.e., that women and men can and should do the same work. (452e–456c). Then, after establishing that what they are proposing is possible, the interlocutors move to the question of whether sharing all work between women and men is best (456c–457a). Only then, does Socrates return to the claim that because the proposal for women and men to be educated together is both possible and optimal, and that one should ignore those who say it is ridiculous (457a–b).

---

completely cut off from knowing if they are sound because it has no access to a reference point for determining whether or not something is true, i.e., it has no access to the Good. When I use "calculating" to describe a psychological power, I mean something very much like, perhaps precisely like, its logical capacity to determine the validity, but not the soundness, of a psychological arrangement. It is the part that can optimize a plan given a set elements, but cannot evaluate those elements except according to how well they fit together.

Much of the argument of this section takes the form of Socrates responding to an objection that he himself raises. The way the objection is presented suggests that Socrates was unwilling to proceed until it was answered, even though none of the interlocutors raised it.[22] The objection is that since men and women are different, and since we established in Book II that different citizens were suited for different sorts of work (the principle of efficiency, introduced at 370c), would it not follow that men and women should do different work (453c)? This is a centrally important objection because, so far, the interlocutors have only added to the model of the city/soul through their dialectic; they have not reversed themselves substantially regarding the nature of any of its structural elements. The development of the city/soul has operated by elaboration, not revision. If a more thorough explanation of the role of women and children in the city/soul implies a contradiction, the interlocutors would be in trouble. Socrates admits, in fact, that they are in trouble, lost at sea, but that perhaps they can hope for an unlikely rescue (453d). Perhaps the model can withstand the storm to come.[23]

---

[22] David Wolfsdorf argues that the imaginary interlocutor Socrates engages in this section is less metaphysically sophisticated than Glaucon and must be convinced by arguments that do not rely on the distinction between ideas and those things that participate in them. For Wolfsdorf, the reason for introducing the imaginary interlocutor is to give Socrates a reason to use a form of argument that would be inappropriate for Glaucon. This does not seem right to me. The room is full of interlocutors, and Plato's mind is full of characters with whom he could have populated the room. There must be some other reason to introduce an imaginary interlocutor, and I think it is to signal that this is an issue that is particularly important to Socrates. David Wolfsdorf, "Plato's Conception of Knowledge," *The Classical World*, 105, no. 1, (Fall 2011): 57–75.

[23] It is interesting that Socrates mentions a dolphin specifically in his account of what their possible rescue might look like. This could be an allusion to Apollo, since he took the form of a dolphin to escape the island where he was born, Delos, and make it to his sanctuary on the mainland, hence its name, "Delphi." It could also be an allusion to the dolphin that rescued the invisible goddess, Aphaia, whom, though obscure, Plato would have known well if he spent some of his childhood on Aegina, as some believe he did (see Diogenes Laertius *Lives*, 3.1). The story of Arion from Herodotus might be in play here, as well, as Mary Townsend suggests. (*The Woman Question*, 35). There could be

Socrates' response to the objection he himself raises—his attempt to rescue them all after he has imperiled them all—has two parts: first, Socrates investigates the nature of the differences between women and men; secondly, he asks what relevance these natural differences have to the sort of work women and men can and should do in the city in speech. It is in the first part of his response to his own objection that Socrates offers his famous and important distinction between *dialectic*[24] and *eristic*[25] (454a). In *dialectic*, interlocutors engage in conversation to get to the truth. They may be impassioned and deeply committed to their positions, but ultimately they would rather be proven wrong than maintain a false opinion. In *eristic*, interlocutors just want to win the argument: they are more attached to besting their opponent than in arriving at the truth. At the moment, according to Socrates, they are in danger of falling into *eristic* if they do not look behind the words they are using to recall the meaning of those words and the role they play in the inquiry. This warning operates on two levels: first, it helps the interlocutors respond successfully to Socrates' objection that giving women and men the same work violates the principle of efficiency. But, secondly, it also serves as a warning to the interlocutors (and to Plato's readers) regarding the dangers of this section of the *Republic*. The larger warning will be clearer if we deal with the smaller one first.

If one operates on the surface of the two claims set in opposition in the objection Socrates raises, then there is a big problem. We established in Book II that citizens with different natures are suited to different work. We asserted in Book V that women and men should do the same work (even though women and men have different natures). Therefore, it seems we can either hold fast to the old principle (different natures imply different work) or the new principle (women and men, despite their different natures, should do the same work), but not to both. But if one asks

---

a Homeric allusion to this shipwreck as well, although Leukothea, not a dolphin, rescued Odysseus from the sea in *Odyssey* Book V. All of these possibilities are provocative, but since the dolphin does not appear again, it is difficult to know what work it is doing in the dialogue.

[24] διαλέκτῳ.

[25] ἐρίζω.

what sorts of differences are relevant to one's work, then there appears to be a way out of the dilemma. If we are attempting to determine whether citizens should be shoemakers or guardians (454b–c), surely it doesn't matter whether citizens are bald or have long hair. If the natural difference between women and men is like the natural difference between long haired people and bald people, then the problem posed in the objection is merely semantic and not worth our concern (if we are committed to *dialectic* rather than *eristic*).[26]

Socrates then turns to the second part of the argument, which asks: are the differences between men and women relevant to the work they pursue (454e)? The answer is: apparently not. The commonplace that all the interlocutors agree to in this passage is that even though there may be certain arts (*techne)* such as baking and weaving that we could quibble about, and even though there may be individual exceptions; in general, men are better at everything than women (455c-d). But, the argument continues, it does not make sense for men to do everything in the city and women to do nothing, so the principle of male superiority in all things actually supports the position of educating women in all things. Plus, women are competent in all things, even if they are not equal to men (456b). For these reasons, Socrates concludes that they were right to say that women and men should be educated together.[27]

---

[26] This part of Socrates' argument is sometimes used to credit Plato with being the first feminist, a claim Julia Annas, among others, rejects outright. She argues that, "his arguments are unacceptable to a feminist, and that the proposals made in Republic V are irrelevant to contemporary debate." Julia Annas, "Plato's *Republic* and Feminism," 307–321.

[27] Several commentators have noticed that Socrates' revision to the status of women does not make them equal to men so much as it makes them identical to them, and yet inferior. Arlene Saxonhouse frames it this way: "Sexual equality is tied to the destruction of what is separate, what is other. On the one hand, in Greek thought the female had always stood for what is private and other. By equating the male and the female, the public and the private are made one. There is no 'other.' But, more basically, the female suggests the divisiveness of the human species, that we are indeed not all the same, that there *is* something that is other. In order to create the unified city, Socrates must destroy the female as female, the female as a threat to the unity of the human species. She is integrated into the political community not as herself, as one with distinctive talents

There is a larger issue operating in this section, though. The interlocutors do not only risk falling into *eristic* on the question of whether or not the differences between men and women demand that they do different work. They risk the whole inquiry devolving into *eristic*. Socrates has been clear since the introduction of the city/soul in Book II that the purpose of the model is to aid in their inquiry into the nature of the human soul, the place of justice within it, and the relative values of justice and injustice for a human life. But, the question posed at the beginning of Book V that Polemarchus, Adeimantus, Glaucon, and Thrasymachus insisted Socrates answer does not seem to be motivated by their interest in the individual soul. They thought a full account of women and children had been left out of the city in speech, but was their concern based on the usefulness of an account of women and children to their inquiry into the soul, or were they focused on too literal a concern for the model itself? The latter seems to be more plausible.

Not only do none of the interlocutors mention the soul explicitly when they insist Socrates compose what he calls the Female Drama, but none of their arguments even seem to allude to the soul by analogy or otherwise. One of the reasons that it is so difficult to see what women and children signify for the structure and activity of the individual soul in the *Republic* is that it is nowhere made explicit in the beginning of Book V how a more detailed explanation of women and children in the city in speech will be relevant to the psychological inquiry they agreed to undertake together. All four of Socrates' most powerful and vocal interlocutors in the *Republic* seem to be in danger of falling from *dialectic* to *eristic* by attaching themselves to the literal meanings of the elements of the city in speech and forgetting or neglecting what makes them relevant to their shared inquiry.

---

or distinctive experiences, but as an inferior male, a physically weaker male." (See Arlene Saxonhouse, *Women in the History of Political Thought*, 47–48). Mary Townsend puts it like this: "All this puts women in a very strange metaphysical position, no less strange than their resulting political one; it demotes them even as it raises them. Their situation is not that of women whose goodness is finally acknowledged as justice might demand; rather they have been given the status of lesser men, people who possess all the qualities of men but in a lesser degree" (Mary Townsend, *The Woman Question*, 38).

Socrates' warning against devolving into *eristic* is explicitly aimed at his imaginary interlocutor who claims to have found an internal contradiction in the constitution of the city in speech, but I also read it to be an implicit warning to Adeimantus, Polemarchus, Thrasymachus, and especially Glaucon. I understand it to be a warning to the readers of the *Republic*, as well. If we want to continue to engage in *dialectic*, which may lead us to the truth, and not *eristic*, we must remember the meanings of our terms and what roles they play in our inquiry. We must try not to get lost in semantics, surface meanings, or side concerns.

Socrates' warning about what could divert us from *dialectic* may serve as a heuristic for approaching the *Republic*, and especially its most confusing arguments. When we seem to be talking about ridiculous or implausible things, it will serve us well to recall how we got to that part of the argument, from where its terms were derived, and what work we were supposed to be doing. But, I believe there is another heuristic of sorts introduced in this section, as well, and it is even subtler. At 456c, Socrates claims to have shown that it is possible for women to do the same work as men and, therefore, for men and women to be educated together. Immediately afterwards, he shifts his focus to a consideration of whether educating men and women together is best. This seems like a sensible and obvious argumentative development: first show that common education is possible, then show that it is optimal. But, this is not how any of the elements in the city in speech have been established before. Throughout Books II, III, and IV we considered the desirability, but not the possibility of each institutional arrangement. Is it possible to constitute a city with only four or five individuals? Probably not. Could we find the perfect balance of citizens with natural talents for each task in the city, each of whom does his work and only his work so that we could constitute a healthy city? Almost certainly not. If we let desires run amok (as in the fevered city) could we set up institutional arrangements and find sufficiently wise leaders to moderate and balance that city into a purged, harmonious whole? Also extremely unlikely.

However, even though the cities in speech of Books II through IV are as implausible as the city in speech emerging in Book V, the possibility of constituting them was never at issue in the dialogue. What explains this, I believe, is the relative plausibility of the souls implied by the cities in speech in Books II–IV versus the soul implied by the city in speech that is beginning to emerge in Book V. If we shift our focus to the individual soul, the prescriptions for shaping up a life of justice are certainly demanding, but they are not implausible. One must cultivate *logismos* so that it is capable of determining the proper internal balances between itself, *thumos*, and *epithumia*. *Logismos* and *thumos* must be allied so that *epithumia* can be controlled and directed toward the good of the whole. These are no small tasks, but they are intelligible and even, to a degree, manageable.

There is also no expectation of perfect achievement of virtue in the city/soul of Books II–IV. The model seems to suggest that the more you achieve the proper interrelationships and internal balances of soul that come to be known as the virtues, the better. The work one should be doing to become virtuous seems fairly clear and the hope for progress seems fairly reasonable. This is a manageable, workable model of the soul on its face, regardless of how far fetched the political analogs might be. In that sense, there is no need for Socrates to defend its possibility.

The city/soul of Book V is different not because the political arrangements it describes are less plausible but because their psychological analogs are. Despite the specter of Sparta that always seems to float around descriptions of the city/soul in the *Republic*, it is indeed difficult to imagine how even these first institutions of the city in speech that will come to be known as Kallipolis could be established and maintained.[28] All of the practical problems of the earlier cities in speech persist, such as how one could accurately and consistently determine what sort of nature and thus education each baby proto-citizen would best be suited for; or, given that our legislative goal is to create a happy city and not necessarily happy citizens (although this will follow if the happiness of the city is

[28] Socrates names the city of the central books of the *Republic* "Kallipolis," the beautiful city, at 527c in Book VII. He and Glaucon have already worked through most of the allegory of the Cave. The detour of Books V–VII has almost looped back to the main path. Socrates is in the midst of his conversation with Glaucon about the mathematical subjects suited to draw our minds up from images to truth. The timing of Socrates' naming is unsurprisingly complicated and provocative, but it is clear that this is the city that is being constructed throughout the central books, that it is not identical to the purged city said to be complete in Book IV, and that it is beautiful.

perfectly instantiated), how to keep potentially unhappy people working well and exclusively at what they are best suited to contributed to the city. These are just low-hanging fruit. The practical problems inherent in this political model are legion. The problems inherent in the psychological model introduced in Book V are worse, though.

Unlike the city/soul of Books II–IV, where the political arrangements were far fetched but the psychological implications were more plausible, Kallipolis is less plausible as a soul than as a city in speech. In order to make this clear, we will have to do quite a bit more work unpacking the psychological implications of the fuller explanation of the role of women and children in the city, but we can begin to sketch the issue before we get into those details.

As I have already noted, at 451d Socrates casts the task of giving a fuller explanation of women and children in the city in speech as the challenge of accounting for the *genesis* and *trophe* of the guardians. And as he begins this account, he immediately adds education (*paideia*) to the list of things about the guardians that this elaboration on the city in speech will have to include. All three of these (*genesis*, *trophe*, and *paideia*) concern, as I have already begun to explain, potency or becoming. At least now the description of the city/soul called Kallipolis will include an account of how each of the parts of the city/soul, but particularly the guardians/*logismos* come to be just. What is the disposition or original condition (*genesis*) of a soul capable of becoming just? What sort of training/formation/upbringing (*trophe*) prepares such a well-disposed soul for education? And, what sort of education (*paideia*) will move a well-disposed, well-formed soul to the actualization of justice?

When we ask about conditions, we bring the thing for which they are the conditions into our consideration, at least implicitly. We may ultimately reject a telelological account, but considering the conditions for the actualization of a thing is a teleological consideration, and it implies at least an inchoate idea of the *telos* of that thing. This dynamic created by the connection in our minds between the minimal conditions specified in a definition and the *telos* those conditions imply plays a central role in the constitution of Kallipolis, the city in speech that is begun after the interruption at the beginning of Book V. The consideration of conditions opens up, by implication, a consideration of the thing for which those conditions are conditions. Now that the interlocutors have begun to consider the minimal conditions for the possibility of justice, the conversation will open to a consideration of the *telos* of justice.

The risk that Socrates seems to fear most acutely is the danger of corrupting his interlocutors. If Glaucon or the others see Kallipolis for what it is—an ideal that can orient their ambitions to become virtuous—and they commit themselves to an attempt to approach the Good, then their successes and failures in that pursuit are not likely to be terribly dangerous, although they might be. The model of the best life, like the more generic model constructed in Books II–IV, will serve as their target, but there may be nothing inherently problematic about a life that misses the target while keeping it in sight and attempting to get closer to it with every "shot," regardless of how one might lament their failures.

On the other hand, if Socrates' interlocutors (or Plato's readers) see that the realm of conventional justice is not truly authoritative, but they do not, for whatever reason, attach themselves to any higher authority, then they will be both politically powerful and morally unfettered. The psychological and political consequences could be catastrophic. Socrates' attempts to contribute to the improvement of his interlocutors' souls cannot help but risk corrupting them in, perhaps, the worst possible way. After they have seen that justice is largely conventional, they could decide that justice is unachievable or not worth the effort. If they cannot see the authority of the Good for their lives, or if they willfully choose to ignore it, they could be diverted from the project of trying to live a good and reasonable life approximating virtue and veer toward a life that embraces injustice, vice, and dissipation. They might not see or care to acknowledge that such a choice would bear any substantial costs, and they might not scratch beneath the veneer that makes such a choice appear to carry with it obvious benefits. The great is often the enemy of the Good, and Socrates knows it only too well. By taking the risk of having great ambitions for the souls of his interlocutors, Socrates makes more modest, less dangerous, more conventional ambitions to approximate goodness in human life unattractive, perhaps even appear to be unacceptable.

The *Republic* was written well after the Peloponnesian War, but it is set before it, so the threat of war and the inevitability of Athens' defeat looms in the background of the dialogue.[29] The ghosts of Alcibiades and Critias lurk not too deeply in the shadows, as well. They were two of Socrates' brightest, most dissipated and, eventually, most catastrophically dangerous students—men who saw themselves and their ambitions beyond justice, but who had no particular attachment to the Good. As Socrates shows Glaucon, Adeimantus, Polemarchus, and Thrasymachus (who certainly already knows) how to detach themselves from convention in order to attach themselves to the Good, he risks leaving them completely unattached. He shows the way for them to become psychologically and politically tyrannical. This is what happened to Alcibiades and Critias, Plato seems to imply, and the promise of educating them for philosophy is why it seemed to be worth the risk.

The risks of composing the Female Drama are significant, but they are also necessary. Socrates cannot keep faith with his interlocutors without responding to their questions about women and children, and there is an important part of the story of the soul that has not yet been told. So, Socrates returns, after his brief excursis on *dialectic* and *eristic*, to the claim that women and men should train and be educated together. Or, more specifically, he returns to a consideration of what instituting this principle would look like and how one should react to those who oppose it.

When Socrates introduced the idea that women and men should pursue their physical training together, the first prompt he gave to Glaucon was to admit that what he was proposing seemed ridiculous (452a). In fact, Socrates didn't just ask for an affirmation from Glaucon that he shared the view that the instantiation of this principle would look ridiculous, he pressed him to think through what its most ridiculous implications would be. This is not a question that was asked about any of the

---

[29] Debra Nails reviews the controversies over the dramatic dating of the *Republic*, and leans tentatively toward 408 BCE, but argues that there will be anachronisms implied by choosing any particular date between 432 and 404, even though dramatic dates outside that range would not be plausible. Debra Nails, *The People of Plato: A Prosopography of Plato and other Socratics*, (Indianiapolis: Hackett, 2002), 324–326.

previous cities in speech, although it could have been. For example, there would have been nothing absurd about Socrates asking "what would the most ridiculous aspects of trying to constitute a city with only four or five men?" or "could we really expect each person to do precisely the work they were best at and only that work?" So, why is Socrates now bringing forward these apparently ridiculous implications of trying to instantiate the city in speech? Why now?

If the Female Drama tells the story of how a soul may become just, then it should begin with what sort of conditions must exist in order for that process of becoming to commence. This is what I believe is beginning to happen when Socrates asks Glaucon to focus on the ridiculousness of the proposal that women and men to should train together. In every society, the conventions of public behavior tend to be formidable. Practices that may once have been a matter of choice or legislation become ingrained over time and enacted unselfconsciously by many members of that society. Others may affirm conventions more, but believe there are rational justifications for maintaining conventional practices whether or not they find them rational. Resisting ingrained conventions tends to be difficult and to come at a high social cost.

If one aspires to be just in the city or the soul, then one must be capable of resisting convention intellectually and in practice. Intellectually, one must be able see conventions for what they are, affirm them when they serve the Good of the whole, and resist them when they don't. In practice, one must be able to withstand the resistance that inevitably will come from those for whom convention is more powerful. In the soul, that resistance comes from habit. In the city in speech, it would come from those who found unconventional behaviors ridiculous.

Socrates' point appears to be that a soul that will be capable of training and education for virtue will be the soul that can manage, among other things, the difficult business of being unconventional. This is precisely the lesson Socrates emphasizes to Glaucon in their consideration of women and men exercising together, that is, in what will soon be named "the first wave" (457a). If training men and women together is the best thing for the city in speech, then one must not be deterred by those who call it ridiculous. Nor should one be moved by the part of oneself that sees it as ridiculous. The part of oneself that understands it to be right must be in control.

In large part, this provision is clear in Book IV where Socrates emphasized the nature of the guardians/*logismos*, and virtue's requirement that it rule in the city/soul. This account in Book V is entirely harmonious with what was presented in Book IV, but it shows the dynamic from a different angle. In Book IV, Socrates elaborated on the necessity of logistic rule. Here, in Book V, the emphasis is on the capacity of the other parts of the soul to be ruled. Successfully controlling the desire to laugh at the ridiculousness of old men and women exercising together is Socrates' image for surviving the first wave. Psychologically, it depicts *logismos* properly containing *epithumia*, which implies both a sufficiently strong calculating faculty (which was treated in the Male Drama) and a sufficiently containable appetitive faculty (which is what is now added to the account by way of the Female Drama).

It is possible to know what is good and yet not to act on it when there are parts of your soul that are stronger than the part that knows what is good. Here, Plato anticipates what, in Book VII of the *Nicomachean Ethics*, Aristotle calls *akrasia.* One can both know the right thing and be dissipated beyond the capacity to act on that knowledge. There are many ways to become one for whom right reason, or even knowledge, is insufficient to guide action. Drug addiction is the easiest example. It is a commonplace that addicts can talk sensibly about their misguided choices, can lament their dissipation, can decide to do what they know to be right, but can then succumb over and over again to urges that overwhelm their resolve. For addicts, the lesson is clear: knowing what is good is a necessary condition for virtue, but it is not always sufficient for putting it into practice.[30]

Knowing that it is best to create a training regimen for men and women together is not sufficient for institutionalizing that arrangement in the city in speech. Having the most knowledgeable person in charge of instituting the right plan is also not sufficient. The rest of the city must also be capable of being led toward arrangements that they find ridiculous. They must have that capacity. The psychological analog to this is

---

[30] For an account of how the structure of the tripartite soul in the *Republic* implies the existence of *akrasia*, see Michael Morris "Akrasia in the *Protagoras* and the *Republic*," *Phronesis* 51, no. 3 (2006), 195–229.

that one who hopes to be trained and educated for virtue must be capable of overcoming those instincts and habits that are not, according to the *logical* soul, best for the whole. One's *thumos* must be willing to align itself with *logismos*. One's *epithumia* must be containable. This is the first lesson of the Female Drama. We have weathered the first wave.

4

Possibility and Becoming

The first act of the first play of Female Drama presents the possibility that a soul could overcome convention and emotion in deference to reason. This possibility is portrayed as the act of overcoming laughter and ignoring ridicule in order to do the right thing for the city, specifically training men and women together as guardians (and auxiliaries). The possibility of overcoming convention and emotion is presented as a necessity for establishing justice in the city in speech and, internally, for anyone with ambitions to be trained and educated for philosophy.

This lesson belongs in the Female Drama because it concerns potentiality and becoming. Only souls capable of being ruled by the calculating (*logismos)* part or power of the soul have the potency for virtue (including the virtue of justice). In the denouement of the Male Drama of Book IV, we learned how and why the calculating part should rule the city/soul. Now, we return to the same dynamic but from the perspective of the parts of the soul that are to be ruled. In a sense, this part of the account was implied from the beginning. Women and children were there all along. As has been true in every previous expansion of the city in speech, Socrates is elaborating on the model, not altering it fundamentally.

At 457b, as Socrates brings the argument about women and men training together to a close, he names it the the "first wave" (*kuma*[1]). Just before he presented the argument, he set up the image by likening the situation of the interlocutors in this moment of the dialogue to having fallen into the sea (453c). The image of being lost at sea is an elaboration on Socrates' sense that the task before them is extremely dangerous. As I

---

[1] κῦμα.

argued in the previous chapter, the danger they face is the corruption of the interlocutors' understanding of justice and its relevance to their lives, which depends upon justice appearing to be possible. So, by implication, saying that they have avoided the first *kuma* means that they have avoided the first threat that the Female Drama poses to making the just life appear possible. The condition for its possibility that Socrates explored in the first *kuma* is the capacity to overcome ridicule for the sake of acting according to reason, both in the city in speech and in the soul.

A centrally important word for my inquiry into the Female Drama of the *Republic* is *kuma*,[2] and it is difficult to translate. "Wave" is conventional, so I will use it throughout my account, and it is not a bad word choice. "Swell" may be slightly better because it may apply more easily to what happens to a woman's body when pregnant, which is another meaning of *kuma*. But, "wave" may be better for the connotation of *kuma* that evokes pregnancy, as well, since it works in English to talk about "waves" of pain in childbirth, that is, contractions. What is important, regardless of word choice, is that the reader of the *Republic* sees the *kumata* both (1) as threats to the stability and safety of the dialogue and (2) as evoking the potientiality or promise of something new coming into the world; as well as, perhaps, (3) the anxiety and pain that attends the transition.

The second *kuma*, which is introduced by name, appears at 457c, and specifies five things, some or all of which overlap with each other: (1) all women should be shared among all men, (2) no individual woman and man should live together, (3) all children should be shared, (4) no parent should know its child, and (5) no child should know its parents. [3]

---

[2] κῦμα.

[3] Socrates: τὰς γυναῖκας ταύτας τῶν ἀνδρῶν τούτων πάντων πάσας εἶναι κοινάς, ἰδίᾳ δὲ μηδενὶ μηδεμίαν συνοικεῖν: καὶ τοὺς παῖδας αὖ κοινούς, καὶ μήτε γονέα ἔκγονον εἰδέναι τὸν αὑτοῦ μήτε παῖδα γονέα. **Glaucon**: πολύ, ἔφη, τοῦτο ἐκείνου μεῖζον πρὸς ἀπιστίαν καὶ τοῦ δυνατοῦ πέρι καὶ τοῦ ὠφελίμου. **S**: οὐκ οἶμαι, ἦν δ' ἐγώ, περί γε τοῦ ὠφελίμου ἀμφισβητεῖσθαι ἄν, ὡς οὐ μέγιστον ἀγαθὸν κοινὰς μὲν τὰς γυναῖκας εἶναι, κοινοὺς δὲ τοὺς παῖδας, εἴπερ οἷόν τε: ἀλλ' οἶμαι περὶ τοῦ εἰ δυνατὸν ἢ μὴ πλείστην ἂν ἀμφισβήτησιν γενέσθαι. **G**: περὶ ἀμφοτέρων, ἦ δ' ὅς, εὖ μάλ' ἂν ἀμφισβητηθείη. **S**: λέγεις, ἦν δ' ἐγώ, λόγων σύστασιν: ἐγὼ δ' ᾤμην ἔκ γε τοῦ ἑτέρου ἀποδράσεσθαι, εἴ σοι δόξειεν ὠφέλιμον εἶναι, λοιπὸν δὲ δή

Socrates assumes that the desirability of this arrangement is obvious,[4] but that he will have to make a case for their possibility. Glaucon tells him that he must argue both for its desirability and its possibility.

Socrates and Glaucon find themselves further apart at this point of the argument than Socrates claims to have anticipated. The dramatic irony of their situation is building. Why would Socrates think the benefits of doing away with the nuclear family are obvious, given that his plan is so thoroughly unconventional? Just as I showed in my analysis in the last chapter of the dramatic set up for the first wave, this growing gap between Socrates and Glaucon seems to emerge because Socrates continues to be focused on the city in speech as an image of the human soul and because Glaucon focuses on the elements of the image as if they had their own reality. Socrates is focused on the soul, Glaucon is focused on the city, and it is becoming more and more difficult for Socrates to be true to the soul without the city in speech falling completely apart. They are, indeed, in deep water.

Readers of the *Republic* interested in philosophical psychology are in deep water here, too, since Socrates offers very little help with our effort to stay focused on the soul. It is easy to identify with Glaucon. It is tempting to continue to pursue questions that the city in speech leads us to without taking the time to think through what their implications are for the soul. But this would be a mistake.[5] What we know is that women and children represent something fundamental to the soul, that women emerge in the city/soul precisely at the same time as the male guardian,

μοι ἔσεσθαι περὶ τοῦ δυνατοῦ καὶ μή. **G**: ἀλλ' οὐκ ἔλαθες, ἦ δ' ὅς, ἀποδιδράσκων, ἀλλ' ἀμφοτέρων πέρι δίδου λόγον. (457c-e)

[4] Perhaps Socrates understands himself to have made the case for their (psychological) desirability in the Male Drama.

[5] That is not to say that it is a mistake to try to understand what the city in speech might teach us about politics or to attempt to understand what the text implies about and for actual women in actual cities. But it is a mistake for one trying to make sense of the *Republic* not to attend to the psychological implications of these arguments, as well.

and that female guardians are to share all pursuits[6] with their male counter parts.

Now we can add to the list of things we have learned about female guardians that Socrates believes that it should be obvious to Glaucon that it would be best for all men in the city/soul to share all women and children in common. As I have argued, I understand women and children in the city/soul to signal issues of potency, potentiality, and possibility. In the first *kuma*, this translates to the claim that the soul with a potency for justice must be capable of being ruled by its *logismos* in the face of ridicule. That seems evident to me in the text. The second *kuma* is more difficult to translate.

Putting together all of the evidence, argument, and speculation listed above, I would like to argue that when one translates the second *kuma* into its meaning for the soul, one arrives at the claim that all of the soul's potencies should be held in common with all of the soul's active capacities, and that the aspects of character that emerge from the activation of each of these potencies should belong to the whole soul and not to any of its particular modes. These claims need a great deal of explanation, and in order to make the logic of this argument explicit, we will have to consider each of its parts in turn: (1) Why should women be understood as potencies in the soul? (2) Why should men be understood as active capacities? (3) Why should children be understood as *aspects of character*? (4) What does it mean for aspects of character to emerge in one's soul from the union of potencies and activities? (5) What does it mean for aspects of character to "belong" either to the whole soul or to one of its particular modes? (6) Why should aspects of character be understood to belong to the whole soul rather than to one of its particular modes?

The first difficulty of the second wave is knowing what Socrates means by "these women" at 457d.[7] The previous argument concerned female guardians primarily, but alluded to female versions of the other members of the city/soul. Does the second *kuma* concern only female guardians or all women? It makes sense to me to argue that the second

[6] κοινῇ πάντα ἐπιτηδεύειν.

[7] τὰς γυναῖκας.

kuma concerns all women and men in the city/soul and not just the guardians. If "these women" refer only to the women in the city who become guardians, then the psychological analog would be only to consider rational potencies. But, if "these women" refer to all of the women in the city then, psychologically, all the potencies of the soul would be at issue. This latter interpretation seems to fit much better with the rest of Socrates' argument, but this is speculative. The text is not clear.[8]

Several different things point to the association of women and children in the city in speech to potency and becoming in the soul, many of which I have already mentioned but will highlight again here. The first and most obvious reason to make this connection is its consonance with the way both Glaucon (at 450b–c) and Socrates (at 451d) frame the Female Drama. Glaucon, in joining his voice to Polemarchus and Adeimantus' petition to revisit the role of women and children in the city in speech (and with Thrasymachus' affirmation), says that what interested him most about what was missing from the model in Book IV was an account of "the time between birth and the beginning of formal education."[9] Glaucon is interested in how one prepares to become a guardian. Likewise, Socrates says they must go back and consider the "rules for birth (*genesis*) and rearing (*trophe*)" that correspond to the account in Book IV (451d). Socrates' interest is also in the origin and development of the guardians in a just city in speech, but his concerns are both deeper and broader than Glaucon's. Socrates, like Glaucon, sees that the Female Drama will require an inquiry into what happens between birth and education, but he knows that it will require them to look into the birth and education of the guardians, as well. They will inquire into *trophe*, and also into *genesis* and *paideia*.

Another reason to read women, children, and the Female Drama as signaling a shift to an inquiry into potentiality and becoming is that the

---

[8] Debra Nails offers several arguments for the first wave applying to all women and girls and not just to those who are on track to become guardians. If she is right, then I think it is even more plausible to argue that the second wave also applies to all women. Debra Nails, "Plato's *Republic* in its Athenian context," *History of Political Thought* 33, no. 1 (Spring 2012): 17.

[9] τω μεταξύ χρονω γιγνομένης γενέσεώς τε και παιδείας (450c).

concept of "possibility" itself becomes a thread that runs through the middle books of the *Republic.* Beginning in Book V, both Socrates' concerns and the interlocutors' inquiries are often versions of the question—"But, is this possible?" Socrates raises the question first at 450a and, as I argued in the last chapter, believes it to be a serious issue for their inquiry. But "possibility" comes up again and again both as a topic of conversation and as a rhetorical move that pushes toward the development of the city/soul which seems uncontroversial (and perhaps is), but which was not a part of the discourse in Books II–IV.

A third reason to associate women in the *Republic* with potentiality is their passive role in ancient theories of reproductive biology.[10] Aeschylus' account of Apollo's defense of Orestes' murder of Clytemnestra to Athena and the jury in the *Eumenides* is a famous example: "The so-called mother is no parent of a child, but nurturer of a newly seeded embryo; the parent is the one who mounts her, while she conserves the child like a stranger for a stranger, for those fathers not thwarted by god.[11] According to Aeschylus' Apollo, men contribute all active life to a child.[12] The role of the mother before the birth is to contain and protect a child as it grows. If the child happens to look like its mother, it is because it took on something of her shape in the womb. But on this ancient model, the mother contributes none of what we would now call genetic material. In the sense of creating activity, the father is the only parent. The mother's role is passive, necessary only insofar as the active capacity of the father cannot operate without the passive containment of the mother. The active role of the father in conception is the obvious corollary to the passive role of the mother. While the female contribution to engendering a child is to provide a passive, protective vessel for prenatal development,

---

[10] For an excellent survey of Fifth Century ideas of reproductive biology, see Andrew Coles. "Biomedical Models of Reproduction in the Fifth Century BC and Aristotle's 'Generation of Animals.'" *Phronesis* 40, no. 1 (1995): 48–88.

[11] Aeschylus *Eumenides*, trans. Collard, line 665.

[12] Apollo certainly has ulterior motives for deploying this argument in the play, but those motives do not undermine my sense that it represents accepted beliefs. Whatever his motives, Apollo uses this account of human reproductive biology because he thinks it will have persuasive power, and Aeschylus presents it as if he were right about that.

the male contribution is to implant an undeveloped, but complete, human seed.[13] Every sense in which a human being is capable of self-movement, i.e. every aspect of soul, comes from the father.

Can this theory of ancient reproductive biology help us to see what Socrates might be suggesting about the *genesis* in this part of the Female Drama? Perhaps. A couple of things are already coming into focus. First, one can see why the Female Drama could be left out of the first constitution of the city/soul without really neglecting anything essential to the question of what justice entailed. If the male is understood to be entirely responsible for the soul of the child, then the Male Drama of the city in speech would, in principle, contain everything necessary for an account of soul. But, secondly, if women are necessary for the potential soul to become actual (i.e. for the human seed to grow into a human being), then one will not be able to account for the development of the city/soul without the Female Drama. This dynamic seems to describe well the structural relationship of the Male and Female Dramas in the *Republic*. The Male Drama was complete in principle, but there was no account given of how it could come to be.[14]

When Socrates introduces the female guardians (or, more precisely, the female puppies well-disposed for training to become guard dogs), he argues that their gender is not relevant to the question of whether they

[13] In her interpretation of the Cave, Eva Brann returns us to the association of feminity with non-being in this way: "When Socrates first introduced the sun, the source of the visible world, as a son, Glaucon had immediately inferred that as a parent the Good was the father (506e6). The Cave image now provides the answer to the obvious question: Who is the mother? It is Nonbeing, the realm in which things are nothing in themselves but only in relation to another; in the terms of the Sophist, it is the realm of the the Other (257b) which bonds beings in the realm of Being, but whose human effects outside that realm are just the opposite: negativity, lack of community, and consequent privacy in the literal sense, namely privation, as well as alienation and ignorance." Brann, *Music of the Republic*, 212.

[14] By "complete" here and throughout my account of the Male Drama, I mean that the Male Drama is complete for their inquiry into the relative values of justice and injustice, I do not mean that the model of the city/soul in Books II–IV is complete in the sense of giving a wholly accurate model of the human soul.

should be educated. We are now in a better position to try to make sense of what this claim might mean for the soul. The parts of the soul are only gendered allegorically, of course. My argument is that femininity signals issues of determinate passivity and masculinity signals activity within the soul. It also seems to be the case that femininity and masculinity can be applied to all parts of the soul (workers/*epithumia*, auxiliaries/*thumos*, and guardians/*logismos*). So, by implication, Socrates would be presenting passivity and activity in every part of the soul. This could mean many different things.

It is important to specify that the passivity suggested by the feminine is determinate. That is, not everyone is capable of everything. We have possibilities for some things and not for others. Puppies do not grow up to be goldfish. So, puppies are not dogs; but, they are not dogs in a very different way than they are not goldfish. They have the determinate potency to be the former, but not the latter. So, the possibilities that women suggest in the philosophical psychology of the *Republic* are not thoroughly indeterminate. They have character and shape. They constrain our activities in determinate ways.

The simplest interpretation of women in the philosophical psychology of the *Republic*, and perhaps the best, would be that every soul has developed and undeveloped potencies. The *epithumetic* soul presents the easiest example, especially in the way that it is presented in the culminating image of the tripartite soul at Book IX, 588c: a "complex, many-headed beast, with a ring of tame and savage animal heads, all of which it can grow and change from within."[15] One of the several lessons that Socrates builds from that image of *epithumia* is that it is the responsibility of *logismos* to determine which of the beast's heads will be fed and which will be starved,[16] and it is the responsibility of *thumos* to control the *epithumetic* beasts, since beasts/appetites cannot be trained or educated.

[15] μὲν ἰδέαν θηρίου ποικίλου καὶ πολυκεφάλου, ἡμέρων δὲ θηρίων ἔχοντος κεφαλὰς κύκλῳ καὶ ἀγρίων, καὶ δυνατοῦ μεταβάλλειν καὶ φύειν ἐξ αὑτοῦ πάντα ταῦτα.

[16] By the time the "man within the man" image of the soul is presented in Book IX, Socrates has introduced and elaborated on the *nous*, as well, but we are not yet there in this account.

The claim that these *epithumetic* animal heads can be fed or starved, controlled or left to wreak havoc suggests that passivity and activity are intelligible options within the *epithumetic* soul. Some of the beast's heads will be actively craving because they are well fed. Others will be weakened by starvation and containment; they will be more passive. But, except insofar as not feeding a particularly dangerous desire might be a matter of exigency, it doesn't matter whether the heads of the *epithumetic* beast are active or passive; the good ones need to be encouraged and the bad ones need to be contained.[17]

If activity and passivity are represented by men and women in the city in speech, then one could rephrase the previous point this way: "it does not matter whether the heads of the *epithumetic* beast are male or female, the good ones need to be fed, and the bad ones need to be starved." Or, taking one more step away from the image of Book IX and back toward the city in speech, one could use the following language to make the same point: "It does not matter whether one's workers are male or female, the good ones need to encouraged and given resources, and the bad ones do not." Or, if one wanted to make exactly the same point in purely psychological terms, one could say "It does not matter whether one indulges one's appetites in everyday life or if they lay dormant; the good ones need to be encouraged, and the bad ones need to be starved if one hopes to live well."

None of the models of the *thumotic* or *logistic* soul suggest an analysis based on passivity and activity as obvious as the *epithumetic* one, but the analogy seems nonetheless to hold. Thumotically, we are apt to be naturally disposed to let many things stir us to action. One person may be naturally forgiving, and another may naturally feel extreme indignation in the face of injustice, etc. Some of these dispositions of spirit will

---

[17] This same dynamic is mirrored in other images of the soul in the *Republic*. In the Ship of State, there is no indication that the sailors can be educated to appreciate the art of piloting, for example. The hope of a well-run, well-directed ship depends on them being directed by the ship owner to support the course charted by the pilot. They can be directed and contained at best, but not educated. Furthermore, in the city in in speech, there is no consideration of educating iron and bronze souls; they must be brought into activities that support the city/soul by some other means.

be important to promoting and preserving the integrity of the just city/soul (perhaps all of them on different occasions), but none of them should be active all the time or dominate. The guardians/*logismos* will determine what the auxiliaries/*thumos* should do to promote and protect the just soul, and the auxiliaries/*thumos* must be ready to be active in the ways that the guardians/*logismos* indicate and passive in all others. Although Socrates does not explicitly play out the psychological meaning of the female for the thumotic and logistic activities of soul, such an account is consonant with the arguments and images of this part of his dialectic.

The image presented in Book III at 413c illuminates passivity and activity of the guardians/*logismos*, and it adds another layer of complexity. This is where Socrates introduces a series of competitions designed to reveal which of the young guardians in training are best at remaining true to their education, since these will also be those who are best at safeguarding the city/soul. There, Socrates says, "They need to be observed right from childhood by those who set the sort of tasks for them in which one would be most likely to forget about their convictions or be fooled about them. And we need to select those who remember and are hard to fool; and reject the others."[18] The added layer of complexity comes here in the suggestion that these guardians in training have an interior life. Some of guardians in training will be able to remember their training and not be fooled when they are tested; others will not be so reliable.

When the rational soul is portrayed in image and argument, an already difficult schema gets much more confusing. But, like the fuzzy complexity of composing the most necessary city (minimal soul) with four or five members, any image of the rational soul must be nuanced if it is to be accurate. The analogy to the soul begins here to repeat itself as microcosm and macrocosm, somewhat like a fractal. This is a pattern that we will see repeated over and over again as the arguments of the *Republic* develop and culminate in the Book IX's image of the soul as the small man inside the larger man. Here, the claim seems to be that a child

[18] τηρητέον δὴ εὐθὺς ἐκ παίδων προθεμένοις ἔργα ἐν οἷς ἄν τις τὸ τοιοῦτον μάλιστα ἐπιλανθάνοιτο καὶ ἐξαπατῷτο, καὶ τὸν μὲν μνήμονα καὶ δυσεξαπάτητον ἐγκριτέον, τὸν δὲ μὴ ἀποκριτέον.

who might become a guardian must be strong in order to serve the city well (and make it strong). So the question of the best organization of the city/soul, at this moment of Book III's account of the character of the guardians, focuses on the question of which part of oneself is strong enough to govern the whole. Which guardian in training is best, presumably given that one has a choice among several? Interpreted psychologically, the question is how one chooses the part of oneself that one will organize one's life around—the part of oneself toward which one will orient one's life; in ancient Greek shorthand, one's *arche*.

Few individuals know their *arche*, the organizing principle and teleological aim of their actions, early in life. Few children know (or are funneled toward) the one, best sort of work they are well-disposed to do, get the proper training and education for it, and then orient their lives to becoming excellent in that activity. Most of us in the contemporary world believe that we could be many things, and not unrealistically. Not all options are open to all people, but many good ones are open to most people in contemporary liberal society. I am a college professor, but I could have been a good physician or architect. My sister is deeply involved in the business of managing touring Broadway shows, but she could have been a performer, a playwright, a director, or a dozen other things.

Each of us needs to focus on something, or some few things (the best city/soul is a monarchy or an aristocracy, not just a monarchy), if we do not want to dissipate our energies. I take that to mean that we all need to choose a pilot for our ship (to anticipate the image from Book VI), and that there may or may not be several good options to choose from. In those cases where a person has the capacity to do many things well, that is, live many possible good lives, then the active organizing principles of those unlived good lives are sort of passive *logistic* souls. If one becomes a college professor at a liberal arts college, has a couple of kids, and buys a big old house, one's logistic soul has a very different set of conditions and challenges in the interest of becoming just than if one became a physician in a huge research hospital, never had children, and rented an apartment. The point is that, for most human beings, there may be many good ways of developing a well-formed and just life, and we must choose. That chosen organizing principle must be active and in charge, and its virtue is wisdom. All the other unchosen organizing principles must be passive or dormant if one is to avoid internal faction.

These attempts to find forms of activity and passivity in the soul that are analogous to women and men in the Female Drama of Books V and VI of the *Republic* are obviously speculative. While Socrates regularly unpacks the allegorical content of the city in speech in Books II through IV (and VIII and IX), we get very little help here, and we must be cautious. We must also, however, try to hold onto the threads we are given to help us find our way out of this labyrinth. As our analysis of the *Republic* progresses, we will continue to return to these speculations on the meaning of the city/soul. If we find that we run into contradictions or inconsistencies, we will have to qualify or even perhaps reject these early speculations, but each time we find confirmation that the city in speech points in something like this direction as an allegory of the soul, we should become more confident of their veracity.

I must extend our speculations a bit more, though, since the second *kuma*, as it is presented at 457c does not only concern women and men, but also children. Socrates specifies not only that children, like women, will be held in common by all men, but that parents will not know who their children are, and children will not know their parents. In order to try to understand children as some sort of imaginary progeny engendered imaginatively by whatever mothers and fathers represent in the soul, we must elaborate a bit more on the passivity and activity that women and men represent.

If we consider the male/active and female/passive versions of each type of soul individually, then it is difficult to extend the image to account for something analogous to procreation and birth within a soul; but if we imagine interactions among parts of the soul, some promising speculative possibilities emerge. If we return to the case of the person who, *logistically*, could be a good college professor or a good physician but also add to the image that, *thumotically*, she is one who has an unusually strong sense of righteous indignation when faced with injustice, then one can also imagine two different unions in the soul that would produce two different "progeny:" the indignant physician and the indignant professor. I will prescind from making a judgment regarding which life would be better; the point is to see that they would both be possible.

On this reading, children within the soul would be the active conditions created by the union of particular parts or functions of the soul. To use some language from Aristotle[19] and the Stoics,[20] the psychological analog in the soul to a child in the city in speech would be a *hexis*. For Aristotle, a *hexis* is developed through deliberate choice and habituation. It is a stable disposition to act in a particular way, particularly in an ethical context. For Aristotle, one who has a *hexis* for courage is one who has attempted to act deliberately with the right amount of fear in her life, at the right times, for the right reasons, and in the right ways. One who has, over a lifetime of serious deliberation, action, and reflection, incorporates those modes of action into her character by habituation. When generosity has become a part of who she is, a stable disposition ready to support generous action at all times, she has developed that *hexis*.

As I read it, the treatment of children in the city/soul has a lot of resonance with the Aristotelian account of *hexis*.[21] When a child is born in the city in speech, the questions are: what sort of child is it; can it be trained; can it be educated; can it withstand the challenges of competition and temptation? In an individual life, the questions posed to proge-

[19] Stephen G. Salkever offers a clear account of the complicated meaning of *hexis* (ἕξις). "[*Hexis*] is a key term in Aristotle's social science, and that science is made inaccessible to us when it is rendered by words like 'characteristic' or 'habit' or 'trained ability.' Perhaps the best way to get at the sense of the term is by example. If I say, 'Mary is courageous,' or 'Mary is a coward,' I am describing Mary's *hexis*, making a statement about those relatively stable qualities that define Mary as a person as far as I can judge. The closest English word to *hexis* is thus 'personality,' if by that word we understand those qualities which define a person and distinguish him or her from other people. To live well for Aristotle is thus to have (or 'be') a good personality, and the primary task of the social scientist is to determine what such a personality looks like, or what sorts of personalities are better than others, in the sense of being better blends or mixtures of those elements (drives and capacities) which constitute us all." Steven G. Salkever "Aristotle's Social Science" 489.

[20] For an interesting account of the role of *hexis* in the Stoic tripartite soul, see Eric Lewis, "The Stoics on Identity and Individuation," *Phronesis* 40, no. 1 (1995): 89–108.

[21] ἕξις. Aristotle, in fact, uses children as an analogy for *hexeis* in *Nicomachean Ethics* I.13.

ny within the soul are not very different: how do my natural dispositions and these ways of organizing my life come together; is this a life worth leading; is it good; is it just, does it suit me; is it sustainable? These are difficult questions, perhaps ultimately impossible to answer, but they are just the sort of questions that Socrates asks of himself and all of his interlocutors. They are precisely the sorts of questions that, in the *Republic*, Socrates continues to bring back to the forefront of their discussion. And, as the conversation moves from the first to the second wave, these questions continue to get more complicated and much more difficult to sort out.

5

The Second Wave

(THE GENESIS OF THUMOS)

At 458a, Socrates asks permission to bracket the question of whether or not the second *kuma* would be possible so that he can focus on the question of whether or not it would be best. If we think of this as a sort of open parenthesis, then one can look forward to it being closed at 472a, the beginning of the account of the third *kuma* (with a sort of stutter step attempt at closing it at 466d). So, the entire account of the second *kuma* concerns whether or not it is best, and brackets the questions of whether it is possible. This also means, as Socrates makes explicit at 473a, that the third *kuma* (that philosophers should rule) is a necessary condition for the second *kuma* (that all women and children should be held in common by all men). I will not attempt to give an account of what this might mean until we have looked at both the second and third *kumata* in detail, but it is important context to have in mind as we proceed.

Socrates begins his account of the second *kuma* with a reminder that the guardians in the city in speech will be prepared to give orders and that the auxiliaries will be prepared to carry them out (458b), and then he moves to the claim that the lawgiver (*nomothetis*) whom he has now explicitly identified as Glaucon, will want to give to them women with similar natures (458c). Socrates asserts that because all of their rearing has been in common[1] (458d), including in the gymnasium, they will be driven by an internal necessity[2] to have sex. Glaucon immediately specifies that this will be an erotic and not a geometric necessity. Socrates does not comment on the nature of the internal necessity that drives

---

[1] καὶ ἐν τῇ ἄλλῃ τροφῇ.

[2] ἀνάγκης οἶμαι τῆς ἐμφύτου.

people to sex; instead he moves to the importance of creating marriage conventions that will guide this internal necessity in a direction that will be beneficial (458e). So, the question for their debate becomes how best to bring about beneficial marriages (459a).

What follows in the section of the dialogue that runs from 459a to 461e are some of the most famous and famously offensive arguments in the *Republic*. It is here that Socrates appears to be recommending eugenics policies as well as every sort of lie, drug, and totalitarian tactic necessary to enact them.[3] In an important sense, these are the arguments for which my reading of the *Republic* offers the most radical reinterpretation, since I do not take Socrates here to be making political policy recommendations. It is telling and important that Glaucon (and perhaps the other interlocutors who are silent in this part of the dialogue) seem to hear Socrates' deeply disturbing political imagery as if it were intended as policy, and that they do not balk more energetically. Perhaps this signals Glaucon's capacity for totalitarian leanings and underlines the dangers implicit in Socrates failing to make himself understood in this part of the dialogue—the fear of which caused him to prostrate himself to Adrasteia at 451a.

If, in this section of the dialogue, Socrates is concerned mainly with the soul and is using the city in speech heuristically, the apparent offensiveness of the arguments is lessened; it might even evaporate. The horror of Glaucon's apparent openness to such terrible policies remains, but that is another story. At 461e, Socrates begins unpacking their meaning, but in order to present what I think these allegorical totalitarian policies have to do with the soul, we will have to consider them one by one as they are introduced at 459 and following.

---

[3] Carolina Araujo argues that these practices, though abhorant to contemporary readers, function as institutional controls of the rulers of Kallipolis. They are essential for the coherence of the constitution of the city in speech. On the level of psychology, this seems right to me. On the level of politics, these policies appear to me not just to be abhorant to contemporary readers, but to Plato as well. Carolina Araujo, "Philosopher-kings: A Communitarian Project," in *Essays on Images from Western Greece*, eds. Heather L. Reid and Davide Tanasi (Fonte Aretusa: Parnassos Press, 2016).

At 459c, Socrates takes up the topic of the necessity of sex in the city in speech by positing that it is best to arrange for the best dogs, birds, horses, and human beings to breed with each other. Socrates immediately acknowledges the deep problem, however, with extending the argument to the human realm. While one can institute a breeding program for animals without disrupting their lives radically, to arrange the unions of human beings according to the principle that the best should breed with the best will require drugs, lies, and fraud. No one in the city except the rulers can know that this eugenics program is in place. If it were conducted openly, the consequence would be faction (459e). So, in order to preserve secrecy, the city will need festivals, sacrifices, hymns, lotteries, and a sexual incentive program for young men who are good at war (459e–460b). The Female Drama has indeed prompted a significant expansion of the city/soul.

Many other institutions also come into being in order to provide the best care for the offspring of these carefully contrived unions, literally the "offspring of the Good."[4] The city will need pens set apart from the city and special nurses who will be responsible for caring for the children, coordinate a nursing schedule with their birthmothers and wet nurses, and ensure that no mother recognizes her biological child. The need to avoid recognition demands that careful timing and good records be kept for both women and men. It also creates a risk for unintentional incest, a problem for which Socrates' calendric response would clearly be insufficient in practice.

The consequences of what Socrates proposes for Kallipolis are much like the consequence of the noble lie for the purged city (414b), both in terms of their political impact and their practical impossibility. The family, as it is constructed within the institutions of Kallipolis at 461d-e, is made up of all brides and grooms married in the same month, and all children born ten months after their marriage. So, every married couple will have many children, and every child will have many parents. The problems with this plan are so myriad and obvious that what is most striking is that Socrates' interlocutors do not balk more obviously. But, of

[4] τὰ μὲν δὴ τῶν ἀγαθῶν (460b).

course, the noble lie of Book III was at least as implausible. The *Republic* is full of such apparently absurd proposals.

In the purged city, the noble lie created a city in speech in which all citizens understood themselves to be brothers, children of the earth. The Female Drama demands that in Kallipolis we create a new world of lies, one that Socrates does not suggest is noble at all, in which again we all understand ourselves to be a part of a large family. And this new set of lies prompts us in Book V to do the same sort of dialectical work that Socrates explicitly walked us through in Book IV. In Book IV, Socrates moved from an account that was politically absurd to one that was psychologically astute by unpacking the city in speech for its psychological content. That is precisely what is called for here in Book V.

Socrates brings the discussion of women and children back to its dialectical purpose at 461e and following when he says, "The next thing we need established by our argument is that this arrangement [of guardians sharing women and children] fits with the rest of the city and is by far the best" (461e).[5] Now that the policy of sharing all women and children in common (i.e. the second *kuma*) is apparently clear enough, Socrates says that the interlocutors must ask whether the new institutional arrangements implied by an elaboration on the role of women and children in the city is consistent with the rest of the constitution that they have constructed. This signals several important confirmations of this reading of the *Republic*. First, Socrates indicates that he has made changes to the constitution of the purged city, and secondly he indicates that those changes will only be acceptable if they are consistent with the way the constitution was constructed earlier. That is, the Female Drama has prompted an elaboration of the city/soul, but it does not imply a repudiation of anything that was previously said of it.

Socrates sets as a standard the fit between the new provisions for women and children in Kallipolis and all of the earlier arrangements made for the institutional design of the city in speech. If the new arguments do not fit within the framework established by the old arguments, then the new arguments will be found lacking. This should remind us

[5] ὡς δὲ ἑπομένη τε τῇ ἄλλῃ πολιτείᾳ καὶ μακρῷ βελτίστη, δεῖ δὴ τὸ μετὰ τοῦτο βεβαιώσασθαι παρὰ τοῦ λόγου.

that Kallipolis is not an entirely new city. We are in a newly elaborated version of the city in speech begun in Book II. In turn, this should remind us that the fundamental issues that were at hand in Books II – IV are still alive. The city/soul begun in Book II was designed as a heuristic for an inquiry into individual justice which, in turn, was the object of inquiry because one needed to know what justice was in order to ask the dialogue's first big question: what sort of life, independent of consequences and appearances, is better: justice or injustice? Socrates reminds us by analogy, the dialectical work of the Female Drama has implications for the individual soul, as well.

Following the analogical connection to the city in speech constructed as a part of the Male Drama, and without introduction or explanation, at 462b Socrates appears to say precisely what women (and perhaps children) stand for in the individual soul. The conversation in this section of Book V has focused up to now on how all women and children might be shared by all men in the city. Then, just after Socrates says the interlocutors must ask whether what they have done dialectically is consistent with the previous constitution, he asks them to focus in particular on the threat of faction and the importance of providing structures in the city/soul to discourage it. Then Socrates says, "Doesn't sharing pleasure and pain bind [the city] together—when, as far as possible, all the citizens feel more or less the same joy or pain at the same births and deaths?[6] Socrates says that the work they have done in the city in speech to make plausible the sharing of women and children is an image of sharing pleasures and pains in the city. Although it will need to be unpacked and explained, it seems obvious that we should begin our attempt to understand the psychological analog to this claim by thinking about how an individual experiences pleasure and pain. Such an interpretive path seems even more justified when immediately after the statement about citizens

[6] οὐκοῦν ἡ μὲν ἡδονῆς τε καὶ λύπης κοινωνία συνδεῖ, ὅταν ὅτι μάλιστα πάντες οἱ πολῖται τῶν αὐτῶν γιγνομένων τε καὶ ἀπολλυμένων παραπλησίως χαίρωσι καὶ λυπῶνται(462b).

sharing pleasure and pains, Socrates explicitly turns the conversation to the soul.[7]

Just as at the end of Book IV, Socrates started with the complete city in speech and began to look for dynamics in the soul that its elements appeared to reflect, here in Book V Socrates takes the city in speech implied by the Female Drama and considers the possible effects of "privatizing" or "sharing" pleasures and pains. Sharing pleasures and pains binds the city together, and privatizing them tears it apart (462b). Since faction is the greatest known threat to the city/soul (462b), sharing pleasures and pains is presented as an essential part of creating internal harmony in the city/soul, that is, virtue.

At 462c, Socrates explicitly connects all of this back to its psychological purpose. Socrates says that the city composed of citizens who share all their pleasures and pains is most like an individual human being. The order of the comparison has been reversed, but the explicit connection is clear. When someone hurts their finger, they say that their finger is hurt, but really the pain belongs to the whole person because something within each of us "binds the body and soul together into a single system under the ruling part within it." (462c)[8]

---

[7] I do not share Cinzia Arruzza's understanding of this passage as a policy recommendation for a city of human beings, so I do not follow her argument to its conclusion in a critique in the ethical and practical problems of creating a city where some citizens (the guardians) can aspire to share the pleasures and pains of the whole city and others (those engaged in economic activity) cannot. Arruzza's analysis of this part of Plato's text is beautifully careful and true to the *Republic*, however, so it is helpful for seeing (1) how the second wave answers one of Thrasymachus' key challenges from Book I, (2) how sharing pleasures and pains is essential to the constitution of Kallipolis, and (3) how this is work that the guardians (*logismos/nous*) and auxiliaries (*thumos*) can do, but that workers (*epithumia*) cannot. Cinzia Arruzza, "The Private and the Common in Plato's *Republic*," *History of Political Thought* 32, no. 2 (2001): 215–233.

[8] οἷον ὅταν που ἡμῶν δάκτυλός του πληγῇ, πᾶσα ἡ κοινωνία ἡ κατὰ τὸ σῶμα πρὸς τὴν ψυχὴν τεταμένη εἰς μίαν σύνταξιν τὴν τοῦ ἄρχοντος ἐν αὐτῇ ᾔσθετό τε καὶ πᾶσα ἅμα συνήλγησεν μέρους πονήσαντος ὅλη, καὶ οὕτω δὴ λέγομεν ὅτι ὁ ἄνθρωπος τὸν δάκτυλον ἀλγεῖ.

The image of the hurt finger should prove to be a great help in our attempt to understand what the second *kuma* means for Plato's psychology and for the elaboration on the model of the soul that is evolving behind the political rhetoric of Book V. When we unpacked the first *kuma* for its psychological content, we found that it concerned the capacity of the non-rational parts of soul to overcome convention or a sense of the ridiculous when directed by the rational soul to institute some particular internal arrangement. The particular example Socrates presented was the unconventional ridiculousness of old women and men exercising together in the gymnasium, and the necessity for a potentially just city to be able to adopt that institution if it were shown to be best. The analogy was the necessity for a potentially just soul to be able to act according to the dictates of reason even when it seems ridiculous or unconventional. This reading fits nicely with the claim that the Female Drama concerns potentiality and becoming; with the narrative frame that indicates that the Male Drama was complete in a sense, and with Socrates' claim that turning to the Female Drama would require the interlocutors to return to the beginning of their dialectical inquiry. I believe I can offer a reading of the second *kuma* that fits similarly well within those interpretative constraints.

Once again, the psychological content of the second *kuma* is much less radical than its political content. The gap between the plausibility of the psychological model and the implausibility of the political model here is even wider than it was for the first *kuma*. On the political level, citizens will be asked to share those things that are in principle shareable, but which seem most naturally one's own. On a political level, overcoming the alliances formed by family ties was always an immense challenge in Athenian democracy, and Cleisthenes' creation of the system of *demes* is considered to be one of the greatest steps in democratic reform precisely because it dealt so deftly with the challenge of breaking up blocks of family power. On a social level, men in Greece are known as their fathers' sons,[9] and elaborate expectations of filial piety frame every part of a man's

[9] And, as in the case of Laertes and Odysseus, some fathers are known by the names of their sons.

individual development. Dissolving the family is a radically unAthenian thing to propose.[10]

But, when the same dynamic is applied to an individual person, the recommendation of the second *kuma* is obviously right, if not as simple to institute as it may at first seem. The claim is that if one's finger hurts, then one should think of the pain as belonging to the whole person and not just to the finger. In practice, that would mean responding to the pain in one's finger in a way that would serve the whole person and not just the finger. If, to use a ridiculous example, that hurting finger were clasping the edge of a cliff, then one would do well not to indulge it. That pain would belong to the whole person, and would be part of a set of considerations that need to be weighed by the rational part of the whole person and enacted by the other parts of the soul in order to preserve the whole individual. One must hold on to the edge of the cliff even if it hurts, because the good of the whole (including the finger) is at stake. It might even include sacrificing the finger entirely. Perhaps one must hold on until one has crippled one's finger forever, but it is still in the interest of the person to hold on. Analogously, it is a necessary condition for the possibility of becoming just that one see one's pleasures and pains in the context of one's whole life, and not as belonging to any one part of it.[11] If one moves from a hurt finger to bruised pride, the principle remains the same even though implementing it would be far more difficult. But, this is what it looks like to be a unified person. Sometimes it is obvious and easy, and sometimes it is difficult, but one always aims to be

---

[10] The history of democratic reform in Athens, beginning with Solon, can be told as an experiment in disentangling politics from family power, with the reforms of Cleisthenes as an apex of sorts. In this sense, Socrates' proposal to subordinate the family entirely to politics could be seen as pushing democratic reforms to their logical conclusion. It could equally be read as a *reductio ad absurdam* argument for thinking that *nomos* could govern *physis*.

[11] As Leon Craig puts it, "Much as the ruling class of the city in *logos* must suppress—and to the extent this is impossible, somehow circumvent, or cleverly 'outwit' (459a–c, 460c–d) natural parental feelings in the interest of a just appraisal of all the city's children…; so must anyone who is serious about wisdom somehow subordinate his natural preference for his "own" ideas to his love of the *best* ideas." Leon Harold Craig, *The War Lover*, 239.

a "unified system" organized under the direction of the "ruling part"—one aims to be whole.

It appears, then, that the second *kuma* concerns the capacity to consider the pleasures and pains of each of its parts in the context of the good for the whole city/soul. Like the psychological content of the first *kuma*, the psychology of the second *kuma* concerns potentiality and becoming in that it indicates the necessity of the potentially just soul to be able to think about and act on its experience of pleasure and pain holistically. And, more generically, it is an account of the place of passion in a life that aspires to be as rational and active as possible. If the claims of particular parts of the soul cannot be brought into perspective by incorporating them in a consideration of the good of the whole soul, then one will not be capable of becoming educated for justice or the other virtues. Furthermore, even if one is capable of reasoning holistically, if one cannot act on one's sense of what is best for the whole city/soul because, for example, the pleasure or pain of one part of oneself is simply too strong to put into perspective, then one will also not be capable of being educated for justice or the other virtues.[12]

A more specific and particular set of implications seem to be emerging from the account of women at this point of the dialogue, as well. Women seem to be associated in the individual soul with the physical body, whereas men appear to represent what animates a human life. Or, perhaps, more precisely, women seem in this part of the *Republic* to rep-

[12] I am hesitant to push quite so far, but this recommendation for putting passions into holistic context may not just widen the divide between the soul and the city in speech; it may suggest the necessity of their structural difference. If one must put one's passions into context in order to be a well-formed human being, and if the end of the ancient *polis* was to promote the formation of shapely souls, then the best ancient *polis* would be committed to the conditions necessary for the formation of the shapeliest human beings. In this case, the best *polis* would need to be committed to the conditions necessary for a person to judge the proper response to one's passions according to the dictates of one's reason and with one's particular situation in mind. In short, the best *polis* would have to commit itself to something like a modern sense of the individual liberty of its citizenry, which is precisely the opposite of telling a citizen that her concerns must be understood only in the context of the holistic good of the *polis*.

resent matter or passion, while men represent form or action. The example of the hurting finger is once again helpful. Our bodies are a necessary part of every aspect of our lives, and the claims of the body demand our attention. If our finger hurts, and we aim to live a good life, we should neither ignore it completely nor obsess over it, but consider the pain in the holistic context of our present situation and larger life goals—then we should act or not based on our reasoned judgment of what that pain means. Because we are embodied, these bodily concerns will come up constantly and need constantly to be contextualized and acted upon.

The claims of the body look like appetites, the *epithumetic* activity of the soul represented by workers in the soul, and in large part they are. But issues of embodiment are not identical with *epithumia*. We have appetites for things that our bodies do not need, or even want. In a different context, Socrates uses the example of the thirst associated with the judgment that one should not drink (perhaps because of illness or of a sense that the drink might be contaminated), as an example of a sort of phantom appetite (439b). In that example, one feels thirsty but drinking is the last thing the body wants. The needs of the body that generate the appetite for liquid are mediated or distorted. In the most extreme example Socrates offers, one can see another rift between appetite and the body in the life of the tyrant. The tyrant's desires are debauched, developed to monstrous depths, and reach to the ancient horror of horrors—the desire to eat one's own children. These tyrannical appetites have no connection to the legitimate needs of the body, and only the most tenuous connection to the body at all.

The body seems to have a role to play in activities of the *thumotic* soul, as well as the *epithumetic*. In the context of the *Symposium*, it seems important to Plato's characterization of Alcibiades that he is tall. In the *Euthydemus*, it certainly matters that Cleinias is beautiful. Charmides' beauty is an essential dynamic in the *Charmides*. Embodiment, perhaps mediated by the way that others respond to these characters, has an impact on how they develop thumotically. Alcibiades' ambitions and recklessness are linked to his physical presence. All of Cleinias' friendships seem to be conditioned by his attractiveness. Charmides' beauty threw Socrates off his game, but just for a minute or two.

With these thoughts in mind, one can see how the body, or the body's claims, might line up with the account of women in the first two waves. The capacity to overcome ridicule and convention in order to be guided by reason becomes, with the frame of embodiment in mind, the capacity of one's passions to become aligned with one's rational actions. Likewise, one can understand the capacity to put the claims of pleasure and pain into the holistic context of the good for one's life as the capacity for one's passions to be brought into harmony with one's rational activity.[13] Understood in these terms, both the first and the second waves concern the capacity of human passions to respond to rational action. The other side of this argument, i.e., the rational soul's proper control of every other part of the soul, was an implicit part of the work of the account in Books II–IV. Once again, it seems that "women" were in the purged city all along, despite the fact that they were barely mentioned before Book V.

If one associates women with passions and men with actions in the city/soul, the argument for the education of women comes into much sharper focus. One must train one's mind to know the good and seek it, but one must also habituate the body to take pleasure in what is good. The body and mind, passions and actions, (men and women) should be trained together because one's pleasures and pains need to be brought into harmony with one's thoughts and intentions if one wants to avoid a life dissipated by factious conflict.

From the point at which they come to agreement on the importance of pleasures and pains belonging to the whole person (462d–466d), Socrates' and Glaucon's focus on playing out some of the details regarding what makes the institutional arrangement of the second *kuma* best for the city/soul. They conclude that "the cause of the greatest good for our

[13] Socrates is, throughout the Platonic corpus, the paradigm case of this dynamic. His physical strength is renowned. He can drink men under the table and go without sleep. He is unphased by the cold and famine that weakens the Athenian troops at Potidea. His swagger is so pronounced on the retreating march from Delium that enemies are discouraged from attacking his section of the line. But, his physical strength is more than matched by his mental or spiritual strength. Like Silenus (or Chiron), the super/sub-human calls of his body are no match for the stronger control of his mind.

city is the sharing of women and children by the auxiliaries" (464b).[14] In a sense, Socrates' interlocutors and Plato's readers should be prepared for this claim about the greatest good for the city/soul, since the explicit question at issue was whether the institution of sharing women and children was best. But, in another sense, Socrates has moved us to this extremely important claim by equivocating on what "best" or "greatest"[15] seems to mean in the context of the argument.

When Socrates raises the question of whether sharing women and children was "best," the context suggests more moderate stakes. The question seems to be, given the elements of the city/soul as they had been presented, whether sharing is or is not the best way to manage women and children. But, when Socrates brings the argument for sharing women and children to a conclusion, he does not just claim that sharing is the best way to manage women and children given those constraints. Instead, he argues that sharing women and children is the cause of the highest good of the city/soul. This is a different meaning of "best." This is a much grander claim.

Judgment regarding what's "best" in the first sense is the work of *logismos*; but, judgment regarding what's best in the second, loftier, sense is not. *Logismos* can take what is given and arrange it optimally by purely internal standards. That is, in fact, its work. As Eva Brann puts it, "the logistikon is a restricted power, a power of planning, whose specific work [is] calculation."[16] But, *logismos* cannot appeal to anything but those internal constraints. It cannot assess the quality of the elements it is given or compare what it achieves to other arrangements of other given sets of elements and constraints. These judgments imply a different meaning for "best" than the one that is intelligible by *logismos* alone. When Socrates says that the community that shares women and children is best in this second sense, i.e. participates in the highest possible arrangement for souls, Socrates is presenting a standard that *logismos* cannot recognize or

---

[14] τοῦ μεγίστου ἄρα ἀγαθοῦ τῇ πόλει αἰτία ἡμῖν πέφανται ἡ κοινωνία τοῖς ἐπικούροις τῶν τε παίδων καὶ τῶν γυναικῶν.

[15] μεγίστου.

[16] Eva Brann, *The Music of the Republic* (Philadelphia: Paul Dry Books, 2004) 163.

enact, at least alone. He implies that there is an activity of soul that is higher than the highest activity apparently possible for the soul as it is presented in Books II–IV. By implication and still unnamed, *nous* has taken the stage in the Female Drama.

It is an essential feature of Plato's dialogic genre to insert centrally important claims in passages where their significance is easily missed. At least many, and perhaps all, of the "elenchic dialogues" offer answers to their guiding questions (what is virtue [in the *Meno*], what is courage [in the *Laches*], etc.), but not at the end, and not in moments where the interlocutors recognize that those answers have been dialectically introduced. One of the important differences between the *Republic* and many (perhaps all) of Plato's other dialogues is that several of Socrates' interlocutors seem intellectually and morally up to the challenge of sticking with Socrates through a long complicated argument; and at least one of them, Glaucon, may be capable of a thorough-going understanding of the deepest matters at hand. But none of Socrates' interlocutors in the *Republic* seems to notice that they have been brought to such a significant conclusion at 464b. Because of that, and of course because of other structural reasons built into the Platonic text, Socrates will not elaborate yet on how exactly the community of women and children is the cause of the greatest good for the city/soul. But, as careful readers, we should be looking for that account and remembering that it originated here. Perhaps, after Socrates refers to children as "offspring of the Good" at 460b, we should already have been expecting it.

At 466d, Socrates voluntarily returns to the question that Glaucon raised at 457d, but that he asked leave to bracket until he had made his case that the arrangement of the city/soul implied by the second *kuma* was best. Now that he has shown it is best to have a city/soul in which all women and children are held in common, he asks, is it possible? Rather than directly addressing the question that he himself just recalled for consideration, Socrates instead turns to the role of women and children in war. At 470b, Socrates explains how war fits into their account of the city/soul. War and faction, he says, are two related things. Faction describes inner conflict. War refers to external conflict. On the level of political discourse, faction comes to mean conflict among Greeks, whether they are citizens of the same city or not, while war means conflict with non-Greeks. On the level of psychological discourse, the analogy for faction has already been made clear several times in the dialogue. It means conflict between the parts or functions of one's soul. Leontius' anger with himself for simultaneously wanting and not wanting to look at the corpses outside the Athenian wall is a reaction to internal faction (and thus proof that the soul has parts). Faction is the generic condition of every form of vice, since it describes the situation in which the parts/powers of the soul do not fully recognize each other's particular sphere of influence (i.e., when the soul is not moderate) and/or in which each of the parts does not do its own work (i.e., when the soul is unjust). Faction is internal conflict. War is conflict with something external to oneself.

If war is to be understood as response to external threats, then there is a sense in which discussing war is, in fact, responsive to the question of whether the shared community of women and children is possible for the city/soul. If the city/soul cannot, in principle, defend itself against external threats, then it will not be possible for it to exist. So, while Socrates may indeed be stalling a bit before he confronts the third *kuma*, he is not entirely off topic.

The particular arrangements for warfare in Kallipolis, like most of what has already been detailed, is fantastically implausible on a political level. It is also tricky to understand psychologically. The main provisions for women and children in war are that (1) women and men should go to war together, (2) children should be observers of war, guided by their (conventional) fathers to avoid excessive risk, and (3) children must be given "wings," that is fast, manageable horses so that they can have a good view of war and a quick, safe escape if it becomes necessary. Socrates goes on to establish conventions for incentivizing bravery, responding to death, and treating enemies appropriately; while none of these latter conventions appears to give women and children special consideration, one must ask why they appear at this point of the dialogue.

In the context of the dialogue, it makes perfect sense that women and men should go to war together. That is what they are trained to do, and the lawgivers of Kallipolis have gone to great efforts to provide the best training to all its trainable citizens so that the best auxiliaries will take the field when needed, regardless of gender. Interpreted for its psychological content, I take this to mean that action and passion, reason and emotion, mind and body should be trained together and take the field together when the soul is faced with an external threat.

What does it mean to say that children should be brought to war as well? First, perhaps we should review what I have argued previously regarding the role of children in the psychological reading of the city/soul. Plato's children represent something similar, I think, to what Aristotle calls "*hexis*:" a stable condition of soul developed by habituation. It is translated into English in several ways including "state," "possession," "disposition," "character," "personality," and "active condition." In the context of my reading of the *Republic*, this would mean that when one's deliberate actions combine with one's embodied passions, that such aspects of character—these active conditions—are engendered. If this is right, then the meaning of taking children to war begins to emerge. When confronted with an external threat, one must defend oneself as well as possible, and such defense may take many different forms. Bringing one's children to war would mean exposing one's developing dispositions to conflict in order to prepare them to one day to be a part of one's rational and passionate defense against such threats.

That brings us to the odd detail we are given about keeping children safe when we bring them to war. Socrates tells us at 467d that they must be given wings (*pteroun*), and then he explains that what he means is that they must be given fast and manageable[17] horses in order that they may have the best possible view of their future job and a safe escape. These are strange and provocative images, and they seem to me to open the door to ideas that Socrates will elaborate on more fully later in the dialogue, but perhaps we can begin to make a bit of sense of them at this point of the argument.

If children are emerging *hexeis*, then they should be brought to battle in the sense that one should develop one's capacities with the assets, liabilities, and challenges of one's situation in mind. Let us return for a moment to the earlier example of the indignant physician—the person who was *logistically* disposed to be a good physician (among other things) and *thumotically* disposed to respond particularly strongly in the face of perceived injustice, and who has put together a life with a clear sense of what both of these dispositions mean for her character. Life is long, and the process of character development is ongoing, as Plato well knew, so our indignant physician will have choices to make every day about how her dispositions may be developed into

[17] ποδωκεστάτων καὶ εὐηνιωτάτων.

hexeis. If she is to live responsibly, she will find ways to test herself along the way.

To extend the example concretely, let us imagine that our indignant physician decides to develop a daily practice in meditation. She might see how being more mindful and in control of her passions could make her a better physician or could improve her life in other ways. At first, such an idea is just an intention. But, if one is capable of acting on that intention over time, it could emerge as a proto-*hexis* of sorts, not a firmly established active condition yet, but something that is on the road to becoming a part of one's character. At that point, any rational, deliberate person would try it out in life—that is, find out if meditation really "works for them." This attempt could take various forms. Perhaps, working in the ER, our indignant physician believes she sees evidence of child abuse and she feels herself becoming enraged, but she needs to keep her passions in check in order to deal most effectively with her patient. Perhaps, she'll give her new proto-*hexis* a try and step into a quiet space for three minutes to meditate. Maybe that will work for her. Maybe it will not. But, she will not know unless she tries.

Although we will not have real clarity until we consider evidence from later in the text, this example appears to me in keeping with Socrates' account of taking children to war. Will a developed disposition for meditation contribute to the holistic goodness of our doctor's life or not? How would one know without trying it out and reflecting on one's experience? One must take one's soul-children to war. But, what could it mean to give them wings? Perhaps it means trying these proto-*hexeis* out in a way that does not put premature pressure on them or depend upon them for more than what they, in their undeveloped state, can reasonably be expected to accomplish. To appeal to our example, our indignant doctor really should have a "plan b" in mind for dealing with her anger at the suspected child abuser in case her emerging capacity for meditation does not work to help her find clarity. But if meditation helps her even a little, she should note it and let it go, let it fly away, and return to developing her capacity for meditation away from conflict so that it will be stronger and more reliable for future conflicts.[18]

---

[18] Jill Frank argues that Socrates is interested throughout the *Republic* in determining what sort of education prepares one for war. She understands this passage (among others) to mean that "[c]hildren should not be exposed to the

After the plan to take children to war on fast horses (which is the last detail Socrates offers specifically about women and children) and beginning at 468a, Socrates presents two arguments about proper behavior for soldiers, in general: (1) how courage and cowardice should be rewarded and punished respectively, (2) how enemies should be treated. Since Socrates broaches these topics as a part of the Female Drama, we should ask both what they mean and in what way they belong to the account of women and children in the city/soul.

If one distinguishes oneself as a brave and honorable soldier, according to Socrates, one should have one's pick of people to show open affection for, perhaps to kiss, whether one desires to direct one's affection toward one who is male or female. And, the reason he gives is clear: "so that if anyone passionately loves another, whether male or female, he will try harder to win the prize for bravery" (468c).[19] If one has passionate love (*eros*), and if this policy is instituted, the power of that passion will be harnessed for the good of the city/soul. The reward takes a pre-existing passion and focuses it in the interest of a rational action, that is, an action designed to contribute to the good of the whole city/soul. So this provision belongs in the Female Drama because it begins with passion (*eros*) and indicates how and why it may be brought into the service of the whole city/soul through *logistic* governance and *thumotic* support.

---

experience of violence on the ground that it deforms their souls and thereby threatens their ability to become virtuous. But this is not true of exposing children to knowledge about war or to knowledge of vice, for that matter (396a). The experience of violence corrupts their capacities for virtue. But a curriculum that insulates children entirely from knowledge of violence is no good either. Neither the experience of violence through war nor the censure of violence through the deception and constraint characteristic of war education, it seems, offers an adequate preparation for the life of philosophy" (453). Although Frank does not address moral psychology in her account, I believe it is entirely compatible with my interpretation of children as *hexeis* and of the value and danger of "taking them to war," which necessitates giving them "wings." Jill Frank, "Wages of War: On Judgment in Plato's *Republic*," *Political Theory* 35, no. 4 (August 2007): 443–467.

[19] ἵνα καί, ἐάν τίς του τύχῃ ἐρῶν ἢ ἄρρενος ἢ θηλείας.

To underline the erotic nature of this part of the argument, Socrates brings Homer and Hesiod into the conversation. When we honor bravery, Socrates suggests, we should model what Homer presents in *Iliad* 7 as the reward of Ajax. And, when brave soldiers die on the battlefield, we should say of them what Hesiod says that they belong to the golden race and have become, in their death, spirits who protect human beings from evil. So, Socrates offers the double recommendation of appealing to passions within the city/soul and of appealing to them with poetry—writing designed to appeal to *eros* for the sake of turning it to rational action.

The final passage of the section of the *Republic* focused on the second *kuma* begins at 469b and offers recommendations for the proper treatment of one's enemies. All of these recommendations begin by making a distinction between Greeks and barbarians. Some threats, it appears, are kindred and others are alien. Both kinds must be defeated, but vanquished kin deserve different treatment than vanquished "others." This is made clear at 470b, where Socrates returns to the distinction between faction and war, suggesting that everything in the argument up to that point may apply equally to both, which makes good psychological sense, as well. Our indignant doctor, for example, may try to use meditation to address an external threat to her virtue or an internal one. Most of the time, including in the case of her anger with a suspected child abuser, we face both, simultaneously. Her anger has an external source, and perhaps a good and legitimate one, but it is *her* anger, too. It is a product of her disposition, and she knows that it must be governed if she is to lead a happy life.

At this point of the dialogue (471c), Glaucon appears to be out of patience with Socrates. He either does not see or does not care that an account of the proper role of auxiliaries in war may have something to do with whether justice is possible in *Kallipolis*. The question that he hoped Socrates would address long ago, and the one that he is no longer willing to wait for, is whether *Kallipolis* is possible at all. When he presses this point, Socrates seems to have no alternative but reluctantly to address the greatest and most profane threat posed by the necessity of enacting the Female Drama—the third *kuma*, which is the subject of the next chapter.

6

The Third Wave

(THE GENESIS OF LOGISMOS)

At 471c, Glaucon seems to be out of patience. Socrates has gone on at length about institutional revisions to the city/soul but he does not seem willing to address the two questions that now interest Glaucon: (1) if Kallipolis is possible, and (2) if it is possible, how Kallipolis could possibly come into being.[1] In order to push Socrates to address his questions directly, Glaucon closes off all the arguments he thinks Socrates might pursue instead. He grants that Kallipolis is best in every imaginable way. He lists all the ways that it would be loveliest and most advantageous for a city to be organized the way Socrates has organized Kallipolis, and he goes on to say that there would be several additional benefits to such a constitution that Socrates has not yet specified. But, he insists that Socrates show, granting all of the above, that Kallipolis is possible and how it could come into being.[2]

Glaucon's interests have shifted again. First, he was interested in (1) whether justice or injustice was better for a human being, then (2)

[1] τὸ ὡς δυνατὴ αὕτη ἡ πολιτεία γενέσθαι καὶ τίνα τρόπον ποτὲ δυνατή.

[2] ἐπεὶ ὅτι γε, εἰ γένοιτο, πάντ᾽ ἂν εἴη ἀγαθὰ πόλει ᾗ γένοιτο, καὶ ἃ σὺ παραλείπεις ἐγὼ λέγω, ὅτι καὶ τοῖς πολεμίοις ἄριστ᾽ ἂν μάχοιντο τῷ ἥκιστα ἀπολείπειν ἀλλήλους, γιγνώσκοντές τε καὶ ἀνακαλοῦντες ταῦτα τὰ ὀνόματα ἑαυτούς, ἀδελφούς, πατέρας, ὑεῖς: εἰ δὲ καὶ τὸ θῆλυ συστρατεύοιτο, εἴτε καὶ ἐν τῇ αὐτῇ τάξει εἴτε καὶ ὄπισθεν ἐπιτεταγμένον, φόβων τε ἕνεκα τοῖς ἐχθροῖς καὶ εἴ ποτέ τις ἀνάγκη βοηθείας γένοιτο, οἶδ᾽ ὅτι ταύτῃ πάντῃ ἄμαχοι ἂν εἶεν: καὶ οἴκοι γε ἃ παραλείπεται ἀγαθά, ὅσα ἂν εἴη αὐτοῖς, ὁρῶ. ἀλλ᾽ ὡς ἐμοῦ ὁμολογοῦντος πάντα ταῦτα ὅτι εἴη ἂν καὶ ἄλλα γε μυρία, εἰ γένοιτο ἡ πολιτεία αὕτη, μηκέτι πλείω περὶ αὐτῆς λέγε, ἀλλὰ τοῦτο αὐτὸ ἤδη πειρώμεθα ἡμᾶς αὐτοὺς πείθειν, ὡς δυνατὸν καὶ ᾗ δυνατόν, τὰ δ᾽ ἄλλα χαίρειν ἐῶμεν (471c-e).

whether the city they were constructing in speech was livable for a man such as himself, then (3) whether the community of women and children was possible, and now (4) whether Kallipolis itself is possible. So, it would be wrong to characterize Glaucon as single-minded. But, on the other hand, he is remarkably focused. His interests shift, but he stays focused on whatever interest he has, and he pushes Socrates to stay with him.

Before looking more closely at Glaucon's questions and working through Socrates' famously controversial response, it is worth taking a moment to consider who Glaucon has revealed himself to be so far and how his character contributes to the nature of the dialogue.[3] Almost halfway through one of Plato's longest dialogues, Glaucon is focused, unshaken, and poised enough to push Socrates back toward the topic that interests him. Without Glaucon's patience and focus, this dialogue would have been much shorter. Like Euthyphro, perhaps Glaucon could have thought of somewhere else he needed to be. Like Meno, maybe his inability to follow the argument could have left him too confused to continue. Or, perhaps like Ctesippus in the *Euthydemus*, he could have become too angry to engage in dialectic. We see versions of these attitudes in the *Republic*, itself, when Cephalus has more important things to do than talk with Socrates about justice, Polemarchus can't quite get himself untangled from the implicit contradictions in the arguments about justice he has heard from others, and Thrasymachus must be made to blush, relent, and retreat to the margins in order for Socrates to proceed with their inquiry. The bulk of the *Republic* could not have been written with interlocutors like those of Book I on center stage. The arguments are too complicated and they need too much time to develop.

Only someone as impressive as Glaucon could sustain the argument of the *Republic* with Socrates. Socrates can begin a conversation with an-

[3] It is interesting that Plato explicitly separates Glaucon's query into two questions: "if" it is possible and "how" it is possible. My interpretation attempts to address both questions even though it collapses them into one some of the time.

yone, but very few interlocutors in the Platonic corpus could have stayed with him to the end of this inquiry.[4]

Glaucon's virtues are central to the structure and content of the *Republic*, but his flaws drive the argument of the dialogue as well. He may be obsessed with politics. According to Xenophon, Glaucon was so impatient for political distinction that he embarrassed himself by speaking publicly before he was twenty years old on matters that he knew nothing about.[5] In most of the *Republic*, he cannot seem to see past the political image that Socrates provides, even though Socrates introduced the image in order to answer Glaucon's own question about justice for an individual person. Or, perhaps, Glaucon is too drawn to political things to focus on the psychological argument, even though he sees it. At no point of the dialogue is Glaucon's overwhelming interest in politics clearer than in 471e and following where, if Glaucon were attending to the purpose for which the city in speech was first introduced, he would see that Socrates had already answered his primary question. Glaucon's question at 358b is not whether justice is possible for an individual—he and Adeimantus seem to presume that it is. Instead, Glaucon asks whether justice is better than injustice for a human life, and he pushes the question by imagining a just life that lacks all of the advantages of seeming just (and an unjust life that enjoys all those advantages).

Had Glaucon remembered the nature of the city/soul at 471e, as he grants point by point the superiority of *Kallipolis* to all other cities, he would realize that he had already, by analogy, been convinced that the life of justice is better in every way than the life of injustice. If he had seen (or cared) that Socrates had provided a convincing answer to his original question, perhaps he would also have been ready to move beyond that important conclusion to another one that Socrates will not explicitly claim until 612c in Book X: that the advantages of the appearance of justice are attached to the reality of justice in such a way that it will be impossible for the perfectly just man to appear perfectly unjust or vice versa. Rightly or wrongly, Glaucon (and Adeimantus) never seemed to doubt

[4] I am indebted to two of my students, Jordin Post and Anna Bates, for bringing Glaucon's virtues into focus for me.

[5] *Memorabilia* 3. 6. 14.

that it was possible for an individual to be just if he chose to be. Glaucon does not insist that Socrates address the possibility of Kallipolis because he is unsure about his capacity to become a philosopher; he does so because he is unsure about his capacity to create a utopia.

Glaucon does not yet know that Socrates is developing the just city/soul of Book IV into Kallipolis, the philosophical city/soul of Books V–VII. It is therefore not yet clear to Glaucon that he has already acknowledged the superiority of the philosophical life to all others. Once *nous* is added to the psychological model, the internal harmony of the just soul from Book IV is not longer the ideal. The model under early stages of development in Book V requires not only internal harmony, but fidelity to a still unnamed external reference point. But this noetic requirement is already in place. Rhetorically, this is a part of what is at stake when Socrates says that the third *kuma* is a prerequisite for the first two *kumata*. In order for any of the institutional arrangements of Kallipolis to be instantiated, a philosopher must rule. Or, put psychologically, in order for a soul to take its best, highest, most beautiful shape, it must be philosophical. It might be the case that this noetic element was implied from the beginning of the construction of the city in speech in Book II—that any vision of internal harmony implies some external reference point in order to be intelligible—but, it is clearly implicit throughout Book V, whether Glaucon has noticed or not.

Perhaps Glaucon does not see that he has agreed that the philosophical life is best because he is not attuned to the psychology of the city/soul at this crucial moment in the dialogue.[6] His mind is on political

[6] There are many theories of the portrayal of Glaucon's and Adeimantus' characters in the *Republic*, and Catherine Zuckert runs through several of the most important and most recent ones in *Plato's Philosophers: The Coherence of the Dialogues* (Chicago: University of Chicago Press, 2009) 336 fn. 102. Most commentators agree that neither of Plato's brothers is portrayed as a potential philosopher-ruler, but I think it is less certain. It seems clear that neither is capable of philosophical rule at the beginning of the dialogue, but I am not convinced that Glaucon is not capable at the end of the dialogue. Neither am I convinced that he is capable, however. Glaucon is presented as a character capable of great things intellectually and morally, and I think he is presented with a choice at the end of the dialogue that we do not get to see him make.

things. He wants to know if it is possible to bring Kallipolis into existence politically. Could one really develop a constitution in which citizens overcame conventions for the sake of a rational conception of the common good? Could one bring into existence a city where the pleasures and pains of each citizen were felt and addressed rationally and holistically by the city as a whole? Could one unify a city to that remarkable degree, get all of one's citizens to act together for common ends, and create a perfectly harmonized political reality?

Socrates has a twofold response to Glaucon's newly refined challenge. First, he announces that Glaucon is forcing the third and most difficult "wave" of objections, the third *kuma*. Secondly, he recalls for Glaucon that it was an inquiry into the nature of of justice and injustice that brought them to where they are in the argument—he reminds him, but perhaps not explicitly enough, that they are working on the pattern (*paradeigma*) of the city/soul, not a city per se. At 472b, before Socrates faces the third *kuma*, he unpacks an important implication of remembering the origins of their dialectic. At this crucial transition in the Female Drama between the second and third *kumata*, Socrates makes an apparent attempt to bring Glaucon back on track—to remind him that the city in speech is an image of the human soul—and he introduces a centrally important principle for their inquiry into the nature of justice and injustice. Should we expect the just man to be perfectly just, he asks, or should we be satisfied if he approximates it? Glaucon immediately says that the approximation, not just the perfection of justice in a human life, will suffice.[7]

With those two points made explicit (i.e., [1] they have been constructing a model of justice, and [2] actualizing the approximation of the model will suffice for justice in a city and in a soul), Socrates goes on to clarify the sort of model or pattern they have been constructing, and the proper way to think about it. He says, we thought

[7] ἀλλ' ἐὰν εὕρωμεν οἷόν ἐστι δικαιοσύνη, ἆρα καὶ ἄνδρα τὸν δίκαιον ἀξιώσομεν μηδὲν δεῖν αὐτῆς ἐκείνης διαφέρειν, ἀλλὰ πανταχῇ τοιοῦτον εἶναι οἷον δικαιοσύνη ἐστίν; ἢ ἀγαπήσομεν ἐὰν ὅτι ἐγγύτατα αὐτῆς ᾖ καὶ πλεῖστα τῶν ἄλλων ἐκείνης μετέχῃ; **Glaucon:** οὕτως, ἔφη: ἀγαπήσομεν. (472b-c)

> by looking at how they appeared to stand in relation to happiness and its opposite, we would also be compelled to agree about our own selves as well, that whoever was most like them would have a life most like theirs. But we were not doing this in order to demonstrate that it is possible for these things to come into being (472c–d).[8]

This passage is particularly important because it is a rare and clear moment in the central books of the *Republic* where the terms of the city in speech are explicitly calibrated to the parts of the individual soul. Here, Socrates tells us (at least part of) what he is up to in the Female Drama. He is still working on the city/soul in order to inquire into the nature of individual justice, and he has been using the model or pattern[9] to create an analogy. He hoped that if they reached certain conclusions about the city/soul, the interlocutors would draw the same conclusions about themselves. That is, if they saw how different arrangements in the city stood in relation to happiness and unhappiness, it would be clear that analogous arrangements within their souls would stand analogously to happiness and unhappiness. He resets the framework of their inquiry, which has grown so substantially and taken so many turns that it is at constant risk of going off the rails, and shows that he has been on the same track for this entire, complicated journey.

In practical terms, Socrates' clarification does two main things. First, it brings Glaucon back to the question of justice for an individual, which he seems to have lost sight of in the argument. Secondly, it provides a heuristic frame for using the city/soul to help clarify moral questions and, ultimately, live the best possible life. Here is what we have been doing, Socrates says, and here's why. Thirdly, it specifies that the frame is not meant to refer to actual cities and people, but to models that need not ever exist in the world in order fully to serve their function in the current inquiry.

---

[8] ἵνα εἰς ἐκείνους ἀποβλέποντες, οἷοι ἂν ἡμῖν φαίνωνται εὐδαιμονίας τε πέρι καὶ τοῦ ἐναντίου, ἀναγκαζώμεθα καὶ περὶ ἡμῶν αὐτῶν ὁμολογεῖν, ὃς ἂν ἐκείνοις ὅτι ὁμοιότατος ᾖ, τὴν ἐκείνης μοῖραν ὁμοιοτάτην ἕξειν, ἀλλ' οὐ τούτου ἕνεκα, ἵν' ἀποδείξωμεν ὡς δυνατὰ ταῦτα γίγνεσθαι.

[9] For more on the meaning of *paradeigma* (παραδείγμα), see Stanley Rosen, *Plato's* Republic (New Haven: Yale University Press, 2005) 201.

This interlude is much briefer than the section at the end of Book IV that takes the structure of the city/soul and unpacks its psychological content explicitly, but it is not less systematic or clear. The work of correlating the parts of the city to the soul was done at the end of Book IV. Here, near the end of Book V, Socrates implies that what the interlocutors have accomplished in the intervening conversation makes their schema deeper, more sophisticated, and better suited to account for the complexities of the human soul.

The most important thing to note about this passage is, perhaps, the most obvious. Socrates is and has been concerned from the beginning of the construction of the city in speech with the city/soul. He continues to think of the city in speech as it has evolved to incorporate women and children explicitly into the life of the city in speech as a useful image in the inquiry into the nature of individual justice and injustice. Now that the city/soul has been elaborated upon almost to the point of completion, and as Glaucon seems to be pushing on points that may or may not be helpful in the inquiry into the nature of individual justice and injustice, it is particularly important to reconnect with the nature and purposes of the image.[10]

Perhaps the most curious thing to notice about Socrates' account of where the city/soul came from and what it will be good for is his claim that it is not important to demonstrate whether or not it is possible for the city/soul to exist (472d). It makes perfect sense for the existence of the city/soul to be irrelevant to using it as a model of justice against which we may judge our own progress towards happiness. But, it is a bit odd to say that the possibility of the city/soul is irrelevant in the context of the arguments about possibility and potentiality that have characterized the Female Drama. What have the first and second *kumata* been about if not possibility? Or, perhaps put more precisely, what sort of pos-

[10] This is not to say that the city is not also important to Socrates. At 472d, Socrates quickly brings the city back into the conversation and raises the possibility of founding a city that approximates the city they are constructing in speech. I do not think the city Socrates has in mind closely resembles the city Glaucon has ambitions to rule, but it is clear, nonetheless, that Socrates, and not just Glaucon, is interested in founding something "in deed."

sibilities have the first and second *kumata* been about if not the possibility of the existence of the city in deed?

The possibilities modeled by the first and second *kumata* are hypothetical possibilities, i.e., necessary, but not sufficient, conditions for something that Socrates seems now to be suggesting will not fully come into being. They take the form of the claim "if p is not true, then q is not true." So, the psychological claim of the first *kuma* could be restated as something like "if the desire to avoid ridicule cannot be overcome by the rational and spirited parts of the soul, then one will not be capable of being trained or educated for virtue." Similarly, the psychological claim of the second *kuma* could take something like the following form "if the pains and pleasures of the particular parts of the soul cannot be brought into holistic perspective and practice by the rational and spirited parts of the soul, then one will not be capable of being trained or educated for virtue."

Neither the first nor the second *kuma* is presented as a sufficient condition for being educable for virtue, much less as a sufficient condition for becoming virtuous. At no point in Socrates' account of the city/soul does he suggest that the one who can overcome the desire to avoid ridicule will become virtuous. Nor does he claim that one who can put one's pleasures and pains into an actionable, holistic perspective will become virtuous. Even collectively they are not sufficient. There is no suggestion that one who shared both of these capacities would necessarily become virtuous or, in particular, just. The first and second *kumata* represent fundamental potencies for virtue, i.e., capacities that signal the possibility of becoming trained and educated for virtue, but they in no way imply that their existence alone will bring virtue into existence.

Because the first and second *kumata* are necessary conditions for the possibility of virtue, they are a part of the ideal model that Kallipolis is turning out to be, but the extent of their outlandishness is not entirely clear until Socrates presents the third and final *kuma*. Socrates has already shown that the first and second *kumata* are necessary conditions for the city/soul to be trained and educated for virtue, but here he admits that the necessary condition for the possibility of the first and second *kumata* is the third *kuma*: philosophers must rule. "Unless either philosophers become kings in their cities or those whom we now call kings and rulers engage philosophy truly and sufficiently, so that political power and philosophy are thoroughly conjoined…there will be no respite from the evil in cities nor, I think, for the human race" (473d-e).[11]

In order to overcome ridicule for the sake of the good of the whole city/soul (the first wave), philosophy and political power must be conjoined. In order to bring the pleasures and pains of parts of the city soul into actionable holistic perspective (the second wave), philosophy and political power must be conjoined. In order, Socrates now clarifies, for cities and human beings to avoid exhausting themselves in the fight against evil, philosophy and political power must be conjoined. In short, no aspect of the city in speech is possible without the conjunction of philosophy and political power. And, as Glaucon and Socrates well know, if Socrates is a model of what the philosophical life looks like, philosophers are never going to rule in Athens. Either Socrates has led Glaucon and the others on (1) an immense wild goose chase, (2) something other than Athenian political policy is at issue here, or (3) the terms of their argument need to be carefully reconsidered and redefined.

Glaucon's response to Socrates' outlandish claim is telling. One can imagine the looks on Polemarchus and Thrasymachus' face at this moment. Polemarchus must be horribly confused. I imagine his jaw dropped open. Perhaps he would be looking around to Adeimantus and the others for confirmation that he just heard what he thought he heard. Thrasymachus, if he has retained any of his character from Book I, must be smirking. Had he not been made to blush, surely he would be yelling or pacing or, perhaps, storming away at this point. One can imagine him calling Socrates a child or a charlatan, or at least thinking it. But, Glaucon reacts differently. His primary concern seems to be Socrates' well-being. Socrates is in danger, Glaucon says, and his only hope for escape is to defend himself by argument. Glaucon reaffirms his commitment to

[11] ἐὰν μή, ἦν δ᾽ ἐγώ, ἢ οἱ φιλόσοφοι βασιλεύσωσιν ἐν ταῖς πόλεσιν ἢ οἱ βασιλῆς τε νῦν λεγόμενοι καὶ δυνάσται φιλοσοφήσωσι γνησίως τε καὶ ἱκανῶς, καὶ τοῦτο εἰς ταὐτὸν συμπέσῃ, δύναμίς τε πολιτικὴ καὶ φιλοσοφία, τῶν δὲ νῦν πορευομένων χωρὶς ἐφ᾽ ἑκάτερον αἱ πολλαὶ φύσεις ἐξ ἀνάγκης ἀποκλεισθῶσιν, οὐκ ἔστι κακῶν παῦλα, ὦ φίλε Γλαύκων, ταῖς πόλεσι, δοκῶ δ᾽ οὐδὲ τῷ ἀνθρωπίνῳ γένει, οὐδὲ αὕτη ἡ πολιτεία μή ποτε πρότερον φυῇ τε εἰς τὸ δυνατὸν καὶ φῶς ἡλίου ἴδῃ, ἣν νῦν λόγῳ διεληλύθαμεν.

stand by Socrates as an ally as he delivers his apology. This time, it is not Glaucon's focused intelligence that keeps the conversation of the *Republic* alive; it is his virtue and friendship.

The first thing to be done if Socrates and his interlocutors hope to survive the third *kuma*—the claim that the possibility of justice in the city/soul is predicated on the union of philosophy with political power[12]—is to define what it means to be a philosopher and to make clear who should and should not engage in philosophy. Only then will it be possible to make the case that they are not simply discussing absurdities. All of Socrates' interlocutors in this dialogue are familiar with political life and what it takes to have power. All of them know Socrates and are familiar with the philosophical life he lives. Blending those two ways of life into one must appear to them as obviously impossible. And, yet, the conversation continues.

The first step Socrates makes in order to begin working toward the definition of the philosopher is to break philosophy down as the love of wisdom and then to define, generically, what it means to be a lover of something. Wisdom will have to wait a moment. He asks Glaucon at 474e whether or not he needs to be reminded that if one is properly to be called a lover of something, one must love the whole of that thing and not just some part of it. Glaucon says that he needs a reminder, and that spurs a few intervening moments of odd dramatic detail before the inquiry proceeds. Socrates voices surprise that Glaucon doesn't remember this premise having been demonstrated already. He says that men like Glaucon who are passionate about boys would do well to remember that they will find all boys attractive. Glaucon deftly avoids affirming or denying Socrates' description of him, though, and they move quickly to the relevance of this principle to developing a definition of the philosopher.

The philosopher, Socrates says, has an appetite (*epithumia*) for wisdom. The surface of the claim is that the philosopher's appetite is for the whole of wisdom and not some part of it. This is what Socrates emphasizes in the comparison to passionate lovers of boys and to the generic clam that those who are truly lovers are those who love all of whatever it is that they love. But it is provocative that Socrates describes this as an

[12] δύναμίς τε πολιτικὴ καὶ φιλοσοφία.

appetite for wisdom, an activity of the lowest part of the soul. Appetites cannot be trained or educated. They may only be fed or starved (to appeal to the image of the soul presented at 588c), and they must be directed by *thumos* and *logismos*. So, in the context of the *Republic*'s treatment of appetite, to say that the philosopher must have an *epithumia* for all of wisdom seems to suggest an original disposition. Perhaps Socrates has already, by implication, pointed to a distinction between those who are disposed to be philosophers and those who are not. This appears to be a bit of foreshadowing, as well, since it will not be until Book IX that Socrates will explicitly add a specific form of appetite to each function of the model of the city soul. Perhaps this appetite for wisdom belongs to *nous*, although Socrates does not say that explicitly since he has not yet built the framework that would make such a claim intelligible.

In the final exchange of Book V, Glaucon raises a concern about the sort of people Socrates seems to be saying are disposed for philosophy. Socrates responds dialectically, bringing Glaucon to see the distinction between belief and knowledge, as well as the difference between the sorts of people who love each of them. It seems implausible and objectionable to Glaucon that philosophers, those who Socrates has now said must rule the city, would be people who lack discernment. If the philosopher who loves all wisdom is analogous to the man who loves all boys, then any boy will do—any speech, any chorus. Shouldn't the philosopher, like the discerning lover of all other sorts of things, have standards?

Socrates' response is careful and, for Platonic dialogues, conventional. He asks Glaucon to take a particular position, i.e., that of the man who is offended by the claim that he loves the images of things in a dream rather than things themselves while awake. Then Socrates engages in a dialogue with that persona. In the course of this dialogue within the dialogue, Socrates makes a few logical distinctions and brings his imaginary interlocutor (played by Glaucon) toward greater self-awareness. The error that the imaginary interlocutor has made is mistaking the many images of a thing for the thing itself, the most common argumentative misstep in the Platonic corpus. And it is the person who is misguided in this particular way—not the person Socrates said had a philosopher's appetite for wisdom—whom Glaucon rightly cannot imagine ruling the city.

The lover of opinion, as he will come to be called at 480a is different from the lover of knowledge. The former loves, for example, apparently beautiful things without knowing or even acknowledging the existence of beauty. The lover of beauty, on the other hand, knows and recognizes beauty. She loves the beauty she sees in all beautiful things. Lovers of belief or opinion are different from lovers of knowledge. The latter are those disposed for philosophy and for the best version of ruling. As Book V concludes, the nature of objects of belief remains an open question. Objects of ignorance clearly do not have being. Objects of knowledge clearly do. But, the objects of belief are more problematic. Whatever they may turn out to be, they seem to partake somehow of both being and non-being.

Before considering the continuation of the account of the third *kuma* in Book VI, we should ask ourselves what the arc of Book V has turned out to be. The dramatic action and the change of the direction of the argument at the beginning of Book V indicate the clear boundary of a new form of inquiry, and Socrates conveniently gives it a name—The Female Drama. But, the curtain has not yet closed on the Female Drama at the end of Book V. Another narrative structure that opens in Book V is the three waves (*kumata)*, but that frame is not yet closed, either. Does Book V not have any psychological work of its own?

If we look back at the ways that the city/soul has developed in Book V, I believe we can see a thread that runs through Book V and that sets up the work of Book VI, but is substantially different from it. Both of the first two *kumata* and the first part of the account of the third *kuma* share a concern with givenness or disposition. The first *kuma* presents the need of the potentially just soul to be able to overcome convention in order to defer to rational direction (451d–457b). The second *kuma* shows that one must be able to incorporate the individual claims of each part of the city/soul into a holistic set of priorities and choices (457c–471c). Now, the third *kuma* claims that one who would be just must have an appetite for wisdom (453c–480a). None of these is presented as something that emerges from training or education. Rather, they describe the preconditions (*genesis*) for the possibility of effective training (*trophe*), which in turn is a precondition for successful education (*paideia*) to virtue.

The psychological work of Book V is an account of the *genesis* of a just soul. The first two *kumata* and the first part of the third *kuma* are the necessary conditions for the possibility of philosophical *trophe* and *paideia*. They are the psychological conditions that must be in place from the beginning in order for a soul to be philosophically trained and educated. What will follow in Book VI will move to an account of the *trophe* of a potentially just soul. It will begin with all of the proper conditions of *genesis* in place, and it will present the conditions of *trophe* necessary to prepare a soul for education (*paideia*), which will be the psychological emphasis of Book VII.

The dispositional conditions presented in Book V may fall roughly into line with the three parts that have framed the structure of the city/soul since Book II: *epithumia*, *thumos*, and *logismos*. The first *kuma* concerns convention, in particular overcoming an aversion to being ridiculed, but it also specifically concerns conventions that emerge in order to regulate and moderate sexual appetites. Why is it unconventional for women and men to participate together in activities where they are scantily dressed? Because women and men distract each other.[13] And why do scantily dressed men and women distract each other? Sexual desire. The ridiculousness of the first *kuma* is not simply a response to breaking convention, it is a blushing, giggling response to breaking a convention that insulates us from a set of interactions that encourage citizens to see each other as potential sexual partners.

Sexual appetite (*epithumia*) must be controlled in order for the first *kuma* to be averted. To translate the point into psychological terms, we might say that one's appetitive nature must be capable of being regulated by reason without the support of conventions. A part of the *genesis* of a just soul is having an *epithumetic* part that can be contained by *thumos* and *logismos*. If *logismos* and *thumos* are not up to the task, the project will of course fall apart; that is the central conclusion of the Male Drama. At this point, the Female Drama adds to the argument the idea that even if the *thumotic* and *logistic* parts of the soul are reasonably strong, if the *epithumetic* part is ungovernable, one's ambition for justice will be, in principle, unachievable.

[13] Men distract men, too, of course, but that is not a matter for the Female Drama to manage; and the possibility that women could distract women seems nowhere to be an issue in the *Republic*.

Similarly, weathering the second *kuma* may be understood as a condition of *genesis* that concerns the *thumotic* soul. The second *kuma* requires that the pleasures and pains of the parts of the city/soul be brought into holistic perspective, i.e., that the city/soul act with each of the parts in mind, but in the interest of the whole. What must be reoriented in the second *kuma* is an understanding of what is "one's own." The pain of the finger is not, first and foremost, the pain of the finger. Instead, it is the pain of the person, which is felt in the finger. The pain is still one's own pain, but not in the sense that it belongs to the finger, only in the sense that it belongs to the whole person. Without the capacity of the parts to let go of the claim that their pleasures and pains are their own in a more particular sense, there is no hope for training or education to virtue.

When we shift the example from the simplistic case of a finger hurting to the much more complicated case of the pleasure associated with a substantial accomplishment being recognized, the connection to *thumos* comes into clearer focus. Let us take, for example, the case of an accomplished athlete who has garnered recognition for her achievements in cross country running. Let us imagine that she takes great pleasure both in the activity of running and in the recognition that she gets for being a good runner. The challenge of the second *kuma* is to subordinate these pleasures to the rational direction of the *logistic* soul, aided by the *thumotic* soul. The pleasures of running and recognition belong to the whole soul, to the whole person, not to the part of her life that competes. When those pleasures contribute to the good of the whole, they should be pursued—but not when they do not. A condition for the possibility of our athlete becoming virtuous is her capacity to be guided rationally with the whole of her soul in mind, rather than being driven to seek the pleasures of competitive running for their own sake. If each part of the city/soul stakes too strongly its claim for what it sees as its own, it will not be possible for it to be incorporated into a holistic sense of what is best for the whole person. If one's *thumos* is too strong for one's *logismos* to bring it into harmony with the rest of one's soul, then one is not disposed for virtue. One lacks the essential *thumotic* aspect of the *genesis* of virtue.

The *epithumetic* and *thumotic* resonances of the first two *kumata* suggest that we should ask whether or not the third *kuma* relates somehow to *logismos*. Thinking about the Female Drama of *logismos* presents some particularly tricky conceptual challenges. From Book II onward, Socrates is entirely consistent in his claim that the *logistic* part of the city/soul must rule. It must be active. Near the end of Book V, he is explicit that the *logistic* ruler in the city/soul must be a philosopher, and that claim is extremely controversial. However, it has never been controversial that *logismos* should be in charge. If *logismos* should rule (and not be ruled), then what could the Female Drama have to add to the male? That is, if *logismos* should be active and not passive in relation to the other parts of the city/soul, what could its Female Drama consist in? What could the Female Drama, the story of the potentially virtuous soul's passive potentialities, possibly say about *logismos*?

The last section of Book V speaks directly to the Female Drama of reason, to the passive, receptive character of the potentially virtuous rational soul. But, *logismos* is not, itself, capable of the sort of passive, receptive role the rational soul is now called on to perform. Like the other parts of the tripartite soul considered in Book IV, *logismos* is only capable of interacting with other parts of the soul. There is no capacity for interacting with anything outside of itself. And, in the case of *logismos*, there is nothing within the soul for it to look to for direction. In a just soul, *epithumia* and *thumos* have active modes, but they are properly passive in relation to *logismos*. But it is not proper for *logismos* ever to be passive in relation to either *epithumia* or *thumos*. If there is to be a Female Drama for reason, *logismos* cannot be cast in a role analogous to *epithumia* and *thumos*.

Rather than recasting *logismos* as a more complicated, double-faceted aspect of soul, Socrates introduces a new part or function of rationality—*nous*. Beginning by implication at the end of Book V and continuing in explicit terms in the rest of the *Republic*, the rational soul has two named modes: *logismos* and *nous*. Similar to the way that Socrates is unclear about whether the divisions of soul in Book IV should be understood as parts or functions, he is unclear about whether *nous* constitutes a fourth part or function of the soul. This fuzziness is, I think, a feature of the model, though, and not a bug. In Kallipolis, the philosopher and the ruler are the same person, but everyone recognizes that the virtues of the philosopher and the virtues of the politician only coincide at the apex of both. *Nous* and *logismos* seem to be presented analogously. In the best life, the capacity to apprehend transcendent ideas and the capacity to organize an internally harmonious and productive life are one and the same. But in most, perhaps all, human lives, these two are not identical.

Here as elsewhere, the revision to the city/soul model is an expansion and not a repudiation of anything that has come before. But, this is the most important revision to the model that occurs in the *Republic*, perhaps the most important element of the psychological model, per se. The noetic soul is passive not in relation to the rest of the city/soul, but instead in relation to "what is," that is, to the objects of knowledge that distinguish the lovers of wisdom from the lovers of opinion. Because of this, it opens up an entirely new set of questions, concerns, and ambitions for the city/soul. The standard is no longer only internal harmony, but an internal harmony that conforms to some external standard. It is no longer the highest possibility of the city/soul to be just; now, it is possible to aspire to be good.

In Book VI, Socrates will begin to elaborate on the implications of adding a receptive, externally oriented function to rationality. We will see it prominently displayed in the images of the Ship of State, the Divided Line, and, later, the Cave; but it is already here, inchoate, at the end of Book V. What distinguishes lovers of wisdom from lovers of opinion is the apprehension of ideas that they see instantiated in things in the world. The lover of beautiful things, for example, may or may not see beauty, per se. She may not even acknowledge the possibility of the existence of beauty. But, the lover of beauty is entirely different. She knows the beautiful and she loves the beauty in the things she sees. She need not have any special love for the things in which beauty is reflected.

So an essential characteristic that distinguishes the philosopher from the non-philosopher is the apprehension of an idea, in this case beauty. The part of the soul that apprehends this idea is *nous*. This is the Female Drama of reason and of *logismos*; for, while *nous* is receptive to Being and the Good; *logismos* is, in the best case, receptive to *nous*. That is, *logismos* organizes the city/soul according to the direction of *nous*. In order for a soul to be disposed to goodness, that is for it to have the best conditions of *genesis* in place, its noetic part must be capable of directing the logistic part in its work ruling the soul, but *nous* must also be capable of apprehending those external ideas that will guide *logismos* toward the best possible regime. As Socrates will say in Book VI, there is something higher than justice, and it is the Good. The two-fold function of reason is to apprehend the Good noetically and to rule the city/soul logistically according to that apprehension.

The proper role of *logismos* within the city/soul continues to be a concern for the whole city/soul that legislates from a holistic sense of the best possible arrangement of its parts. *Thumos* continues to be the ally of *logismos* in its attempt to protect the city/soul from internal (faction) and external (war) threats. *Epithumia* continues to be the untrainable, uneducable set of appetites that *logismos* and *thumos* must work to assimilate into the best possible, least factious, scheme of internal organization. But, the Female Drama tells us that reason has an additional function, as well. *Nous* must orient itself to those ideas that exist independently of the city/soul and direct *logismos*'s government of the city/soul with them in mind. What this means, how it works, and how one may train such a well disposed city/soul to be ready for an education in virtue is the work of Book VI.

As we come to the end of Book V, the city/soul has been substantially revised. It now has three or four parts or functions: *epithumia*, *thumos*, *logismos*, and *nous*. If *nous* is a separate part of the soul from *logismos*, then there will be four parts. If the same part of the soul functions noetically and logistically, then there will be three parts of the soul. The precise number cannot be specified because the possible unification of the *nous* and *logismos* is precisely what is at stake in the question of whether philosophers can be rulers. If one claims that *nous* and *logismos* can be unified, then psychologically one has said there are three parts of the soul, and one of them has two functions. If, on the other hand, one thinks that politics and philosophy cannot be unified in the city/soul, then the psychological implication is that we each have four parts of soul—that *logismos* and *nous* will be separate, and the soul will have four parts. "Three or four?" is a question that sits behind the entirety of the Female Drama.

The first short section of Book VI (484a–d) reviews the dispositional conditions necessary for the possibility of the development of a virtuous city/soul that were demonstrated in Book IV. Then the focus of the dialogue turns from *genesis* to *trophe* when Socrates says that "right from childhood, a true lover of learning must strive above all for every kind of truth." (485d).[14] What follows this claim is a list of qualities that should be cultivated in philosophers—a list of moral habits, which are precisely the sorts of character traits one would think a well-disposed child should develop in order to become educable. Then Adeimantus interrupts. It is after this interruption, I will argue, that the real work of book VI begins.[15] Before we turn to the account of philosophical *trophe* that runs through most of Book VI, it is worth taking a look at this short, transitional, section at its beginning both to suggest what is to come and to shed light back onto what has been accomplished so far in the Female Drama.

At the end of Book V, Socrates and Glaucon agree that philosophers seek knowledge of what they love, while others can have no more than belief or opinion. Now, at the beginning of Book VI, Socrates presses this distinction to its extreme by characterizing non-philosophers as blind (484c). And, although he phrases it as a question, Socrates goes on to present a clear, strong case for why non-philosophers are not fit to rule. He asks,

---

[14] τὸν ἄρα τῷ ὄντι φιλομαθῆ πάσης ἀληθείας δεῖ εὐθὺς ἐκ νέου ὅτι μάλιστα ὀρέγεσθαι.

[15] The breaks between Books V and VI and then VI and VII are both soft. The end of V already begins the work of VI, and the beginning of VI is still playing out some of the implications of the arguments of V before it gets down to the work that seems to me to define Book VI. I will argue that a similar thing happens in the transition from Book VI to Book VII as Socrates moves from the Divided Line to the Cave. These smooth transitions make the hard turns at the beginning of V and the end of VII even more pronounced. And, although each of these transitions (hard and soft) make good sense, it is worth remembering that the Book divisions are probably not Plato's own, but were instead imposed by Alexandrian librarians centuries later. See Debra Nails, "Plato's *Republic* in its Athenian Context," *History of Political Thought*, 33, no. 1 (Spring 2012): 4.

> Do they seem any different from blind people, those who lack knowledge of what the being of each thing really is, who have no clear model of it in their souls, who cannot refer like painters to what is most true, so neither can they establish laws for beautiful, just, or good things based on their constant reference and exacting study, nor can they guard and preserve those that have been established? (484c–d)[16]

Non-philosophers have no knowledge of what things really are. They cannot have models in their souls of what each thing really is. They cannot appeal to knowledge of the beautiful, the Good, and the just, so they lack an essential condition for the possibility of creating *nomoi* (laws and norms) that are reflections in the world of true beauty, goodness, and justice.

Likening the capacity of apprehending knowledge to sight (an image that has been with us since as early as 369d and will be with us throughout the remainder of the *Republic*), the philosopher is described here as the one with the capacity to know, just as a sighted person is one with the capacity to see. This is the work of *nous*. The matter at hand is still the disposition of the proto-philosopher, although Socrates is giving us a glimpse of what might become of a person with this disposition and what she might be able to achieve. Socrates is here reviewing the *genesis* of the philosopher, the necessary dispositional conditions for the possibility of philosophical *trophe* and *paideia*.

Socrates locks in the exact nature of what has (and hasn't) been demonstrated in Book V by recalling the analogous relationship between philosophers (*philosophoi*[17]), honor-lovers (*philotimon*[18]), and passionate

---

[16] ἤ οὖν δοκοῦσί τι τυφλῶν διαφέρειν οἱ τῷ ὄντι τοῦ ὄντος ἑκάστου ἐστερημένοι τῆς γνώσεως, καὶ μηδὲν ἐναργὲς ἐν τῇ ψυχῇ ἔχοντες παράδειγμα, μηδὲ δυνάμενοι ὥσπερ γραφῆς εἰς τὸ ἀληθέστατον ἀποβλέποντες κἀκεῖσε ἀεὶ ἀναφέροντές τε καὶ θεώμενοι ὡς οἷόν τε ἀκριβέστατα, οὕτω δὴ καὶ τὰ ἐνθάδε νόμιμα καλῶν τε πέρι καὶ δικαίων καὶ ἀγαθῶν τίθεσθαί τε, ἐὰν δέῃ τίθεσθαι, καὶ τὰ κείμενα φυλάττοντες σῴζειν.

[17] φιλόσοφοι.

[18] φιλοτίμων.

men (*erotikon*[19]) at 485b. Although the conversation will go on to track the development of the soul disposed for philosophy, and although the dialogue has suggested many things about the developed philosopher's character, the interlocutors really have demonstrated very little about the philosophical soul so far. Many of the characteristics of the philosophical city/soul (Kallipolis) are identical to the just city/soul, so those qualities will be called up into the conversation for confirmation as the dialogue proceeds. To use the language of the city in speech, the argument being developed in this part of the dialogue is that the guardians should be philosophers, not that the earlier arguments for the rule of the guardians are moot.

In terms of arguments specifically concerning philosophers (i.e., the arguments that have followed from the third *kuma*), only a few things have been demonstrated. At 475b, we learn that the philosopher must have an appetite for wisdom. At 479e, we see that philosophers seek to apprehend things in themselves, which are unchanging regardless of the particular ways they may be reflected in the world. Socrates calls the apprehension of things in themselves "knowledge" rather than "belief." The second point could be stated more simply as the claim that philosophers seek knowledge, and not just opinions, about what they love. Putting these two claims together, it appears that the philosopher seeks knowledge of wisdom. This is an apparently odd claim, since wisdom seems either to involve knowledge or to be a species of knowledge. To translate once more, this appears to mean that the philosopher seeks knowledge of (a kind of) knowledge, and that she loves it.

The philosopher is like the lover of honor and the lover of love in that she loves all of the things that reflect what she loves. It seems open to argument at this stage of the dialogue whether or not the lover of honor and the lover of love may also have knowledge of the object of their love. In fact, it seems plausible that they would. How else would the lover of honor love all honor, except that he recognizes it wherever it appears? How else would the lover of love love all love except that he recognizes it wherever it appears. By definition, it appears, each of these

[19] This is also the word Socrates uses to describe Glaucon when he uses his love of boys as an opening to discuss love in general.

three seek knowledge, rather than opinion, So, all that seems currently to distinguish the philosopher from the other two is that the desired object of her knowledge is knowledge. Why this might be a superior disposition for the capacity to rule is not at all clear, yet.

The last element of the discussion of the *genesis* of the philosopher is, appropriately, also the first element of the discussion of the *trophe* of the philosopher: her natural disposition for truthfulness. Truthfulness is presented at 485c as a feature of the nature of the philosopher. And, at 485d, Socrates says that genuine lovers of learning should strive for truth in all forms. So truthfulness is presented both as a disposition that one has or does not have and as something that can be cultivated with practice. The rest of the qualities of philosophical character that Socrates rattles off before Adeimantus' interruption at 487b are not presented as natural. Rather, they are at least in part the consequence of the cultivation (*trophe)* of the natural disposition (*genesis*) for truthfulness. So, truthfulness is the last word on philosophical *genesis*, and the first on philosophical *trophe*.

The work of Book V has been to bring the proto-philosophical soul into the world, to give an account of its *genesis*. *Kuma*, as we have seen throughout Book V, means "wave," and our interlocutors have, indeed been at sea during this part of the dialogue. *Kuma* can also be translated as the swell of a pregnant woman's body or a painful contraction in childbirth. Plato's account of Kallipolis is not finished at the end of Book V, but something new is in the world of the *Republic.* Someone has been born, and she has the *epithumetic*, *thumotic*, *logistic*, and *noetic* dispositions necessary for the possibility of becoming a philosopher (and, thus, also be the best possible ruler of the city/soul). Inquiring into what her childhood will have to entail if she is to convert those philosophical dispositions into an educable set of habits will be the work of the next chapter.

Part Three

Philosophical *Trophe*, Book VI

7

The Ship of State and the Corrupt City/Soul
(The Trophe of Epithumia and Thumos)

After a brief moment of synopsis and review (484a–d), Socrates takes up one of the most essential questions implied by the third *kuma*: how could the same person possibly possess the qualities required of the philosopher and of a ruler, since they seem to be so different? The qualities of the best ruler of the city/soul have been under consideration since Book II. At the end of Book V, Socrates began to demonstrate the qualities of a philosopher. So, Socrates has described both types, and they seem very different, indeed. The inquiry that opens at the beginning of Book VI asks how one man could fit both descriptions. Glaucon has already agreed that philosophical rule in the city/soul would be best, but he wonders if it is possible for these qualities all to exist in one person.

The first premise Socrates asserts in this new part of the inquiry is that philosophers love the sort of "being" that is unchanging—being that does not undergo a process of becoming or of decay (485b). The second premise he presents is that philosophers love all of that sort of being (just like the honor-lovers and love-lovers love all of what they love [485b]). With those points stipulated, Socrates asks Glaucon to consider whether or not philosophic natures must be truthful (485c). Glaucon immediately affirms that it is plausible, but Socrates insists on a stronger formulation. It is not possible, he says, for a lover of wisdom also to be a lover of falsehood (485d). Truthfulness is an essential, not accidental, feature of the philosophical character.

From the start of the Female Drama near the beginning of Book V (451c) to this point in the dialogue near the beginning of Book VI (485d), Socrates has kept the inquiry focused on the nature of the philosophical city/soul, that is, on all of those features that must be a part of its *genesis*. At this moment, he shifts the conversation from the nature of the philosophical city/soul to its childhood training or formation, its *trophe*, when he asserts that "right from childhood, a genuine lover of learning must strive above all for all kinds of truth" (485d).[1] This is the first time we have been presented with something that a proto-philosophical person needs to *do*, rather than something she needs to *be*. This signals the beginning of the second play in the Female Drama, and its theme is philosophical *trophe*.

The next premise Socrates introduces involves something like a principle of scarcity. He says that when one's appetites are inclined in one direction, they will become weaker in other directions (485d).[2] Whether or not one finds this principle controversial, for Socrates it seems to be a commonplace that requires no argument or evidence. It has a significant impact on the course of the inquiry, though. With this principle in place, Socrates infers that the one who is naturally disposed to philosophy will be drawn away from the pleasures of the body. He draws this conclusion because philosophers have been shown to be naturally drawn toward the pleasures of the soul. So, in one quick movement, Socrates claims to have established a principle from which the philosopher's ethical orientation can be derived. Then he immediately begins to derive the specific moral characteristics of the philosopher from this principle.

The philosophical nature is temperate, and not avaricious (485e). She is not petty-minded, or illiberal (486a), not afraid of death or cowardly (486b). She is just and gentle (486b). She learns quickly and has an excellent memory (486c). The philosophical nature is musical, graceful, and drawn to what is proportionate (486d). We are told this last characteristic, in particular, "makes it easy to lead to the form of each thing which is."[3]

Glaucon immediately assents to all of these virtues of the philosopher, each of which follows from the characteristics of the philosophical nature and the idea that when one's energy is focused in one direction, one will have less energy for other things. The love of wisdom, according

[1] τὸν ἄρα τῷ ὄντι φιλομαθῆ πάσης ἀληθείας δεῖ εὐθὺς ἐκ νέου ὅτι μάλιστα ὀρέγεσθαι.

[2] ἀλλὰ μὴν ὅτῳ γε εἰς ἕν τι αἱ ἐπιθυμίαι σφόδρα ῥέπουσιν, ἴσμεν που ὅτι εἰς τἆλλα τούτῳ ἀσθενέστεραι, ὥσπερ ῥεῦμα ἐκεῖσε ἀπωχετευμένον.

[3] ἣν ἐπὶ τὴν τοῦ ὄντος ἰδέαν ἑκάστου τὸ αὐτοφυὲς εὐάγωγον παρέξει.

to this argument, is the mother of virtue. And, as Socrates brings his list of the philosopher's virtues to a close, there seems to be no question about whether such a person would be fit to rule. All of the qualities of the best possible ruler seem to have been summarily deduced from the philosopher's nature. Then, Adeimantus jumps in.[4]

Adeimantus' intervention at 487b is not as dramatic as the interruption Polemarchus triggered at the beginning of Book V (449b), but it is striking. He implies that he does not have any words to counter the words of Socrates' argument (although he does not admit it directly), but that the facts do not seem to support Socrates' claims about the philosopher, especially about the philosopher's usefulness to the city.

According to Adeimantus, the facts seem to suggest that most philosophers are not worth taking seriously at all, and that those few who are best at philosophy seem to be rendered useless to the city by virtue of their philosophical activity. It is fine to do philosophy when one is young, but continuing with it into adulthood seems to corrupt men's souls. If you look at people who have gone on to study philosophy beyond their youth, you find people who are anti-social[5] and thoroughly depraved.[6] If we look at the facts, Adiemantus says, we see nothing like the conclusion to which Socrates' argument seems to have arrived.[7]

Glaucon has continually pushed the city in speech to generate answers to his political questions, but he has been amenable every time Socrates has nudged him back to a consideration of the city/soul that focuses on supporting their inquiry into individual justice and whether or

---

[4] A former student of mine, Anna Bates, has developed a compelling interpretation of Adeimantus' interventions in the *Republic* that has yet to be published.

[5] ἀλλόκοτος.

[6] παμπόνηρος.

[7] λέγω δ' εἰς τὸ παρὸν ἀποβλέψας. νῦν γὰρ φαίη ἄν τίς σοι λόγῳ μὲν οὐκ ἔχειν καθ' ἕκαστον τὸ ἐρωτώμενον ἐναντιοῦσθαι, ἔργῳ δὲ ὁρᾶν, ὅσοι ἂν ἐπὶ φιλοσοφίαν ὁρμήσαντες μὴ τοῦ πεπαιδεῦσθαι ἕνεκα ἁψάμενοι νέοι ὄντες ἀπαλλάττωνται, ἀλλὰ μακρότερον ἐνδιατρίψωσιν, τοὺς μὲν πλείστους καὶ πάνυ ἀλλοκότους γιγνομένους, ἵνα μὴ παμπονήρους εἴπωμεν, τοὺς δ' ἐπιεικεστάτους δοκοῦντας ὅμως τοῦτό γε ὑπὸ τοῦ ἐπιτηδεύματος οὗ σὺ ἐπαινεῖς πάσχοντας, ἀχρήστους ταῖς πόλεσι γιγνομένους (487c–d).

not it is more choiceworthy than individual injustice. Adeimantus has also pushed for their shared inquiry to migrate more and more toward politics, notably at the beginning of Book V when he supports Polemarchus's desire to hear more about the roles of women and children in the city in speech. But no interlocutor has been as bold or unflinching in his insistence that their inquiry into the city in speech become an inquiry into the politics of a city in deed than Adeimantus is at this moment. Words are fine things to play with if you have the leisure, he seems to say, but facts are facts, and philosophers, in fact, render themselves useless to the city by doing philosophy.

Socrates predicts at 477d that his response to this challenge will surprise Adeimantus—Socrates agrees with him. We must be careful, though, to discern just what their point of agreement is. Socrates does not agree that the inquiry must leave the realm of words and enter the realm of facts in order to make progress. Rather, he agrees that the activity of philosophy renders the philosopher useless to the city. Socrates has not and will not abandon the city in speech, but he will take Adeimantus' concerns to heart. He agrees to explain how it could be true both that there will be no end of evil in the city until philosophers rule and that philosophers are useless to the city. Adeimantus will hear the argument as if it were relevant to actual Athenian politics—and it is—but Socrates will present it as fundamentally responsive to a dynamic within the soul that has only recently emerged. To underline his continuing commitment to the city in speech, Socrates presents his response in the form of an image.

The Ship of State, one of the most famous and powerful images in the *Republic.* It emerges in response to Adeimantus' challenge, but it also elaborates on a dynamic within the soul that could not have been addressed before facing the third *kuma*. Looking at the structure of the dialogue as a whole, Plato has placed this image of a particular part of the inner workings of an individual soul at practically the first moment it was possible to present it. One of the main psychological implications of saying that a philosopher must rule the city/soul is that the ruler of the city/soul must apprehend the idea of the Good and use it to form a model for creating good institutions within the city/soul. It is only with the introduction of the philosopher at the end of Book V that we are given an image of a part of the city/soul apprehending something outside of itself. The model of the soul that is "completed" in Book IV is only capable of looking inward. So, psychologically, we may say that only with the third *kuma* do we see that reason has an outward- as well as an inward-looking aspect. *Nous*, like the true pilot, looks above and beyond itself to find fixed stars to steer by. *Logismos*, also like another aspect of the true pilot, organizes the crew and steers the ship to follow the course set by *nous*. It is possible for these two functions to be served by two different parts of the soul, but the implication is that it is better if they are unified. The image of the Ship of State addresses the dynamics (and problems) that emerge when we recognize this double-function of reason.

Socrates asks Adeimantus to consider an image that he stipulates at the outset is drawn not as a description of one thing but as a composite of many things. This qualification alone seems to imply that Socrates does not mean to be giving an account of a dynamic that exists anywhere in the world between philosophers, politicians, and citizens; but this is not entirely clear. He also says, however, that what the philosopher experiences in relation to cities is uniquely difficult to bear, which seems to suggest that he is speaking from experience (488a). Here, the lines between the city in speech and the city in deed are at least as blurry as ever.

The first of the well-known elements of the Ship of State that Socrates constructs is the tall, strong, deaf, myopic, deficiently educated ship-owner (488a–b). Next, he describes the sailors who quarrel with each other about who should be control the ship. The sailors, each of whom thinks he should be captain, are entirely untrained in the art of captaining. They not only reject the notion that there is a teachable craft of captaining, they are ready to kill anyone who says there is. And, the sailors relentlessly crowd the ship owner, using various strategies and pleas in their attempt to take control. Sometimes, if one sailor is successful at getting control of the ship from the ship owner, the other sailors will kill him. And, in the moments that the sailors are successful at holding the control of the ship they wrest away from the ship owner, they feast on whatever cargo is aboard rather than transporting it to its proper destination. Since they recognize no art of captaining, they call anyone "captain" who is successful at seizing and holding control, and they praise him as an expert about ships. Anyone unsuccessful or uninterested in seizing power, they call useless (488b–d).

As Socrates finishes his description of the sailors on the Ship of State, he elaborates a bit on what the sailors do not know about the true art of being a captain. By implication, Socrates begins at this point to introduce the third element of the image—the true pilot. What the sailors do not realize, according to Socrates, is that "a true captain must pay attention to the seasons of the year, the sky the stars, the winds, and all that pertains to his craft if he is really going to be expert at ruling a ship" (488d).[8] The sailors, who only want what they want and who only see the dynamics on the ship as reflections of the dynamics they see among themselves, cannot imagine that one of the activities of the man truly fit to pilot the ship is to attend to things far above and beyond the activities on deck. If they were to hear or see of such a person, Socrates says, the sailors would call him a "stargazer," a "useless babbler" and a "good-for-nothing" (488e–489a). Piloting has no place in their conception of captaining, so the framework itself and not just the content would be incomprehensible to the sailors.

Socrates assumes that Adeimantus immediately sees the relevance of this image to the political question that he had posed, and he enlists him in the effort to defend true philosophers against the accusations of uselessness that are levied against them. Adeimantus wanted to know how it could both be true that cities should be ruled by philosophers and that philosophers were useless to cities; the Ship of State is an answer to that question. The one who knows how to pilot a ship is its true pilot whether or not others on the ship recognize him as their captain. Popular standards for selecting the ship's captain may neglect entirely the most important qualifications for that position. In the more sanguine interpretation of the image, it is possible for the true pilot to become captain of the Ship of State, but there is nothing in the image (at least so far) to prevent the darker interpretation that contends that it is not possible for the true pilot ever to have control.

Socrates goes even further than this to cater his response to Adeimantus' questions and concerns. At 489c, he makes the connection be-

[8] ὅτι ἀνάγκη αὐτῷ τὴν ἐπιμέλειαν ποιεῖσθαι ἐνιαυτοῦ καὶ ὡρῶν καὶ οὐρανοῦ καὶ ἄστρων καὶ πνευμάτων καὶ πάντων τῶν τῇ τέχνῃ προσηκόντων, εἰ μέλλει τῷ ὄντι νεὼς ἀρχικὸς ἔσεσθαι.

tween the Ship of State and the city in deed perfectly clear when he tells Adeimantus to pass the following message along to the unnamed critic whose position he supposedly is espousing: "You will make no mistake if you liken our current political rulers to the sailors we were just describing, and if you liken those who the sailors call useless stargazers to the ship's true captains" (489c).[9] There is no room for misunderstanding at this level of the image. Philosophers are marginalized and maligned by politicians because of the deficiencies of those who hold political power and not because of any deficiency in philosophy or philosophers. Socrates wants to make this point clear. Perhaps he wants Adeimantus (and the other interlocutors) to spread the word.

The next step Socrates proposes to take in the argument and in the process of unpacking the implications of the image of the Ship of State for the city/soul is to show that it is not just an unhappy coincidence that "the many," (i.e., the sailors) are bad. The sailors' badness is not a bug; it is a feature of the dynamic Socrates is working to describe. To make this argument, he returns to the first principle introduced in Book VI, the truthfulness of the philosopher. He also reminds Adeimantus that earlier (in Book V), they had agreed that the philosopher loves the truth and follows it unequivocally and wholeheartedly, just like lovers of honor and the lovers of love follow the objects of their love wholeheartedly and unequivocally. This truth, alone, about the truthfulness of philosophers shows that their unflattering reputation is undeserved.

At 490b and following, Socrates underlines the fact that he is reviewing the argument of Book V with Adeimantus by returning to the images of procreation and birth that ran throughout that part of the *Republic.*

> Won't it be a reasonable plea for his defense, then, that the true lover of learning strives by nature for what is? He does not linger over each of the many things that are believed to exist, but keeps on going, without blunting or lessening his passion, until he touches the nature of each things itself with the element in his soul that is fitted to grasp

[9] ἀλλὰ τοὺς νῦν πολιτικοὺς ἄρχοντας ἀπεικάζων οἷς ἄρτι ἐλέγομεν ναύταις οὐχ ἁμαρτήσῃ, καὶ τοὺς ὑπὸ τούτων ἀχρήστους λεγομένους καὶ μετεωρολέσχας τοῖς ὡς ἀληθῶς κυβερνήταις.

> that sort of thing because they belong to each other. Once he has approached true reality, has intercourse with it, and has given birth to intelligence and truth—only then does he attain knowledge, live fully, find sustenance, and find relief from his labor pains. (490b)[10]

In other words, Socrates says, were we to offer an *apologia* for the philosopher, we could say that he single-mindedly pursues the nature of each thing like a lover until reality is joined with the the part of his mind it belongs to. He does not let go until their union produces understanding and truth. Only then is the philosopher truly and fully alive. (One cannot help but think that this odd apology might have been even less successful than the one Socrates actually chose to give in 399 BCE.) Socrates' central image is clear and consonant with the account in Book V: the lover of learning has an appetite, a passion, for the nature of each thing in itself. He pursues this passion and procreates with it. The children born of the union of the philosopher with philosophy are truth and understanding.

Adeimantus' intervention prompts Socrates to review the topics and images of Book V, but Plato must have created this return in order to make the connection between the work of Book V and the emerging project of Book VI clear. Nowhere in Book V do we hear about the "element in [the philosopher's] soul that belongs to" the nature of a thing in itself. It is implied by the description of the lover of love and the lover of honor, as well as by the description of the philosopher, that there must be some element in the soul that is fitted to grasp things beyond itself. Likewise, it is logical that the philosopher's capacity to grasp something beyond himself would be more specifically fitted for reality, per se. The Ship of State has also introduced, just a few lines earlier, this capacity to see beyond oneself in the form of the image of the true pilot/stargazer.

---

[10] ἆρ᾽ οὖν δὴ οὐ μετρίως ἀπολογησόμεθα ὅτι πρὸς τὸ ὂν πεφυκὼς εἴη ἁμιλλᾶσθαι ὅ γε ὄντως φιλομαθής, καὶ οὐκ ἐπιμένοι ἐπὶ τοῖς δοξαζομένοις εἶναι πολλοῖς ἑκάστοις, ἀλλ᾽ ἴοι καὶ οὐκ ἀμβλύνοιτο οὐδ᾽ ἀπολήγοι τοῦ ἔρωτος, πρὶν αὐτοῦ ὃ ἔστιν ἑκάστου τῆς φύσεως ἅψασθαι ᾧ προσήκει ψυχῆς ἐφάπτεσθαι τοῦ τοιούτου—προσήκει δὲ συγγενεῖ—ᾧ πλησιάσας καὶ μιγεὶς τῷ ὄντι ὄντως, γεννήσας νοῦν καὶ ἀλήθειαν, γνοίη τε καὶ ἀληθῶς ζῴη καὶ τρέφοιτο καὶ οὕτω λήγοι ὠδῖνος, πρὶν δ᾽ οὔ.

But this is the first we have explicitly heard about the existence of that element of the soul. It has not yet been named, but this is the first account in the *Republic* of the work of *nous.*

Within only a few more lines, Socrates comes back to the point in the inquiry that he and Glaucon had reached before Adeimantus' interruption. They agree that "when truth takes the lead, we would never say that a chorus of evils would follow behind" (490c).[11] And, with that principle re-established, Adeimantus agrees that there is no need to go back through the list of all of the particular virtues that are natural consequences of the philosopher's fundamentally truthful nature. So, at 491e, the conversation moves forward from the point where Glaucon and Socrates left it before Adeimantus' interruption, but Adeimantus is now Socrates' main interlocutor and the concerns he voiced in his interruption are very much an influence on the direction of the inquiry. [12]

It seems fair to say that Socrates could not have developed the issues illustrated by the Ship of State until precisely this moment in the dialogue, but is also the case that its seeds were planted much earlier. We cannot see how philosophy and politics function in the Ship of State until we see why philosophical rule might be desirable. We do not hear that political rulers should be philosophers until late in Book V because that case cannot be made until the nature of political rule and philosophy have at least been sketched. In order for the normative part of that claim to have meaning, one needs the definitions of individual and political virtue presented in Book IV. And those arguments, in turn, depended on the development of the city in speech and, particularly, the idea of the guardians.

---

[11] ἡγουμένης δὴ ἀληθείας οὐκ ἄν ποτε οἶμαι φαμὲν αὐτῇ χορὸν κακῶν ἀκολουθῆσαι.

[12] Anna Bates, in an unpublished essay entitled "Adeimantus and the Meaning of Interruption," argues that Adeimantus' interactions have a different character than Glaucon's. Glaucon expresses a desire to be convinced and makes an effort be sympathetic with Socrates' arguments, while Adeimantus is more critical. His "questions are about the value and validity of Socrates' arguments." Adeimantus' comments function as interruptions to the order of ideas Socrates seems to intend and, as such, influence the course of argument at least in a different way, if not straightforwardly more, than Glaucon's comments.

So, in order to get to the Ship of State, you must start with guardians. But, in a sense, the story of the Ship of State is already suggested by the word Socrates uses for "guardian" in Book II, *phylax*.[13] "Guardian" is a fine translation for *phylax*, but it could also be "sentinel" or "watchman." I do not propose that we attempt to overturn the established convention of translating *phylax* as "guardian," but considering these alternatives suggests that the dynamic Socrates presents in the Ship of State may already be a version of the rule of the guardians in the just city of Book IV. Already in that earlier version of the model, before philosophers, before the need for *nous* and before the limits of *logismos* have emerged in the inquiry, the possibility of the true pilot being mistaken for a stargazer is already there. He is the "watchman" looking to nature to predict a famine or perhaps reading Homer to manage his own ambitions—the one who knows that the best sort of political rule requires him to look beyond the city to things that seem to have nothing to do with politics. There is no way for Socrates to have elaborated on that possibility or those problems earlier in the dialogue, and they were not necessary for the Male Drama of the *Republic*, but they seem to have been there already in principle—tucked into the word *phylax*—ready for the Female Drama to bring them into being.

The next questions Socrates faces at 491a are: (1) what sort of corruption generates false, useless philosophers, and (2) why only a small number seem to escape such corruption? The truthful, virtuous nature of the philosopher has now been argued twice and can serve as a premise shared by Socrates, Glaucon, and Adeimantus. But, Socrates and Adeimantus have also explicitly agreed that although it is the fault of the many (i.e. the sailors) that true philosophers (i.e. the true pilot) are thought to be useless, most of those who claim to be philosophers are bad, false, corrupt imposters.

Socrates wants to work toward an account of the origin of false philosophers, and he posits two possibilities: (1) they have good philosophical natures that somehow get corrupted or (2) they do not have the right sort of nature to do philosophy, but they pursue it anyway (491a). Once again, Socrates shifts from an account of philosophical *genesis* to philo-

---

[13] φύλαξ.

sophical *trophe*, that is, from a consideration of the dispositions necessary for the possibility of becoming trained and educated for philosophy to an inquiry into the proper form of that training. In this passage we see that shift from two angles. First Socrates asks how one with a good philosophical *genesis* can be corrupted by bad philosophical *trophe*. Second, he asks what it would look like for one with a deficient philosophical *genesis* to attempt philosophical *trophe*. The assumption of this second question is that philosophical formation is bound to fail if philosophical disposition is lacking.

In order to explain the sorts of corruption that he has in mind, Socrates suggests that Adeimantus grasp a general principle that will help him understand the particulars of their inquiry. For every growing thing, Socrates says by way of illustration, the more vigorous the seed, the more it is injured by deficiencies in what it needs to thrive, such as food, climate, and location (491d). He then formulates the general principle from this example: "So it is, I take it, natural that the best nature should fare worse than an inferior one if it receives improper nurture" (491d).[14] Just as a particularly vigorous seed needs more nutrition than a less vigorous seed in order to thrive, and just as it will suffer more acutely from deficient nutrition. Likewise, a soul that is disposed to philosophy needs more of what other, less virtuously disposed, souls need, and it will suffer more if those needs are not met. The more vigorous the nature (*physis*), the more important the nurture (*trophe*). Not many souls have a philosophical *genesis*, that is, not many begin with a disposition to develop a philosophical nature (*physis*). Only a few of those, if any, undergo the *trophe* necessary to nurture their philosophical nature into readiness for philosophical education.

The psychological and political consequences of poorly nurturing good-natured souls are dire. Just as Socrates shifted to a clearer, less ambiguous political discourse to answer Adeimantus' question about why philosophers seemed to be useless for politics, Socrates' political exemplification of this new principle leaves very little room for misunderstanding. His first step is to make explicit the connection between the meta-

[14] ἔχει δὴ οἶμαι λόγον τὴν ἀρίστην φύσιν ἐν ἀλλοτριωτέρᾳ οὖσαν τροφῇ κάκιον ἀπαλλάττειν τῆς φαύλης.

phor of the seed and the case of the good natured young soul in the city: "Well, then, if the nature we proposed for the philosopher comes to learn properly, it will inevitably grow to attain every virtue. But if it is not sown, planted, and grown in a proper environment it will come to the very opposite end, unless one of the gods comes to its rescue (492a)."[15] There is no room for ambiguity here. The philosophical nature is the seed. The nurture it receives is the environment in which that seed is sown, planted, and grown. If the good philosophical nature lands in a proper environment, it will develop virtue; but, if it lands in an unsuitable environment, it will develop into something far worse than what becomes of less impressive seeds under the same circumstances.

Socrates does not let the implications of this principle for Athens go unsaid. His next point makes it perfectly clear that Athenian democracy creates a terribly inhospitable environment for philosophical *trophe*, and that it is practically hopeless for a philosophical nature not to be corrupted there.

> Whenever a crowd of them sit together in assemblies, courts, theaters, army camps, or any other gathering of a mass of people in public and loudly and excessively object to some of the things that are said or done, then approve of others, shouting and clapping; and when the rocks and the surrounding space itself also echo and magnify the din of their praise or blame. In such a situation, what do you think, as the saying goes, a young man has in his heart? How will any kind of private education he may have received protect him, and not let him get swept away by such praise and blame? How will he not be washed away by the flood to wherever it goes, so that he will call the same things beautiful or ugly that these people do, practice what they practice, and become like them (492a-d). [16]

---

[15] ἣν τοίνυν ἔθεμεν τοῦ φιλοσόφου φύσιν, ἂν μὲν οἶμαι μαθήσεως προσηκούσης τύχῃ, εἰς πᾶσαν ἀρετὴν ἀνάγκη αὐξανομένην ἀφικνεῖσθαι, ἐὰν δὲ μὴ ἐν προσηκούσῃ σπαρεῖσά τε καὶ φυτευθεῖσα τρέφηται, εἰς πάντα τἀναντία αὖ, ἐὰν μή τις αὐτῇ βοηθήσας θεῶν τύχῃ.

[16] ὅταν, εἶπον, συγκαθεζόμενοι ἀθρόοι πολλοὶ εἰς ἐκκλησίας ἢ εἰς δικαστήρια ἢ θέατρα ἢ στρατόπεδα ἤ τινα ἄλλον κοινὸν πλήθους σύλλογον σὺν πολλῷ θορύβῳ τὰ μὲν ψέγωσι τῶν λεγομένων ἢ πραττομένων, τὰ δὲ ἐπαινῶσιν, ὑπερβαλλόντως

Sophistry, according to Socrates' account of it here, is not an unfortunate accident in the Athenian political system created by marginal foreign characters who disrupt the process by clever argumentation and unconventional thinking. The real sophistry of Athens exists in the democratic system itself which empowers mobs to assert the power in their numbers instead of empowering those (few) who are capable of seeing and acting on behalf of the good of the city.[17] On the rare occasion that one is born in Athens with the capacity to develop into a wise and virtuous ruler, democratic institutions work on that nature from birth to corrupt those capacities and render that promising youth not just useless, but bad.

Our first clue in this passage that Socrates has shifted to a more aggressive rhetorical position with Adeimantus than he had been taking with Glaucon is that he asks Adeimantus if he is one of the many (*hoi poloi*)—if he believes what "the many" believe about the sophists (492a), an accusation that Adeimantus would resist as strongly as Glaucon, but that Socrates has not ever made (and seems would not ever make) to Glaucon. The many believe that there are a small set of private individuals called sophists who corrupt the youth. Those few with greater under-

---

ἑκάτερα, καὶ ἐκβοῶντες καὶ κροτοῦντες, πρὸς δ'αὐτοῖς αἵ τε πέτραι καὶ ὁ τόπος ἐν ᾧ ἂν ὦσιν ἐπηχοῦντες διπλάσιον θόρυβον παρέχωσι τοῦ ψόγου καὶ ἐπαίνου. ἐν δὴ τῷ τοιούτῳ τὸν νέον, τὸ λεγόμενον, τίνα οἴει καρδίαν ἴσχειν; ἢ ποίαν ἂν αὐτῷ παιδείαν ἰδιωτικὴν ἀνθέξειν, ἣν οὐ κατακλυσθεῖσαν ὑπὸ τοῦ τοιούτου ψόγου ἢ ἐπαίνου οἰχήσεσθαι φερομένην κατὰ ῥοῦν ᾗ ἂν οὗτος φέρῃ, καὶ φήσειν τε τὰ αὐτὰ τούτοις καλὰ καὶ αἰσχρὰ εἶναι, καὶ ἐπιτηδεύσειν ἅπερ ἂν οὗτοι, καὶ ἔσεσθαι τοιοῦτον.

[17] Arlene Saxonhouse puts it this way: "Claims of equality necessarily entail claims of inequality, of who is not equal. *Eidê* enable us to typologize, to define equal and unequal, but *eidê* also can tyrannize. The openness of democracy is the escape from that tyranny, but at the same time it may leave us lost without the grounds to make choices or structure the world in which we live" (274). In democracy, the well-disposed proto-philosopher may be more likely to emerge in democracy because of its openness, but she will be extremely unlikely to get the cultivation prerequisite to a philosophical education in a democracy because of that very same openness. (Arlene W. Saxonhouse, "Democracy, Equality, and Eidê: A Radical View from Book 8 of Plato's *Republic. The American Political Science Review* 92, no. 2 [June 1998]: 273–283.)

standing see that the real sophists in Athens, the real corrupters, are the democratic assemblies who use all of the powers of the mob to compel the few to capitulate to them.

The real danger of the Female Drama and, particularly, the third *kuma* is now coming sharply into focus. One of the clear implications of saying that philosophers should rule is that non-philosophers should not. The argument for a philosopher-ruler is an argument against all regime types that marginalize the philosopher, but it implies a particularly scathing critique of democracy. Socrates forcefully makes this point to Adeimantus. Not only are the wrong people in charge of Athens, but the system is built never to let the right people mature into readiness to lead.

Socrates continues to explore the first of the two problems of philosophical *trophe* that he introduced at 491a, namely the case of a philosophically disposed soul who is not properly nurtured for philosophy. He shifts at 492d from a consideration of what "educators and sophists" say about philosophers to a consideration of how they act towards them, which is to punish them. The consequences of speaking and acting philosophically in Athenian democracy are, according to Socrates at this moment of the *Republic*, disenfranchisement, fines, or death. The only way for a philosophical nature to survive such treatment seems to be a divine rescue.

This horrible treatment of the philosopher, which also turns out to be self-defeating for the city that aspires to be well governed, should not just be blamed on a few educators or sophists, though. As Socrates made clear regarding those responsible for the corrosive things said about the philosopher, the city as a whole and its constitution is to blame, not a few individuals. These educators and sophists who act violently toward philosophy are simply articulating a position the masses (*hoi poloi*) already hold to be true.

> None of these private teachers-for-pay—the ones whom the people call sophists and consider to be rival craftsmen—teaches anything other than the opinions the crowds share when they are assembled together. The sophist calls that wisdom. It is just as if someone were learning the habits and appetites of a huge, strong beast that he is rearing—how to approach and manage it, when it is hardest to deal with or gentlest and what makes it so, what sounds it utters in either

> condition, and what tones of voice soothes or incites it. Having learned all this by spending time with the beast and his experience with it; he calls his familiarity wisdom, organizes his experience as if it were a craft, and starts to teach it. But, he really knows nothing about which of these habits or appetites is beautiful or shameful, good or bad, just or unjust; he uses all these terms in to describe the big beast's beliefs. He calls the things the beast likes good and the things that anger it bad. He would have no other account to give of them. But, when it came to the nature of the necessary and the Good, and the way that their beings differ widely, he would neither have recognized those things or be able to show them to anyone else (493a-c).[18]

Within the democratic regime, those who are honored for their wisdom are those who reflect the will of the masses. Socrates tells us that they are like those who have become familiar with the behaviors of a huge, strong beast. Because of their familiarity with the beast's behaviors, they can anticipate its actions, soothe it, enervate it, etc. Because they have this knowledge, sophists have the power to train the citizens of a democratic regime to act in certain ways, just as an animal trainer has the power to modify a beast's behavior. This power, they call wisdom.

---

[18] ἕκαστος τῶν μισθαρνούντων ἰδιωτῶν, οὓς δὴ οὗτοι σοφιστὰς καλοῦσι καὶ ἀντιτέχνους ἡγοῦνται, μὴ ἄλλα παιδεύειν ἢ ταῦτα τὰ τῶν πολλῶν δόγματα, ἃ δοξάζουσιν ὅταν ἁθροισθῶσιν, καὶ σοφίαν ταύτην καλεῖν: οἷόνπερ ἂν εἰ θρέμματος μεγάλου καὶ ἰσχυροῦ τρεφομένου τὰς ὀργάς τις καὶ ἐπιθυμίας κατεμάνθανεν, ὅπῃ τε προσελθεῖν χρὴ καὶ ὅπῃ ἅψασθαι αὐτοῦ, καὶ ὁπότε χαλεπώτατον ἢ πρᾳότατον καὶ ἐκ τίνων γίγνεται, καὶ φωνὰς δὴ ἐφ᾽ οἷς ἑκάστας εἴωθεν φθέγγεσθαι, καὶ οἵας αὖ ἄλλου φθεγγομένου ἡμεροῦταί τε καὶ ἀγριαίνει, καταμαθὼν δὲ ταῦτα πάντα συνουσίᾳ τε καὶ χρόνου τριβῇ σοφίαν τε καλέσειεν καὶ ὡς τέχνην συστησάμενος ἐπὶ διδασκαλίαν τρέποιτο, μηδὲν εἰδὼς τῇ ἀληθείᾳ τούτων τῶν δογμάτων τε καὶ ἐπιθυμιῶν ὅτι καλὸν ἢ αἰσχρὸν ἢ ἀγαθὸν ἢ κακὸν ἢ δίκαιον ἢ ἄδικον, ὀνομάζοι δὲ πάντα ταῦτα ἐπὶ ταῖς τοῦ μεγάλου ζῴου δόξαις, οἷς μὲν χαίροι ἐκεῖνο ἀγαθὰ καλῶν, οἷς δὲ ἄχθοιτο κακά, ἄλλον δὲ μηδένα ἔχοι λόγον περὶ αὐτῶν, ἀλλὰ τἀναγκαῖα δίκαια καλοῖ καὶ καλά, τὴν δὲ τοῦ ἀναγκαίου καὶ ἀγαθοῦ φύσιν, ὅσον διαφέρει τῷ ὄντι, μήτε ἑωρακὼς εἴη μήτε ἄλλῳ δυνατὸς δεῖξαι.

The word that Socrates uses for what the sophists call wisdom is *tribé*,[19] which is often translated "knack," but which literally refers to rubbing or massaging something. To have acquired the *tribé* of something is to have a feel for it, to have massaged it thoroughly. Having the sort of familiarity and power associated with *tribé* contrasts sharply with acquiring a *techné*.[20] In order to have a *techné* for something, one must not just have developed a capacity for engaging with it in practical terms, but that capacity must also be grounded in knowledge of that thing.

By likening the sophist to an animal trainer in this passage, Socrates has created an opportunity to calibrate several different levels of the *Republic*'s immense argument to one other. In this exchange with Adeimantus, which is undeniably concerned with contemporary Athenian politics, Socrates appeals to an image that will later (588c) be undeniably concerned with the structure of an individual soul, thus suggesting an analogical relationship between the two. Additionally, the comparison between the *tribé* of the sophist/animal trainer in the passage above and the *techné* of the philosopher/true pilot from the end of Book V and beginning of Book VI shines light back on the city/soul from Book IV, and illuminates at least one way that it is structurally deficient, i.e. the absence of any capacity to see beyond itself. The city/soul of Book IV can only have a *tribé* of itself. It lacks the capacity for *techné*; its approach to self-governance cannot be based on knowledge, but only on having a feel for what it is. In order to have knowledge of something, one must be able to apprehend the unchanging ideas that it instantiates, and the city/soul of Book IV lacks the capacity for that sort of apprehension.

Much later in the dialogue, in Book IX at 588b, Socrates suggests that the conversation return to the first things that led them to this point of the argument.[21] The proposition he has in mind, he says, is that doing injustice profits an unjust person who is believed to be just.[22] In order to address that claim, which Socrates is now (finally) ready to refute, he

[19] τριβή.

[20] Τέχνη.

[21] ἀναλάβωμεν τὰ πρῶτα λεχθέντα, δι᾽ ἃ δεῦρ᾽ ἥκομεν.

[22] αὐτῷ διαλεγώμεθα, ἐπειδὴ διωμολογησάμεθα τό τε ἀδικεῖν καὶ τὸ δίκαια πράττειν ἣν ἑκάτερον ἔχει δύναμιν.

fashions an "image of the soul in words." [23] So, we return to the image in Book IX, the culminating image, I believe of the three or four-part soul. The first part of this image of the tripartite soul in Book IX is a many-headed beast, the second is a lion, and the third is a human being. All three grow naturally together and exist within an image of human being, so the whole resembles one of its three parts. Tending to the details of this powerful image would take us too far off track from our consideration of psychology of Book VI, but making the connection between the beast of Book VI (493a) and the beast of Book IX (588c) is important.

Socrates describes the sophist in Book VI as the one who can tame the beast (i.e. the democratic populace) because of his familiarity with its habits, his *tribé*. He claims that the sophists' capacity to do so is mistaken for wisdom. In the image of the Ship of State, the analogous character would be the sailor who, by appealing to his knack for the ways of sailors, learns to sway them to do what he wills. As the Ship of State makes clear, the true captain of the ship possesses a thoroughly different kind of knowledge, *techné*. He knows how to set a course by the stars. His practical plan for the course of the ship is informed by his knowledge of realities above and beyond the ship itself. The sophist and his apparent wisdom are false friends to the city; he appears to be wise, and his ideas have a certain efficacy, but they are really just projections and manipulations of the appetites of the many. The true captain of the ship is like the philosopher; he appeals to his knowledge of the Good, not a familiarity with the many, in order to determine what is best for the city.

When the beast returns in Book IX, it is clear that taming it does not simply mean predicting its reactions. It requires that it be trained toward what is good for the whole soul of which it is a part. In Book IX, the beast is clearly an image of the appetitive/*epithumetic*, soul. And the lion and the little man are clearly spirit/*thumos* and reason/*logismos-nous*. If the beast of Book IX is to be a harmonious part of the whole, some of its heads must be fed and others starved. And, in order to know which beasts/appetites should be encouraged and which others should be thwarted, one must have an image of the whole harmonious soul which contains an image of the version of the beast that contributes best to it.

---

[23] εἰκόνα πλάσαντες τῆς ψυχῆς λόγῳ.

One must have an idea of the Good in order to make good versions of those choices.

As Adeimantus and Socrates continue to develop their account of how and why those with philosophical natures are rarely, if ever, nurtured into an educable philosophical character, they take up the imaginary case of a young person with a philosophical nature, what his experience might be in Athens, and how that experience might mold his character. They are still considering the boy at the assembly who aspires one day to be able to move the crowd—to direct that beast—but now the case is refined to specify that this particularly ambitious boy is also well disposed in every way for philosophy. At 494b, Socrates reminds Adeimantus, "we agreed that ease in learning, a good memory, courage, and high mindedness belong to the philosophical nature."[24] Starting from this list of his virtues, they speculate that such a person would start life by being honored by other children, then pressured by his family to do them services. He would be constantly flattered, become rich, and, while still a young man, be full of exaggerated expectations of his capacities, in large part because he would never have experienced failure or dishonor.

Socrates asks Adeimantus to suppose someone gently approaches a young man in that state of mind and tells him he has no sense, although he needs it, and that it cannot be acquired unless he works like a slave to attain it" (494d).[25] They agree immediately that it would be completely unlikely that such a person would respond well to that message. Nothing would suggest that the person offering that criticism and advice was being reasonable. How could one who has been universally honored and consistently successful begin to imagine that he has been entirely on the wrong track?

Socrates brackets the practical impossibility of such a philosophically-disposed, democratically-honored young man recognizing that he should reorient his life, though, and goes on to imagine that the is

[24] ἐκ τῶν ἔμπροσθεν. ὡμολόγηται γὰρ δὴ ἡμῖν εὐμάθεια καὶ μνήμη καὶ ἀνδρεία καὶ μεγαλοπρέπεια ταύτης εἶναι τῆς φύσεως.

[25] τῷ δὴ οὕτω διατιθεμένῳ ἐάν τις ἠρέμα προσελθὼν τἀληθῆ λέγῃ, ὅτι νοῦς οὐκ ἔνεστιν αὐτῷ, δεῖται δέ, τὸ δὲ οὐ κτητὸν μὴ δουλεύσαντι τῇ κτήσει αὐτοῦ.

"turned around and drawn toward philosophy" (494e).[26] (The allusions to the cave in this passage are clear.) Even in the unlikely case of a chain of events bringing a philosophically disposed soul to an appreciation for pursuing a philosophical education, things look bleak. Everyone in that nascent philosopher's life will be committed to dissuading him from his philosophical pursuits. Every pleasure he has experienced will be at risk. Every form of success and approbation that he has enjoyed will have to be abandoned. Everything that makes him capable of becoming a philosopher will work within his life to make that prospect painful and unattractive. Like the man seeking the kingdom of heaven in Chapter Nineteen of the Gospel of Matthew, it may be easier for a camel to go through the eye of a needle than Plato's rich, handsome, brilliant boy to become a philosopher.

As bleak as the prospects already seem to be for the person born with a disposition for philosophy, Socrates is not finished. At 495b he goes on to say that once such a person has rejected the philosophical life, and it seems inevitable that he will go on to do terrible harm. Those who have great natures do great things, Socrates says. And those who are unattached to the Good are likely to do bad things. Therefore, those who are born with the capacity to be the best are also those who can and will become the worst, especially when all of the characters and conditions of their lives conspire to incentivize their vice.[27] Once again, we have run into the horror that prompted Socrates to prostrate himself to Adrasteia, the terrible risk that philosophical education might create ethically unhinged monsters.

---

[26] τῶν λόγων εἰσαισθάνηταί τέ πῃ καὶ κάμπτηται καὶ ἕλκηται πρὸς φιλοσοφίαν.

[27] I find it impossible not to have Alcibiades in mind when I read this section of the *Republic*. As Debra Nails highlights, Alcibiades' power as an orator and democratic politician and the vulnerability of the Athenian *demos* to poetry and rhetoric combined to send the Athenian Navy to Sicily for its most devastating defeat. See Debra Nails, "Plato's *Republic* in its Athenian Context," *History of Political Thought* 33, no. 1 (Spring 2012): 11.

Socrates' account of what happens when a soul with a philosophical *genesis* undergoes a radically unphilosophical *trophe* ends here, but he goes on to address the other perversion of philosophical *trophe* with which he began this section of argument (491a)—those who are not well disposed for philosophy (i.e. do not have a philosophical *genesis*), but attempt a philosophical *trophe*, anyway. For this part of the discussion, Socrates returns to the sexual imagery he used to describe the philosopher's "intercourse" with philosophy at 490b. If all goes well, the philosophically disposed soul is erotically drawn to philosophy and has intercourse with it, then the union of philosophy and the philosopher give birth to understanding and truth. But when this union doesn't happen, and we have just seen how unlikely it is that it ever will, something very different is born. When unworthy men have intercourse with philosophy, their children are sophisms. Understanding and truth are the children of philosophical souls who procreate with philosophy, and sophisms are the children of non-philosophical souls who procreate with philosophy. The latter are what give philosophy a bad name.

The plight of the tiny group of people who are naturally philosophical and who have wed themselves to a life of philosophy is terribly constrained in the city in deed. Constantly at risk of drowning in sophisms, slander, and threats to their life, they withdraw from the public sphere and limit their ambitions to avoiding injustice and impiety in their private lives. Socrates only gives two examples, Theages and himself, and he laments that neither of them live in a city (literally, a constitution) where they could do more good. The psychological analog to this dynamic seems to be the person for whom *epithumia* is just too strong for *logismosnous* and *thumos* to contain, regardless of their philosophical nature. This is still the Female Drama, after all, even though Socrates has not reminded his interlocutors and readers of that in quite some time. Theages represents that person whose appetites (*epithumia*) have constrained opportunities to take control of his life because of his physical disabilities. Socrates offers himself as an anomaly who, because of his *daimonion*, is uniquely and mysteriously capable of philosophical self-governance despite his hostile environment.

Presumably because Adeimantus can no longer think of anything that might be said in defense of a democratic constitution, he asks Socrates which of the constitutions extant in the Greek world might offer a philosophical nature a promising philosophical *trophe*, and Socrates replies—none of them. A philosopher cannot rule a Greek democratic regime because the many are too strong. He can also not rule in any other extant regime because their non-philosophical, non-democratic rulers are also too strong in their own particular ways. This situation creates an apparently inescapable cycle because regimes that cannot be ruled by philosophers are also incapable of nurturing young philosophical natures into mature philosophers who are capable of ruling. Not only are there no philosopher rulers in Greek cities, unless divine providence intervenes, none can ever emerge. From this moment forward in the exchange with Adeimantus, Socrates is clear that he is no longer talking about cities in deed. If they are to continue their conversation, and they are, they will have to return to the city in speech.

8

Philosophical *Trophe* in *Kallipolis*

(The Trophe of Logismos/Nous)

At 497b in Book VI, Adeimantus and Socrates seem to have exhausted all of their options for imagining the possibility of a philosopher-ruler developing to maturity within an actually existing *polis*. They have considered in some detail why the Athenian democratic regime can neither nurture a philosophical nature nor a non-philosophical nature into philosophical maturity. Socrates then presses the point and claims that these conclusions apply to all extant regimes in the interlocutors' world. What the city/soul needs is to be ruled by a philosopher, but the actual conditions of all the cities in Greece exclude this possibility. The psychological analog holds, as well. There seem to be no human beings, perhaps with the exceptions of Theages and Socrates, whose appetitive (*epithumetic*) and sprited (*thumotic*) souls are ruled by reason (*logismos* and *nous*). And neither of them are viable candidates for political rule. Despite Adeimantus' drive to bring the conversation out of the world of words and into the world of facts, at 497c he follows Socrates back into a consideration of the city in speech.

Socrates assumes that when he has closed off all possibilities for philosophical rule in existing cities that Adeimantus will ask him what the best possible constitution would be. Adeimantus tells Socrates that he has made the wrong assumption, though. He was not planning to ask what the best possible city would be, he says; instead he wants to know whether the constitution they have already described would be a city fit for a philosopher. And Socrates says it would be, except in one way. "In all other respects, it is the same. But, as we already said, there must always be someone in the city who has a rational account of the constitution—the very same understanding that you, the lawgiver, had when you made these laws [for the city in speech] (497c–d).[1] Adeimantus has served as a lawgiver for the city in speech (as has Glaucon) from outside the city, but a city capable of raising a philosopher would have to have a lawgiver within it who had a rational understanding of the constitution.

This brief exchange between Adeimantus and Socrates suggests several things. First, we see that Adeimantus probably does not think of the purged city in speech as the best possible city. If Adeimantus thought that city in speech were best, he presumably would not have disagreed with with Socrates' assumption that his next question would be about the best possible city, since it would be one and the same as the one he claims to be interested in. Secondly, it appears that with one important exception, Socrates seems to believe that the purged city in speech provides a framework for the best possible city, since we already know that he believes that the city ruled by a philosopher is the best possible city and we see that the city founded in Book IV is almost that city. Finally, we can see, at least in sketch form, what Socrates thinks the Book IV model lacks, i.e, "there must always be someone in the city who has a rational account of the constitution—the very same understanding that you, the lawgiver, had when you made these laws."

Although Socrates says he alluded to such a person earlier in their conversation (perhaps at 412a-b), he claims that there is no one within the Book IV city-soul who has a rational account of the constitution. This is the missing piece, and we already know from the end of Book V what it entails. In order to have a rational account of something, one has to have knowledge of it. Knowledge is grounded in the apprehension of the unchanging idea that makes something what it is. Opinion, on the other hand, is based on an apprehension of a multiplicity of things that resemble each other but it lacks an idea of what they share (479e). For someone within the city in speech to have a rational account of the constitution, that person must be able to apprehend the unchanging idea that makes that constitution what it is.

[1] τὰ μὲν ἄλλα, ἦν δ' ἐγώ, αὕτη: τοῦτο δὲ αὐτὸ ἐρρήθη μὲν καὶ τότε, ὅτι δεήσοι τι ἀεὶ ἐνεῖναι ἐν τῇ πόλει λόγον ἔχον τῆς πολιτείας τὸν αὐτὸν ὅνπερ καὶ σὺ ὁ νομοθέτης ἔχων τοὺς νόμους ἐτίθεις.

From Book II to Book IV, Glaucon and Adeimantus serve as the law-givers to the city in speech, with Socrates as their very active guide. They see the city in speech and they discuss its constitution in relation to various principles that then orient their law giving and, ultimately, its founding. However, as Socrates' interlocutors, they do not reside within the city in speech. What Socrates now tells Adeimantus at 497c–d is that there must be someone within the city in speech that functions in the role that Glaucon and Adeimantus have been playing. The best city in speech must be self-governed, not legislated from without. The psychological analog seems clear. The philosophical soul must also be self-governed, autarchic. It must be capable of apprehending the idea of the Good, which exists outside of itself and to use its apprehension of the Good to organize all the parts of itself into a harmonious, thriving whole. This part of oneself that has the capacity for external apprehension should also be the same part responsible for internal organization. The true pilot should both gaze at the stars in order to chart the Ship of State's course, and he should also take charge of all of the operations on board in order to keep the ship on that course. In the language of the city in speech, the philosopher must rule. By saying that the only thing the fevered city lacks is a lawgiver, and by pointing out that Adeimantus and Glaucon have been playing that role, Socrates also implies that all of the essential parts of the best city were already present in the dialogue in Book IV; they just were not yet present in the city/soul model.

Once all of the possibilities for philosophical rule in an existing *polis* have been exhausted, Adeimantus and Socrates turn back to a consideration of the city in speech. The first question Socrates takes up is how a city can "engage in philosophy without being destroyed" (497d),[2] and the first claim he makes in this inquiry is "beautiful things are difficult" (497d).[3] We already have seen many reasons why Socrates might understand philosophical rule to be beautiful; the question now is why he here emphasizes its difficulty. The next several arguments in Socrates and Adeimantus' shared inquiry are at least as concerned with establishing the possibility of philosophical rule as with developing strategies for

[2] τίνα τρόπον μεταχειριζομένη πόλις φιλοσοφίαν οὐ διολεῖται.

[3] τὰ καλὰ τῷ ὄντι χαλεπά.

helping a city accept such a regime. It seems important to Socrates to make the case that although there is no extant regime in which it would be possible for a philosopher to rule, it is not impossible in principle.

One of the most difficult aspects of developing a psychological reading of the middle books of the *Republic* is figuring out how to approach the account of the philosopher, especially in Book VI. On the one hand, the philosopher is presented as the proper ruler of the best city, so if the city is presented as an analog for the soul, then the philosopher should be understood as a part of that soul, as *nous* (combined, in the best case, with *logismos*). On the other hand, when we read of the education of the philosopher, the account appears to make good literal sense; that is, the account of the education of the philosopher seems consonant both with other sections of the *Republic* and with discussions of philosophical nature, activity, and practice in the larger context of the Platonic corpus. So, which is it? Is the philosopher of Book VI a philosopher per se, or an image of the proper role of *noetic* activity in a philosophical soul?

Perhaps obviously, the answer is both. As I read it, the difficulty of making sense of the psychological content of this section of the *Republic* stems not from stretching the analogy too far, but instead from how perfectly it holds. Part and whole are so similar in this case that there is little or no "unpacking" to do, and that turns out to be a bit confusing. Like a fractal repeating itself in microcosm and macrocosm, the part of the soul that rules a philosophical life is analogically identical to the person who runs the city philosophically.[4] So, the account of the nurture of the part of the soul capable of such self-rule is the same as the account of the nurture of the person capable of the best political rule.[5]

---

[4] This seems closely related to what Eva Brann describes as a "particular kind of philosophical imaging which makes the Whole reappear as embedded within itself." Eva Brann, *The Music of the Republic* (Philadelphia: Paul Dry Books, 2004), 206.

[5] Jessica Moss finds the usage of "*epithumia*" in the *Republic* to be consistent with its usage in the *Charmides*, where it is explicitly defined as "desires for pleasure." This suggests the possibility of a fractal-like repeating pattern on the appetitive end of the soul, as well. As Socrates makes clear in Book IX, all parts of the soul have their own appetities, so what makes the lower part of the soul distinctive is not that it has appetites, but rather what kind of appetites it

The essential relationship between the best city and the *trophe* of the philosopher exacerbates the confusion even more at this part of the argument, but not because the analogy is weaker or more tenuous; rather, because it is so tight. One can develop theories about what Plato thought were the determining factors in philosophical *genesis*, and they will be both antiquated and almost certainly offensive. Of all the wisdom we have to glean from the ancients, they are not our best teachers on matters of disposition.[6] But, even bracketing the prejudices of ancient culture, the Platonic account of philosophical *genesis* is full of mystery. Socrates can describe the sort of nature (*physis*) that is trainable and educable for philosophy, but his account of the external conditions for bringing such a nature into the world is grossly and necessarily underdetermined. Soon, when we get to the account of philosophical education (*paideia*) in the *Republic*, I will argue that the external conditions necessary for it are actually fairly minimal. It is premature to try to make that argument here, but the basic point is: if one has a philosophic nature (*physis*) engendered by a good philosophical *genesis* and nurtured by a good philosophical upbringing (*trophe)*, then one will be in the best possible position to find and to benefit from a good philosophical education (*paideia*), regardless of the external conditions one enjoys or suffers. This is, of course, not to say that external conditions are not relevant to philosophical *paideia*, only that the one who has a good philosophical *genesis* and *trophe* will be less vulnerable to external impediments and less reliant on external props.

---

has either in terms of the objects of those appetites or the way in which its objects are desired. From this perspective, *epithumia* looks something like appetite for appetite. Jessica Moss, "Pleasure and Illusion in Plato," *Philosophy and Phenomenological Research* 72, no. 3 (May 2006): 503–535.

[6] Rigid cultural norms made it difficult to discern the differences between human beings that were products of nurture (*trophe*) from those that came down to nature (*physis* and *genesis*). As Bertrand Russell famously quipped, "Aristotle maintained that women have fewer teeth than men; although he was twice married, it never occurred to him to verify this statement by examining his wives' mouths." Bertrand Russell, *The Impact of Science on Society* (Matchette Foundation Lectures, Number III. Delivered at Columbia University, 1950. New York: Columbia University Press, 1951) 7.

For philosophical *genesis*, external conditions are mysterious, and for philosophical *paideia*, external conditions are less relevant; but, for philosophical *trophe*, external conditions are centrally important. Because the constitution of one's city serves as an important set of external conditions for individual development, one side of the city/soul analogy becomes relevant to the other side of the city/soul analogy in this section. While in most parts of the *Republic*, it seems important either to be exploring the constitution of the city in speech or its psychological analog, but not to let the two overlap in one's analysis; here, it appears to be impossible to maintain that separation.[7] What the philosophically disposed soul needs in order to be ready for a philosophical education is philosophical *trophe*, nurture. One must develop the habits and values that will best support one's future education by being immersed in a culture that sets those pre-rational defaults properly. One's family, friends, society, and, city provide the structure within which one's pre-rational preferences develop; they are the mechanisms by which a philosophical nature will either be nurtured or corrupted. And, according to Socrates in his exchange with Adeimantus, if one's city is a corrupting influence, there is practically no hope.

The city that will provide a proper philosophical *trophe* for a well-disposed philosophical nature is the philosophical city. Our analogy is

[7] Although I argue that the philosopher is a special case, in general I agree with G. R. F. Ferrari and others who argue that it is a mistake to treat the citizens in the city in speech as individuals whose souls have a tripartite constitution. He puts it this way: "Certainly, each person in the city performs his own task (ὅτι τὸ αὑτοῦ ἕκαστος εἷς ὢν ἔπραττε, 433d); but this is not to say that each is a just individual. As the just city is one in which each element performs its proper task, so too with the just individual (441de). But the elements of the just individual are the parts of his soul; he is the person in whom reason, spirit, and appetite perform their proper tasks; and this is not at all what it means for an individual in the just city to perform *his* proper task. That task is simply the job that society requires of him and to which his abilities fit him. One man will make a good potter, another a good soldier, yet another a good ruler. If each does what he is fit to do and in particular does not attempt to do a job that is the prerogative of a different class (434b), the city is just, and its analogy with the just individual is complete. That analogy does not peer into the souls of the individual to whom the just city is analogous (Ferrari, *City and Soul*, 44–45).

still in place, but we cannot stay neatly on one side of it or the other for this part of the argument. Whether or not a philosophical city has ever existed or will ever exist, and whether or not a good philosophical nature will ever be born in it, the recipe for becoming educable for philosophy is for the philosophically disposed soul to be born into the philosophical city. In the philosophical city, the philosophically disposed soul will become habituated to virtue and experience justice, moderation, courage, and wisdom. She will not be flattered by corrupters or find success in vice. When she is ready to engage the world rationally, she will not have to overcome a lifetime of experiences that have made true things appear false, good things appear naïve, and the most important things appear trivial.

Is philosophical *trophe* impossible because no city in the world is governed philosophically? And, since philosophical *trophe* is a necessary part of becoming philosophical, is Socrates describing the tragic reality that it is not possible for one to become philosophical in his world or ours? I do not believe so. I think that Socrates turns his attention to the possibility of philosophy in the last part of this exchange with Adeimantus in order to suggest a way through this apparently inescapable predicament. No one can re-live one's childhood and reset the values and assumptions that one's pre-rational experiences established, but one can reconsider those assumptions and values, and one can work to develop new habits. The conversation of the *Republic* seems to imply three particularly powerful ways for one with a philosophical *genesis* to overcome an inferior philosophical *trophe*: following a philosophical guide/teacher, engaging in conversation with others who have a philosophical *genesis*, and exploring powerful, illuminating images.

Socrates sums up this part of the argument by saying that it seems impossible for a philosopher to take a fifth-century Greek *polis* in hand for two reasons. The first reason is that the masses have never seen a person who was virtuous in word and deed. Plato's language here is complicated and interesting.

> However, it is no wonder that the masses are not convinced by our arguments. I mean, they have never seen a man that matched our plan—though they have more often seen words purposely chosen to rhyme with one another than just happening to do so in the present case. But a man who, as far as possible, matched and rhymed with

> virtue in word and deed, and wielded dynastic power in a city of the same type—that is something they have never seen even once (498d–499a).[8]

The passage is tricky because Socrates is making fun of sophistry in both form and content, and a translation that preserves the joke is (almost?) impossible. The masses are used to sophists who make words and phrases resemble each other (*homoiomena*[9]), which Reeve smartly translates as "rhyme." What the masses have never seen is a person who has power in a city and who is equal and similar to himself in word and deed.

It is a problem that the many (*hoi poloi*) have not seen a philosopher with political power. It is also a problem that they have not heard good arguments. "Neither have they, my good man, spent enough time listening to beautiful and liberating arguments that strain in every way to seek the truth, in order to acquire knowledge; nor have they kept their distance from all the sophistries and eristic contests that strive for nothing except reputation and disputation, whether in public legal proceedings or private gatherings" (499a).[10] The parallels between what the many have not seen and what they have not heard are clear. Because sophists do not acknowledge the possibility of apprehending an objective reference point for judgment, the many in the regime controlled by sophists only see power wielded and justified by reference to itself and its efficacy. Analogously, because sophists do not acknowledge the existence of truth or its choiceworthiness, the many do not hear arguments that acknowledge the

[8] Here, I have used the Reeve translation instead of my own. τὸ μέντοι μὴ πείθεσθαι τοῖς λεγομένοις τοὺς πολλοὺς θαῦμα οὐδέν: οὐ γὰρ πώποτε εἶδον γενόμενον τὸ νῦν λεγόμενον, ἀλλὰ πολὺ μᾶλλον τοιαῦτ᾽ ἄττα ῥήματα ἐξεπίτηδες ἀλλήλοις ὡμοιωμένα, ἀλλ᾽ οὐκ ἀπὸ τοῦ αὐτομάτου ὥσπερ νῦν συμπεσόντα. ἄνδρα δὲ ἀρετῇ παρισωμένον καὶ ὡμοιωμένον μέχρι τοῦ δυνατοῦ τελέως ἔργῳ τε καὶ λόγῳ, δυναστεύοντα ἐν πόλει ἑτέρᾳ τοιαύτῃ, οὐ πώποτε ἑωράκασιν, οὔτε ἕνα οὔτε πλείους.

[9] ὡμοιωμένα.

[10] οὐδέ γε αὖ λόγων, ὦ μακάριε, καλῶν τε καὶ ἐλευθέρων ἱκανῶς ἐπήκοοι γεγόνασιν, οἵων ζητεῖν μὲν τὸ ἀληθὲς συντεταμένως ἐκ παντὸς τρόπου τοῦ γνῶναι χάριν, τὰ δὲ κομψά τε καὶ ἐριστικὰ καὶ μηδαμόσε ἄλλοσε τείνοντα ἢ πρὸς δόξαν καὶ ἔριν καὶ ἐν δίκαις καὶ ἐν ἰδίαις συνουσίαις πόρρωθεν ἀσπαζομένων.

existence of truth. Instead, all they hear are *eristical* attempts to outdo each other with cleverness. Without an external reference point for judgment, all authority dissipates into power and all argument is reduced to cleverness.

These comments on what the many have not seen and have not heard point precisely to the issue of inner and outer reference points that Socrates has been emphasizing throughout his account of philosophical *nous* and *trophe*. The sophist, like the sailor on the Ship of State who manages to seize and hold power over the over sailors, lives in an apparently self-contained world. His only standards are self-referential. They "rhyme" only with themselves like their clever speech. So, the masses have never seen someone whose words match his deeds and not just his other words. They've never experienced the possibility of an external standard for speeches, so they do not believe one could possibly exist. The idea that argumentation might be oriented to a quest for truth rather than to the conquest of one's opponent is thoroughly alien to them. And, really, they cannot be blamed. No one with their experiences could be expected to do differently. Their upbringing and enculturation (*trophe)* has made the possibility of philosophical insight (*noesis)* completely implausible. Not only do the sophist and philosopher appear identical to those who do not acknowledge the existence of something beyond themselves to be apprehended (like the stars), without the proper *trophe* it is impossible for them, in principle, to tell them apart.

It is important to note that Socrates is not primarily focused here on constructing a critique of sophistry, although that is clearly a part of his point. His main focus is to explain why the masses cannot be expected to entertain the possibility of a constitution ruled by a philosopher. In a way, Socrates offers a defense of the masses in these passages, and it is presented very much in the mode of the Female Drama. Why can a philosopher not come into political power in Athens or any other extant regime? Because the many lack the capacity, the potency, to be ruled by a philosopher. And why do the many lack the potency for philosophical rule? Because, whether or not they had a good philosophical *genesis*, the *trophe* provided by Athenian democracy undermines their philosophical development in every possible way. One is neither nurtured with philosophy in sight nor in earshot. One develops all of one's pre-rational assumptions about the world with philosophy either absent or maligned.

How could such a one ever be expected to pursue a philosophical education? How could one not mock and malign such an alien prospect?

The psychological analog to the political situation described at 499a is fairly straightforward. If one's epithumetic soul (one's appetite) is not nurtured with a reference to the Good, then it will be profoundly difficult not to let one's appetites take over one's life. If one has no idea of health, then the question of whether one should eat potato chips or a green salad is simply a matter of taste. And if one's appetites have never been indulged or denied according to their contributions to health, then one cannot expect those appetites to recognize good health or to pursue the foods that might contribute to it. Until one sees the the life of one who eats well and hears an account of how her choices of foods connect directly to health, one cannot expect to believe that health is a possibility or that it has anything to do with how one comports oneself to one's appetites. Appetites are not just for food, of course. Precisely the same dynamics explain why one who has not seen a virtuous person or listened to an account of how her choices contributed to the development of her virtue cannot be expected to develop virtue.

It is a sad fact that the many are incapable of acknowledging the difference between sophistry and philosophy, according to Socrates, and this sad fact is one of the things that made him reluctant to begin the Female Drama at the beginning of Book V. But, just as Socrates seems to be closing off every avenue that might lead to a regime of a philosophical ruler, he insists on arguing that such a regime, however implausible, is not impossible:

> If sometime in the boundless past, some necessity forced those who best at philosophy to take control of a city, or if that it is happening now in some barbaric place beyond the known world, or if happens in the future; we are prepared to fight for the argument that the constitution we have described has existed, does exist, and will exist whenever the muse of philosophy controls a city. It is not impossible for

> this to happen, so we are not speaking of impossibilities, but we agree that it is difficult. (499c–d)[11]

Socrates' defense of the possibility of a philosophical city pushes the limits of credulity. Within the defense, he admits that no one has seen such a regime and that perhaps it has not ever existed. But, it is possible, he insists, and if it ever has, does, or will exist, it will take the shape he has described. Then, dramatically, he says that he is prepared to fight with anyone who denies it.

Adeimantus, who is now careful to distinguish himself from the masses, agrees with Socrates on the possibility of establishing a philosophical regime, however difficult, but he cannot imagine that the masses could be brought into agreement with them on that point. This is a self-refuting position, since if it is impossible to bring the masses into agreement with philosophical rule, philosophical rule would be impossible; but Socrates does not point out Adeimantus' incoherence. Instead, he attempts to enlist Adeimantus into his project to disabuse the masses of their misconceptions about philosophy, soothe their prejudices, and reform their opinions about philosophers. Both the form and the content of the argument Socrates makes to Adeimantus here are helpful to our attempt to make sense of the psychological content of this section. The argument takes the form of *nous* guiding *logismos* in its reasoning with *thumos* about *epithumia*, i.e., a true pilot using his knowledge of fixed things and his management skills to attempt to convince a ship owner about how to organize the crew or a guardian attempting to persuade an auxiliary to help him govern the workers in a city. The content of the argument builds upon the description of the philosophical nature from the beginning of Book VI.

At 485c, Socrates introduces an axiom of sorts: "when one's appetites are strongly inclined in one direction, they will be more weakly in-

---

[11] εἰ τοίνυν ἄκροις εἰς φιλοσοφίαν πόλεώς τις ἀνάγκη ἐπιμεληθῆναι ἢ γέγονεν ἐν τῷ ἀπείρῳ τῷ παρεληλυθότι χρόνῳ ἢ καὶ νῦν ἔστιν ἔν τινι βαρβαρικῷ τόπῳ, πόρρω που ἐκτὸς ὄντι τῆς ἡμετέρας ἐπόψεως, ἢ καὶ ἔπειτα γενήσεται, περὶ τούτου ἕτοιμοι τῷ λόγῳ διαμάχεσθαι, ὡς γέγονεν ἡ εἰρημένη πολιτεία καὶ ἔστιν καὶ γενήσεταί γε, ὅταν αὕτη ἡ Μοῦσα πόλεως ἐγκρατὴς γένηται. οὐ γὰρ ἀδύνατος γενέσθαι, οὐδ' ἡμεῖς ἀδύνατα λέγομεν: χαλεπὰ δὲ καὶ παρ' ἡμῶν ὁμολογεῖται.

clined in others." At 500b, he brings the same point back up with more detail and then elaborates on it further.

> Without a doubt, Adeimantus, someone whose thoughts are truly focused on being does not have the leisure to look down at human things, get involved in their disputes, and develop malice and resentment for them. Instead, as he looks at and contemplates orderly and fixed things that neither do injustice to nor suffer injustice from each other, being all in a rational order, he imitates [these orderly and fixed things] and tries to become as like them as he can. Or do you think there is any way to stop someone from imitating the things he loves and spends time with?[12]

The philosopher who contemplates reality is not drawn into the disputes of those who live entirely in a world of competing opinions. First of all, according to the axiom at 485c (i.e., that if one's appetites are strengthened in one direction, they will be weakened in another), the philosopher's appetite for knowledge weakens his appetite for the things that others quarrel about. Socrates introduces a second axiom here as well: one who associates with something he admires will imitate it. The philosopher who is drawn to and associates with reality, which is constant and orderly, will himself become more constant and orderly by virtue of imitating it.

This passage and the axiom that it introduces serve as an important transition to the idea of imitation and to themes that will dominate the rest of Books VI and VII. Socrates has famously scathing things to say about imitation and its perils, but his praise of imitation is less well explored. Here, the philosopher ruler imitates the constancy and order of the reality he apprehends and attempts to "stamp" (*plattein*[13]) that image

---

[12] οὐδὲ γάρ που, ὦ Ἀδείμαντε, σχολὴ τῷ γε ὡς ἀληθῶς πρὸς τοῖς οὖσι τὴν διάνοιαν ἔχοντι κάτω βλέπειν εἰς ἀνθρώπων πραγματείας, καὶ μαχόμενον αὐτοῖς φθόνου τε καὶ δυσμενείας ἐμπίμπλασθαι, ἀλλ᾽ εἰς τεταγμένα ἄττα καὶ κατὰ ταὐτὰ ἀεὶ ἔχοντα ὁρῶντας καὶ θεωμένους οὔτ᾽ ἀδικοῦντα οὔτ᾽ ἀδικούμενα ὑπ᾽ ἀλλήλων, κόσμῳ δὲ πάντα καὶ κατὰ λόγον ἔχοντα, ταῦτα μιμεῖσθαί τε καὶ ὅτι μάλιστα ἀφομοιοῦσθαι. ἢ οἴει τινὰ μηχανὴν εἶναι, ὅτῳ τις ὁμιλεῖ ἀγάμενος, μὴ μιμεῖσθαι ἐκεῖνο;

[13] πλάττειν.

on the character of the people he rules. Psychologically, the analog would be to *nous* apprehending constant and orderly external reality and, with the help of *logismos* and *thumos*, attempting to form his *appetites* in its image: "And if he should be required to make a habit in private and in public—of stamping what he sees [in fixed and orderly things] into people's characters, instead of shaping only his own, do you think he will be a poor craftsman of temperance, justice, and the whole of democratic virtue?"[14] Imitation, here, is not only not maligned, it is the central dynamic in the process of becoming virtuous. The essential activities of the philosophical ruler are his apprehension and imitation of fixed and orderly being and his attempt to impose on those in his charge the Good order that he knows and embodies.

At 500c Socrates sets the stage to move on from his account of philosophical *trophe* and to begin his inquiry into philosophical *paideia*. The curtain is not quite down on the drama of *trophe*, and the drama of *paideia* is not quite ready to begin, but elements of both are woven into the remaining lines of Book VI. Like a cycle of Attic tragedy, each of the three parts of the Female Drama stand alone, but each also contributes to a whole they come together to form.

Just in case Adeimantus has forgotten that their inquiry has closed down any possibility of the philosophical regime being engendered in an extant *polis*, Socrates adds the point that the philosopher who will attempt to impress the orderly image of the Good on a city will insist that the characters of the citizens that he is to rule come to him as clean slates. For the third time (414c, 461d–e, and 501a), Socrates has insisted that citizens in the city in speech leave the past entirely behind. This appears to be something that may or may not be possible in speech, but cannot be accomplished in deed. Here, for the first time, Socrates gives an account not just of the necessity of creating a political and psychological clean slate, but of how it might be possible.

[14] ἂν οὖν τις, εἶπον, αὐτῷ ἀνάγκη γένηται ἃ ἐκεῖ ὁρᾷ μελετῆσαι εἰς ἀνθρώπων ἤθη καὶ ἰδίᾳ καὶ δημοσίᾳ τιθέναι καὶ μὴ μόνον ἑαυτὸν πλάττειν, ἆρα κακὸν δημιουργὸν αὐτὸν οἴει γενήσεσθαι σωφροσύνης τε καὶ δικαιοσύνης καὶ συμπάσης τῆς δημοτικῆς ἀρετῆς.

In Book III, 414c, Socrates presents the noble lie as an essential step in bringing the city/soul into harmony. Given that there are natural differences between gold, silver, and bronze citizens, he argues that the only way to avoid envy and to encourage cooperation is to convince everyone that they are siblings. But, no part of the myth of metals seems plausible, nor is there a persuasive account of how it is to be made plausible to the citizens of the city/soul. Likewise, in Book V, 461d, Socrates claims that all parents will think of all children who are born during a particular interval as their own children, and all children born during that time will be told whom to call father. But, again, there is no sense of how that story will become plausible to the citizens of Athens. They may see its utility, but it seems unlikely that they would genuinely come to believe that such parent/child relationships truly exist.

At 501b, however, Socrates describes the process by which the citizens of Kallipolis would come to leave their old habits and opinions behind:

> As they did their work, [the philosopher rulers] would, I suppose, often look in each direction: on the one hand, up toward what is just by nature, and beautiful, temperate, etc.; and, on the other hand, down toward what is in human beings, mixing and blending those practices to produce a human likeness, taking their cues from the human likenesses that Homer called divine and godly when they appeared among human beings....[The Philosopher ruler] would erase one thing, I suppose, and draw in another, until they had made people's dispositions as beloved by the gods as possible.[15]

When Socrates suggests that the lawgiver must work with citizens who are "clean slates," it appears that he is talking about about something ob-

[15] ἔπειτα οἶμαι ἀπεργαζόμενοι πυκνὰ ἂν ἑκατέρωσ᾽ ἀποβλέποιεν, πρός τε τὸ φύσει δίκαιον καὶ καλὸν καὶ σῶφρον καὶ πάντα τὰ τοιαῦτα, καὶ πρὸς ἐκεῖν᾽ αὖ τὸ ἐν τοῖς ἀνθρώποις ἐμποιοῖεν, συμμειγνύντες τε καὶ κεραννύντες ἐκ τῶν ἐπιτηδευμάτων τὸ ἀνδρείκελον, ἀπ᾽ ἐκείνου τεκμαιρόμενοι, ὃ δὴ καὶ Ὅμηρος ἐκάλεσεν ἐν τοῖς ἀνθρώποις ἐγγιγνόμενον θεοειδές τε καὶ θεοείκελον....καὶ τὸ μὲν ἂν οἶμαι ἐξαλείφοιεν, τὸ δὲ πάλιν ἐγγράφοιεν, ἕως ὅτι μάλιστα ἀνθρώπεια ἤθη εἰς ὅσον ἐνδέχεται θεοφιλῆ ποιήσειαν.

viously impossible. But here, when he describes the philosopher ruler's process, it seems far more plausible. Here, the lawgiver (as painter) encourages some habits and opinions and discourages others. Those she encourages, she "paints." Those she discourages, she "erases." It is still difficult to see how any process of erasure could make one into a purely clean slate, but the process itself is not only plausible, it is familiar. Everyone who has studied something practical, such as learning a sport or playing a musical instrument, is familiar with the teacher's work to undo a student's bad habits and inculcate new, better ones. And, if one focuses on the psychological half of the analogy, rather than the political, the process Socrates describes seems not just plausible, but obviously right. It also seems clearly to be a precursor to Aristotle's presentation of the role of habituation in ethical development.

If one has decided to become a guitar player, then one will be well-served by indulging those desires that contribute to that endeavor and attempting to "erase" those that don't contribute. If one has been taught that long fingernails and soft skin are beautiful, one will need to do one's best to erase those opinions as well as the habits that contribute to them so that one can have the callouses and unobtrusive fingernails of a guitar player. If the would-be musician enjoys being recognized by her teachers for her progress in a new endeavor, then she should indulge that desire by employing a good and effusive teacher. And, over time, if she is consistent, she will likely be able to erase the old, unproductive appetites at least to some degree, and to strengthen the helpful ones. Her reasonable ambitions guiding deliberate action, and aided by the part of her that loves honor and recognition, can and will manage her appetites. The bronze workers/sailors/masses/appetites will become mangageable if the philosophical ruler handles them well.

With the process by which the masses may be manage in place, Socrates claims to have shown both that the regime of the philosopher is best and that it is possible, however difficult it may be. He proposes next, at 502c–d, in what turns out to be the last part of his direct conversation with Adeimantus, to investigate what sort of curriculum will support the proto philosopher-ruler's development. Although Socrates' language and imagery does not immediately recall the themes of Book V, he is taking the conversation back into the framework of the three *kumata.* In order to make that context clear, Socrates adds that the accounts of women and children (the first two *kumata*) have been completed, and what remains is to go back and take up the subject of rulers (the third *kuma*) from the beginning (*ex arches*[16]) (502e). Specifically, their task is to show that philosophers are "guardians in the most precise sense" (503b).[17]

Very quickly, Adeimantus and Socrates' discussion moves from a review of why it would be difficult and unusual for one person to embody the character of a guardian and a philosopher simultaneously to the question of whether or not there is something higher than justice, one of the most important inquiries within the *Republic*. A proper guardian must develop all of the virtues, including justice. That was established in Book IV. Now, as a part of his review, Socrates reminds Adeimantus that a proper guardian must get to those virtues by "tak[ing] the longer road and putting no less effort into learning than into physical training" (504d-e).[18] But, Adeimantus asks, why? If the guardian of Book IV can achieve all of the virtues, what is he missing? What is he lacking? What subject will he never approach unless he "takes the long way around?" And Socrates answers: "the form of the Good" (505a).[19]

Socrates and Adeimantus have only a brief exchange about the form of the Good. Their conversation consists of Socrates making a series of claims about disagreements about the Good, thinly veiled as questions, and Adeimantus making just enough short, affirmative responses to keep the conversation moving. Socrates begins with the admission that we have no adequate knowledge of the Good, and he ends with a touch of exasperation that Adeimantus would still want to hear his opinion on the Good just after he had confessed that he had no knowledge of it. Then, perhaps just in time, Glaucon jumps back in to revive his role as Socrates' immediate interlocutor.

When Glaucon steps back into the foreground of the dialogue at 506d, he signals the beginning of the most famous sections of the *Republic*: the account of the Divided Line at the end of Book VI and the Cave immediately following it at the beginning of Book VII. In the next chap-

---

[16] ἐξ ἀρχῆς.

[17] τοὺς ἀκριβεστάτους φύλακας φιλοσόφους.

[18] περιιτέον τῷ τοιούτῳ, καὶ οὐχ ἧττον μανθάνοντι πονητέον ἢ γυμναζομένῳ.

[19] τοῦ ἀγαθοῦ ἰδέα.

ter, I will focus on the the Cave and its presentation of philosophical *paideia*, which will involve looking carefully at its resonances with the Divided Line. But, here, as I bring to a conclusion the discussion of philosophical *trophe*, it is important to think clearly about the arguments and images out of which the Divided Line emerges. We must consider how it fits both in the context of the immediately preceding inquiries of Book VI, and also in the larger "Female Drama" of Books V–VII. First, a bit of review is in order.

As Book VI opens, Socrates has largely finished his account of philosophical *genesis*, that is the way that each of the three parts of the city/soul must be disposed in order for philosophical upbringing (*trophe*) and education (*paideia*) to be possible. Insofar as we understand our "nature" (*physis*) deriving from a starting place that is entirely out of our control (*genesis*) or the control of those who raise us, Book V tells the story of what it means to have a philosophical nature. Book VI, then, takes up the question of philosophical nurture (*trophe*). It gives an account of how a philosophically disposed soul, one with a philosophical nature, must be nurtured in order to for it to be educable for philosophy.

The account of philosophical *trophe* in Book VI begins with Socrates' reminder that in Book V, they had reached the conclusion that those with a philosophical nature were deeply attached to the truth. From there, at 485d, Socrates said that children with a philosophical nature should, above all, strive for truth in every form.[20] When that child who is naturally disposed to truthfulness strives for truth, she will develop a number of virtues, which Socrates goes on immediately to enumerate. She will be temperate (485e), high-minded (486a), courageous (486b), gentle (486b), and a fast learner (486c). She will have a good memory (486c) and a good sense of proportion and grace (486d).

Adeimantus interrupts just after Socrates and Glaucon complete this list, and the inquiry into philosophical *trophe* takes a few steps backwards before it begins to move forward again, but this first step is important. The virtues on this list are not presented as a part of a philosophical nature. Rather, they are generated by the activity of truth-

[20] τὸν ἄρα τῷ ὄντι φιλομαθῆ πάσης ἀληθείας δεῖ εὐθὺς ἐκ νέου ὅτι μάλιστα ὀρέγεσθαι.

seeking undertaken by one who has a natural disposition for truthfulness. In other words, the virtues are not presented as a part of philosophical *genesis*. Instead, they are products of philosophical *trophe*. The love of truth is a part of one's philosophical nature, but the search for truth is an activity that one may or may not pursue, and which can either be bolstered or squashed by one's upbringing. So, the philosophical virtues Socrates enumerates are in one sense a fulfilment of what is natural to the philosophically disposed soul, but they are not characteristics that develop automatically from its nature. A philosophical soul needs to be nurtured in order to develop the virtues that are, in the sense above, natural to it.[21]

Each of the virtues that emerge in the character of the philosophical person who is nurtured to strive for truth serves as a check on the proto-philosopher's appetites. In this sense, the account of the development of philosophical virtue is an account of philosophical *trophe* for the epithumetic part of the city/soul. In Book V, the first *kuma* described the *genesis* of the philosophical epithumetic soul: it has to be capable, by nature, of being curtailed by *logismos* and *nous*. Now, at the beginning of Book VI, we learn that the *trophe* necessary for the epithumetic part of the philosophical soul is habituation to virtue. The given (by *genesis*) aspects nature (*physis*) of the epithumetic part of the philosophical soul must be nurtured by the activity of truth-seeking into a character amenable to philosophical education (*paideia*).

Adeimantus' interruption at 487b prompts Socrates to present the Ship of State, which first answers the question of why, if the philosopher is so virtuous, he tends to be so maligned by politicians. It also frames a direct critique on extant philosophical regimes and makes clear that the city/soul under discussion in the dialogue is not one that exists in the world, although it is possible that it might. Starting at 494b, Socrates asks Adeimantus to imagine what it would be like for a proto-

[21] Because Aristotle later described virtues as neither natural nor opposed to nature, this may perhaps seem obvious. But the *Republic* likely precedes the *Eudemian* and *Nicomachean Ethics* by more or less thirty years, so it is important to highlight that we can find that teaching here, as well. *Nicomachean Ethics* Book II, Chapter 1.

philosopher whose epithumetic soul has been nurtured for virtue to grow up in Athens. He would be admirable in every way. Everyone, both in his family and in society at large, would want him to use his power to their advantage. He would be smothered in flattery and spoiled by effortless success. In short, his spirit would be thoroughly ill-disposed to philosophical education, which would require humility, patience, and readiness to be misunderstood and maligned by just about everyone.

The thumotic *trophe* required for philosophical education is almost precisely opposed to what Adeimantus and Socrates imagined would happen in Athens to a philosophically disposed soul. By implication, Socrates suggests that the child should be encouraged to pursue truth, independent of its apparent value for practical matters, and he should be taught that the opinions of the masses cannot be trusted. Later, the philosophically disposed child (i.e., the one who is epithumetically nurtured to virtue and with the beginning of the nurturing of his spirit in place) should practice soothing the masses, disabusing them of their false ideas about philosophers. He should lay the foundation for the possibility of philosophical rule.

When Glaucon interrupts at 506d, Socrates has begun to suggest the proper nurture (*trophe*) for the noetic soul. Adeimantus does not seem up to the inquiry, though, or perhaps Socrates is not prepared to engage in it with him, as he signals with his impatience and frustration. Once again, Glaucon plays the role of Socrates' encourager and would-be protector. He insists that Socrates continue and he again reassures him not to be derailed by his fear of disgrace or ridicule (506d). When the other interlocutors interrupt, it is to challenge Socrates or accuse him of being coy (or worse), but Glaucon's interruptions are always encouraging.

The last time Glaucon coaxed Socrates through his fear of acting hubristically (451b), Glaucon laughed,[22] and what followed was the Female Drama. This time (506d), Glaucon is not laughing, and Socrates' concerns are both more and less serious. Since he flatly refuses to do

[22] For a helpful account of the meaning of Glaucon's laughter at this crucial moment in the dialogue see, Leighton Moore, "Laughing at Logoi: Laughter, Persuasion, and Glaucon's Courage," *Interpretation* 26, no. 3, 1999: 315–332.

what Adeimantus asked, which was to give an account of the Good, it seems reasonable to infer that his reservations about giving such an account are more serious than any others he has mentioned before in the dialogue. But, his reluctance to discuss "an offspring of the Good" seems to be based on less dangerous grounds. Rather than prostrating himself to Adresteia to forfend a punishment for *hubris*, this time Socrates merely fears disgracing himself and looking ridiculous.

Socrates' first foray into his account of "the offspring of the Good" is the image of the sun. This also introduces Socrates' account of the *trophe* appropriate to the noetic part of the philosophical soul. Predictably, the sort of nurture appropriate to *nous* (in a philosophically disposed soul that has been "raised right" epithumetically and thumotically) is concerned with acquainting the mind with the best, highest, and truest things. The form of the inquiry that leads to the conclusion that light, and not just vision and visible objects, are necessary for something to be seen, serves as an important model for noetic *trophe.* Glaucon's first thought is that vision only requires two things: a visible object and someone capable of vision. Socrates prompts him to acknowledge the necessity of light to vision and of the sun as the source of light.

Socrates imbeds several important intellectual exercises in the dialectical discovery of the necessity of light (and the sun) for vision. First, he prompts Glaucon to consider the conditions that underpin human action. Even in an activity as simple as seeing, it is easy to neglect to acknowledge the conditions that make it possible—to recognize that the observer is not entirely autonomous in his vision, but requires the existence of light in order for his eye to function. He also encourages Glaucon to push toward a knowledge of causes. Recognizing the necessity of light for vision triggers the inquiry into the source of light, its cause, and a subsequent acknowledgment of its necessity to vision. Finally, Socrates walks Glaucon through this argument intellectually. Even though they are considering sensible phenomena, the inquiry that leads from vision to light to the sun operates solely by appealing to the relationship between those ideas. So, when Socrates makes the analogy of vision to knowledge, light to truth, and the sun to the Good, Glaucon is already acquainted with the thoroughly non-empirical argumentative pathway that leads up to those conclusions.[23] This account of the sun and its light will guide Glaucon through the increasingly complicated images that build upon it.

Right after introducing the sun as the offspring of the good—the closest object of inquiry to the good Socrates claims to be able to consider—he puts the sun into a two-dimensional mathematical structure. He constructs the Divided Line. The line between noetic *trophe* and noetic *paideia* for the philosophical soul is a fine one. The structure of the Divided Line is mirrored in the structure of the Cave, which I will consider in the next chapter, but the distinction is important. The allegory of the Cave is, explicitly, an image of education, and it is an image in motion. One must follow a person through his journey up, down, and back up again out of the Cave in order to understand philosophical *paideia*. The Divided Line is an image of the last step of pre-educational upbringing necessary for the journey through the Cave to be possible. It consists in finding plausible, but not entirely having an understanding of: (1) the importance of inquiring into the necessary conditions for what one experiences as true, (2) the drive to uncover the causes of those conditions, and (3) the analogical relationship between the visible and the intelligible. These are not things that can be taught, but they can be habituated. And they are not a part of philosophical education, per se, but instead conditions for its possibility. The sufficient conditions for one who is chained at the bottom of the Cave to stand up, turn around, and begin her upward journey are still mysterious, but these necessary conditions, at least, are clear. One who has not been nurtured to find these things plausible and important, regardless of how well disposed one might be by nature, will, absent divine intervention, never be able to pursue a philosophical education, never be able even to begin to climb up out of the Cave.

---

[23] As Stanley Rosen notes, "Plato nowhere explains, except by metaphors of vision, how the intellect apprehends Ideas. This is a problem separate from that of how the intances of an Idea participates in the Idea itself." Rosen, *Plato's* Republic*: A Study*, 255.

9

The Divided Line and the Allegory of the Cave

Book VI of the *Republic* ends with the image of the Divided Line and Book VII begins with the allegory of the Cave, two images that map precisely onto one other.[1] The former is static and schematic, and the latter is full of motion and rich detail; but they share the same elements and structure. Together, they complete the model of the soul that Socrates constructs in the *Republic*.[2] The model of the city/soul that Socrates says was finished in Book IV was sufficient for an inquiry into the nature of justice for an individual and a city; but it was incomplete in itself, and it

---

[1] Rosen thinks "it is a mistake to press the correspondences between the two images of the sun and the divided line and the image of the cave," and I am not sure if he would count my claim of their structural identity as pressing the correspondence too far or not. In the same passage, he also says, "On my reading, the cave represents various and not entirely consistent stages of the human soul," which is very similar to my reading. Structural identity is not the same thing as identity. The Divided Line and Cave are very different in essentially important ways, but they share a structure. In fact, it may be that their shared structure is a part of what makes those important differences between them intelligible to us. (Stanley Rosen, *Plato's* Republic (New Haven: Yale, 2004) 271.)

[2] For a survey of the appearance of caves in ancient Greek history and literature and their resonnances with Plato's images of the Cave, Divided Line, and Ship of State, see Marie-Elise Zovko, "Of Caves, Lines, and Sea Travels: Plato's Syracusan Voyages and the Central Analogies of the *Republic*," in *Politics and Performance in Western Greece*, eds. Heather L. Reid, Davide Tanasi, and Susi Kimbell (Fonte Aretusa: Parnossos Press, 2017), 313–227. In particular, Zovko notes, "Caves occupy a limnal zone or boundary region between everyday consciousness and what lies beyond, whether dreams, death or the transcendent source of all, a realm of forces which arouse a sense of awe or terror and which need to be approached, honored, or appeased in a specific way" (319).

was insufficient for an inquiry into the nature of the best life for an individual (philosophy) or the ideal constitution (philosophical rule). The city/soul of Book IV was, in principle, capable of achieving internal harmony, but it lacked the capacity to acknowledge the Good. In Book V, we learn what sort of basic characteristics a philosophical soul must start with, including the capacity to attend to ideas external to oneself. In Book VI, we see the ways that those basic characteristics must be nurtured into a character suitable for philosophical education and, importantly, the centrality of the philosophical soul's yearning for truth. As Book VII opens, we have before us a soul that has both the *genesis* and the *trophe*, the nature and the nurture, necessary for a philosophical education.

The Divided Line[3] is both the last word on philosophical *trophe* and the framework within which Socrates will present philosophical *paideia*. Analogical thinking is one of the *noetic* capacities necessary for philosophical *paideia*, and it is not something that one can have naturally from birth (by *genesis*), it must be formed by habit (by *trophe*). In a sense, this lesson has been foundational to the whole of the dialogue, since the analogy of the city to the soul has been operating since Book II. If one is not able to think of the discussion of the city as an analog of the soul, then the inquiry falls apart. Since it has been operative from near the beginning of the dialogue, by the time analogical thinking becomes an explicit topic of concern the interlocutors have been engaged in it (with varying levels of success) for quite a while. So, the habit of analogical thinking has been nurtured throughout the *Republic.* Socrates has modeled how *trophe* operates.

When Socrates brings Adeimantus and then Glaucon to the point of the inquiry where he must say something about noetic *trophe* (i.e., after he has presented the forms of *epithumetic* and *thumotic trophe* necessary for a philosophical life), he gives an explicit account of the necessity of analogy to their inquiry. He will not inquire directly into the nature of

[3] For a careful parsing of the Greek text of the Divided Line and subtle arguments about how best to imagine its structure, see Franco Trabattoni, "What Role do the Mathematical Sciences Play in the Metaphor of the Line?" in *Essays on Plato's Epistemology* (Leuven: Leuven University Press, 2016) 167–188.

the Good, he says, but he will take their present discussion into a consideration of "an offspring of the Good" (506d).[4] The point of this, of course, is not just to better understand the "offspring of the Good," but to understand "the Good" better by analogy.

With the introduction of the Divided Line, Socrates makes the analogy itself a concern of their inquiry. At the same time, the interlocutors are working towards a better understanding of the Good by considering what light, the offspring of the Good, can reveal; they are also working towards a better understanding of analogical thinking, itself: how it is structured, what faculties it employs, and how those faculties and activities of soul can be integrated into a functioning, self-aware whole.

Before we delve into the structure and meaning of the Divided Line and then move our inquiry into the allegory of the Cave, I would like to take a moment to notice that at this point the city in speech appears to disappear almost entirely from the foreground of the dialogue. Appearances can be deceiving, though. Just as the soul had not ceased to be a genuine concern in Book V when it seemed to disappear, the city in speech continues to be important at the end of Book VI and the beginning of Book VII even though it has receded from the foreground. One of the challenges of analogical thinking is keeping both parts of the analogy clear and present in one's mind. The inquiry into the city/soul that is presented in the *Republic* serves over and over again to test our capacity to do just that.

The *noetic* soul that the Divided Line analyzes belongs to the Philosopher Ruler, so, it concerns both the individual *noetic* soul and the soul of the one best suited to rule the city in speech, since they are one and the same. As I argued in the previous chapter, the analogy is easy to lose track of here not because it has been stretched too thin, but instead because it is so perfect that it appears to collapse into an identity. This will continue to be an issue throughout the inquiry into philosophical *nous*. It is a feature of the structure of the *Republic*, not a bug, and it is replayed in several of its key images, which serve as milestones for inter-

[4] ἔκγονός τε τοῦ ἀγαθοῦ.

pretation and checks against mistaken readings of this magisterially structured book.[5]

Here are a few examples of the way some of the key images in the *Republic* embody this overlapping, repeating pattern. The structure of Kallipolis, the best possible city in speech, which is an image of the best possible individual soul, is mirrored in the soul of the ruler of Kallipolis, the Philosopher-Ruler. In the the Cave, the realm of shadows stands in for the actual realm of visibility and the realm of visible things stands in for the actual realm of intelligibility—the analogy intentionally overlaps itself. And in the synoptic image of the soul presented in Book IX (588b), the mirroring occurs again when the whole soul and the rational part of the soul are both said to have the same look or likeness. These images and others suggest that mirroring or, as I called it earlier, a sort of fractal repetition of microcosm and macrocosm, is an important part of the way Socrates presents reason in the *Republic*'s inquiry into the nature of the city/soul.

All of the habits of philosophical *trophe* emerge and develop from the philosophical soul's attraction to truth (475b). From that natural attraction, the philosophical soul develops the habit of striving for truth (485d), and from that striving emerges all of the virtues listed at the beginning of Book VI. Those first habits concern the way that someone with a philosophical nature needs to become habituated to managing its appetites—the *epithumetic* part of her soul. In the conversation with Adeimantus, Socrates explains both why no extant *polis* could nurture a philosophical soul properly and what sort of nurture (*trophe*) the *thumotic*

---

[5] Danielle Allen's careful analysis of Plato's terminology for forms, paradigms, types, shadows, phantasms and images is helpful for making sense of how a dialogue that contains so many scathing criticisms of "image-thinking" is also a dialogue that employs, recommends, even demands "image-thinking" in order to see it whole. Allen argues the *eikon* is the term Socrates consistently uses for the sorts of images that he endorses, although she finds one exception in his account of the lowest region of the Divided Line. My reading of the *Republic*, which includes the necessity of working back through the images at the bottom of the Cave before one can make one's second ascent to the light, removes the need to see that instance of *eikon* as an exception to Allen's rule. Danielle Allen, *Why Plato Wrote* (Malden MA: Wiley-Blackwell, 2013) 148.

part of the philosophical soul requires. The presentation of the Divided Line, which does not occur until Glaucon takes back the role of chief interlocutor from Adeimantus, presents the form of proper upbringing for the *noetic* philosophical soul.

The account of visibility that Socrates begins at 507b is the framework for the introduction of the Divided Line, and it develops in explicit analogical relationship with the idea of intelligibility.[6] The objects of the activity that Socrates described as belief or love of opinion at the end of Book V (i.e., beautiful things and good things) are now set into the class of visible things, while beauty and goodness are classed among the things that are intelligible. Socrates does not offer any revision to his previous account. This is an elaboration. Instead of talking about vision or intelligence as the defining activity of a particular person's character, Socrates now makes it clear that the rational part of the soul is capable of many things and that it is important both to keep them straight and to see how they relate to one another.

The Divided Line is a schematic account of the key modes of human perception and how they relate to one another. In one dense, geometrical image, which begins at 509d, Socrates lays out the relationship between the visible and the intelligible realms and then, within them, parallel subdivisions between indirect and direct apprehensions of each. By using a mathematical image, Socrates is able to emphasize the formal relationships and proportions between each of its parts. Like the other images mentioned above, the Divided Line involves a fractal-like pattern that repeats itself in microcosm and macrocosm, in part and whole. The whole line is divided unevenly, and each of its two sections is subdivided according to the same proportion. It is unclear in the text whether the intelligible part of the line is shorter or longer than the visible part—and for good reason I believe, since that detail is not built explicitly into the image.[7] Socrates does not specify which region is larger and which is

[6] According to Stanley Rosen, "Plato nowhere explains, except by metaphors of vision, how the intellect apprehends ideas." *Plato's* Republic (New Haven: Yale University Press, 2005) 255.

[7] Danielle Allen has a helpful footnote in that summarizes the dispute among Plato scholars about whether the realm of the intellect should be assigned to the top or bottom section of the Divided Line. The argument turns on

smaller. Apparently any proportion will do, as long as it is repeated in part and whole. This is a key feature of the mathematical image.

Within the realm of the visible the two subdivided parts of the line represent (1) shadows or reflections in water and (2) the things of which they are shadows and reflections. The former are derivative of the latter. In the realm of the intelligible, two parallel forms of apprehending things are specified.

> In one part, the soul uses images of things that were previously imitated, and it must base its inquiry on hypotheses that proceed not to a first principle, but to a conclusion. In the other part, [the soul] moves from a hypothesis to an unhypothetical first principle, but without the images the other part [of the soul] uses. Instead, it uses the ideas of things themselves and proceeds methodically (507b).[8]

There are (1) things that we understand hypothetically according to assumptions from which we move "down" towards conclusions, rather than "up" towards first principles. We'll call these theories or hypotheses. And, (2) there is another kind of knowing that also begins with hypotheses, but moves methodically upward by using the ideas of things themselves (i.e., forms) to come to know those things. We will call the objects of this kind of knowing "ideas themselves." Socrates tells us that the former are derivative of the latter, the same way that shadows are derivative of the objects that cast them.

At least, this is the case Socrates is trying to make, since the existence of ideas in themselves is controversial. Clearly, Thrasymachus thought them absurd or, at best, irrelevant in Book I. The sophists to whom Socrates regularly alludes deny their existence. Now, Glaucon admits to not really understanding Socrates' account. The analogy pre-

---

whether the largest part of the line should be assigned to appearances; or, on the other hand, whether that part should be given to the intelligible realm since it is the highest as well as the largest segment of the model. Danielle Allen, *Why Plato Wrote*, fn.2, 176.

[8] τὸ μὲν αὐτοῦ τοῖς τότε μιμηθεῖσιν ὡς εἰκόσιν χρωμένη ψυχὴ ζητεῖν ἀναγκάζεται ἐξ ὑποθέσεων, οὐκ ἐπ᾽ ἀρχὴν πορευομένη ἀλλ᾽ ἐπὶ τελευτήν, τὸ δ᾽ αὖ ἕτερον—τὸ ἐπ᾽ ἀρχὴν ἀνυπόθετον—ἐξ ὑποθέσεως ἰοῦσα καὶ ἄνευ τῶν περὶ ἐκεῖνο εἰκόνων, αὐτοῖς εἴδεσι δι᾽ αὐτῶν τὴν μέθοδον ποιουμένη. (510b)

sented in the Divided Line is a proof that begins with an uncontroversial phenomenon and an analogical relationship as premises. From these it concludes with an assertion of the (controversial) existence of the cause of that (uncontroversial) phenomenon. It takes the following form: if vision is analogous to intelligence, and if shadows in the visible realm are made by visible objects, then theories and hypotheses in the intelligible realm are made by intelligible objects. Therefore, intelligible objects exist.

Furthermore, Socrates argues that vision is only possible because of the existence of light, which is caused by the sun; so, analogously, intelligibility is only possible because of the existence of truth, which is caused by the Good. Therefore, truth and the Good must also exist. And finally, just as the sun is the source not just of the visibility of visible things, but also their existence, the Good is not just the source of the intelligibility of intelligible things, but of their existence as well. All of the elements described in the visible realm are familiar, as are the relationships among them. The only uncontroversial element on the intelligible side of the line is theory/hypothesis. Every other element of the line concerned with intelligibility and all of the relationships among those elements are conclusions being drawn from this analogical argument.

The argument does not stop at establishing the existence of intelligible objects, truth, and the Good. It goes on from its metaphysical claims to unpack their epistemological implications. The unstated and perhaps uncontroversial premise of the epistemological argument of the Divided Line seems to be: if we apprehend each of these different sorts of things, we much possess the faculties required to apprehend them. As always, the dynamics on the visible side of the line are clear. Since we see objects and shadows, we must possess the capacity to see objects and shadows. That is, we must have the capacity (or potency) for apprehending objects and images of objects. The implication, based on the analogy between visibility and intelligibility, is that we must also have the capacities necessary to approach ideas themselves and the theories/hypotheses that are images of them. Although it has been quite a long time since Socrates offered any reminders, Book VI is still a part of the Female Drama, the story of the capacities of the city/soul and what their fulfilment would mean.

The four "conditions of soul"[9] (511d) established by the analogical argument of the Divided Line are: *nous*,[10] *dianoia*,[11] *pistis*,[12] and *eikasia*.[13] A significant part of my interpretation of the allegory of the Cave will be to think carefully about the meaning of each of these "conditions of soul" and the relationships that exist among them, but it is possible to offer tentative definitions of each of them that I will work to refine later. *Noesis* has been an important part of this account since the beginning of my interpretation of Book VI, and it is generally translated it as "reason," but also sometimes as "intellection" or "apprehension of reality." *Noesis* is fundamentally different from *logismos*, or calculation. The work of *nous* is to apprehend being, and the work of *logismos* is to put things in order. They work together when the order that *logismos* imposes is a reflection of the order *nous* apprehends, but they may operate independently, as well. *Noesis* is the function of soul that was missing from the purged city/soul of Book IV and that was most clearly added to the *Republic's* ever-developing psychological model when the Ship of State was shown to need a stargazer to be its true pilot—the capacity to look outside oneself for guidance. *Dianoia* has only been a part of my reading implicitly, just as I believe it has only up until this point of the *Republic* played an implicit role. "Understanding" is a conventional and fine translation of *dianoia*, although I also like "theorizing," "hypothesizing," and "modeling," as well.

The conditions of soul described on the visible half of the Divided Line have been with us, too. *Noesis* generates knowledge. *Pistis* generates belief. Rosen describes it as "the affection of the soul that treats images as originals."[14] In that sense, both the intelligible and the visible parts of the Divided Line have been our constant companions since late in Book V, whether or not we have known their names. After Plato's time, *pistis* came conventionally to be translated "faith," which is not quite right for

---

[9] παθήματα ἐν τῇ ψυχῇ.

[10] νοῦς.

[11] διάνοια.

[12] πίστις.

[13] εἰκασία.

[14] Rosen, *Plato's* Republic*: A Study*, 273.

its usage in the *Republic*, but thinking of *pistis* as faith is not entirely unhelpful, either, in the Platonic context. If one only apprehends beautiful things or true things, but not beauty or truth itself, then on what basis does one claim to recognize those things as beautiful or true? What beautiful and true things have in common is something that is unseen (to the one who does not apprehend beauty or truth in themselves), and religious faith, perhaps among other things, is belief in things unseen. We would probably be drawn off-track too often by translating *pistis* as faith, but in that important sense it fits nicely with the epistemology of the *Republic*.

Eikasia is the last of the four conditions of soul presented on the Divided Line. It has been with us, too, from the beginning of the dialogue, but more in terms of the form of the *Republic* than its content. Often *eikasia* is translated as "imagination," which is probably the best choice in English, but it is a bit misleading. "Imagination" often evokes "invention," which is also not wrong in the context of the *Republic*, but not quite right either. The key issue is that *eikasia* is an image of something that could also be apprehended with *pistis*. It is an invention of a way of illustrating something that could be observed. It is not imaginative creation out of nothing or invention of something wholly alien to the visible world. Stanley Rosen provocatively describes an eikones (an object of *eikasia*) as "the presence of something that is absent, but not invisible."[15] One's theory of imagination might include the condition that it is always working on objects of sense or reflection (internal objects of sense), in which case such provisions are already built in conceptually; but one may have different theory of imagination that does not include such limits. So, we must be careful.

For Socrates, *eikasia* is not wholly untethered from observation (and intellection). Failure to stay clear on this point does not much inhibit interpretation of the critiques of imagination in the *Republic*, but it renders one entirely incapable of appreciating the goodness, power, and beauty inherent in images that Socrates presents. It dulls almost to the point of invisibility the brilliance of dialogue form itself. One of the greatest ironies in the history of philosophy is that the philosopher who

---

[15] Stanley Rosen, *Plato's* Republic (New Haven: Yale University Press, 2004) 269.

wrote in the genre most sensitive to perspective, most suggestive of the indispensability of context, most attuned to the relevance of individual experience to theoretical activity is cast as the paragon of abstraction, insensitivity to culture, and monolithic thinking.

There is no break in the dialogue between Book VI and Book VII. To underline the continuity between the two books, Socrates first word in Book VII is "next" (μετά). The allegory of the Cave follows immediately after the image of the Divided Line.[16] This is how it is introduced: "Next, then," I said, "compare the effects of education and a lack of education on our nature to a condition like this" (514a).[17] While it may be somewhat controversial to argue that *genesis* is a central theme of *Republic* Book V and that *trophe* is central to Book VI, the centrality of *paideia* (education) to Book VII seems almost too obvious a point to make. What I hope to accomplish in this chapter is not to offer a substantially new account of the Cave, but to situate it differently in the text based on my understanding of the context in which it is presented. Book VII is the third "play" in the trilogy of Female Drama introduced in Book V. It is concerned with the final layer of potencies necessary for a city/soul to install the philosopher-ruler.

Although the details of the allegory of the Cave are not all drawn in the first few lines, and although the image has not yet been set in motion, the basic elements of the Cave are all either explicitly or implicitly contained in the preliminary sketch presented at 514a–515a. (1) People are fettered and imprisoned in the bottom of a Cave where (2) they can only see what is ahead of them. (3) Light in the Cave is being provided by a fire far above and behind the prisoners. (4) People likened to pup-

---

[16] Seth Benardete notes that ending Book VI with the Divided Line and starting Book VII with the Cave signals a connection and a separation between the two images, which he characterizes in this way: "The division between Books VI and VII, which separates the sun and line from cave is a fortunate reminder of the fact that Socrates offers the line from the start as a continuation of his account of the good, but the cave gets tied in with them only after it has been given by itself." Seth Benardete, *Socrates' Second Sailing* (Chicago: University of Chicago Press, 1989), 166.

[17] μετὰ ταῦτα δή, εἶπον, ἀπείκασον τοιούτῳ πάθει τὴν ἡμετέραν φύσιν παιδείας τε πέρι καὶ ἀπαιδευσίας.

peteers carry objects between the fire and the prisoners, and some of them make noises.

After more elaboration, Socrates will make the connection between the Divided Line and the Cave explicit, but we can see most of the parallels now, and infer the others easily. There are two sources of light in the image: the fire, which provides light to the prisoners and puppeteers, and the sun, which is the source of light outside the Cave and to which its mouth is opened. The fire is described. The Sun is implied. These two sources of light imply two different realms of apprehension; the area illuminated by fire, i.e., the interior of the Cave is one realm, and the area illuminated by the sun, i.e., the world external to the Cave, is another. Later, Socrates will say it straightforwardly, but we can already see now that the part of the Divided Line that describes the realm of the visible is analogous to the interior of the Cave, and the part of the Divided Line that describes the realm of the intelligible is analogous to the area outside the mouth of the Cave—the part illuminated by sunlight.[18]

Here we have another image with a repeating fractal-like structure, an overlapping analogy that necessarily introduces confusion by not keeping its terms separate. Formally, it looks like this: Fire : Sun :: Sun : the Good. Within the Cave, both realms are described as visible, but as

---

[18] Seth Benardete offers two alternatives to superimposing the Divided Line and Cave (and Sun) directly on top of each other because he sees problematic implications following from such an interpretation, even though he acknowledges that Socrates explicitly tells Glaucon that they should be superimposed. "...Socrates tells Glaucon that the sun, line, and cave are to be superimposed on one another (517a8–b6)...Such a superimposition, however, is difficult to interpret, for in the ascent from cave to sun, there is no place for thought. Once one leaves the cave, one first sees most easily shadows and then phantoms in water, afterwards the sky at night, and only then the sun itself in its own place (516a6-b7). Mathematics and its visible constructions along with its intentional objects have vanished, for the city in which the arts are perfected has vanished too. The difference between the natural and the conventional horizon is ignored, and becoming and making are identified. Socrates, it seems, wanted to indicate that the mathematicians are prisoners, too, and their constructions and theorems duplicate the cave and do not transcend it." I believe my reading avoids these problems and offers an opening to take Socrates at his word at 517a. Benardete, *Socrates' Second Sailing*, 176.

having different sources and qualities of light. Within the Divided Line, one realm is visible and the other is intelligible. Within the Cave, the Sun is the source of the higher form of illumination. Within the Divided Line, the Sun is the source of the lower form of illumination. The analogy is clear, consistent, and helpful in illustrating Socrates' account of the nature of the Good and its relationship to truth and human intelligence. But, it is also extremely confusing because of the different roles played by the sun on either side of the analogy in the two images.

As I argued above, the Divided Line operates as an argument. The elements of the visible part of the line are familiar and the relationships among them are uncontroversial, unlike the elements on the intelligible part of the line and the relationships among them. Socrates establishes the analogy in order to move the interlocutors from familiar premises to new conclusions. If the analogy holds between the visible and intelligible realms, and if the visible realm is clear, one has all one needs to draw conclusions about the intelligible realm. Here again we see the pedagogical wisdom of introducing the image of the Sun first. Socrates has given Glaucon the best possible footing for keeping these overlapping images straight. With the Sun, Glaucon has both the highest, most archetechtonic idea in mind first, and he is familiar with the most confusing part of the image—the part most likely to lead him into confusion.

The Cave does not just employ elements analogous to the Divided Line; it presents a parallel argumentative process as well. Even though Socrates narrates the description of the Cave from the perspective of one who is unfettered, or perhaps even from the third person omniscient view of the lawgiver that he has been using since the city/soul was introduced in Book II, the first description of the Cave comes from deep inside—from the point of view of the prisoners. That is where the interlocutors must begin. The lower parts of the Cave and its basic structure are what is given, and an apprehension of the upper realms of the Cave and whatever might lie exterior to it must be achieved. This structure mirrors precisely the way that the analogical argument of the Divided Line begins with premises in the visible realm and works toward conclusions in the intelligible realm.

These early parallels between the Divided Line and the allegory of the Cave will be joined by many others, but already the structures are clear enough to unpack the elements of the interior of the Cave in terms of the psychological distinctions presented in the Divided Line and to speculate about what elements will have to exist outside the mouth of the Cave in the allegory in order for the analogy to continue to hold. The first part of the Divided Line is the realm of *eikasia*, picture-thinking, imagination; and the lowest part of the Cave is populated by people who can only see shadows (and hear echoes) on a wall.

If the parallel between the Divided Line and the Cave is to hold, we should be able to find a division in the interior of the Cave that lines up with the division between *eikasia* and *pistis* on the Divided Line, and indeed we do. Above and behind the prisoners in the realm of *eikasia* at the bottom of the Cave, there is a wall; and behind that wall there is a road where the puppeteers carry the objects whose shadows appear on the wall of the Cave. The man-made wall between the fire and the prisoners is our dividing line between *eikasia* and *pistis*. The realm of *pistis*, populated by puppeteers in the Cave, is perhaps the most interesting and difficult part of the image to unpack, so we will do well to wait until Socrates has developed the allegory a bit more; but we can conclude from the analogy to the Divided Line that this is the realm of sophistry (among other things, perhaps)—of attention to things believed to be true or good or beautiful, but not to truth, goodness, or beauty itself. It is the realm of opinion, not knowledge.

The final structural element of the interior of the Cave is the fire itself. Here, we can see a parallel to the Divided Line clearly, but cannot avoid a bit of murkiness in describing it because this is the point at which the elements of the analogies overlap and, if we are not careful, collapse into one another. The fire within the Cave is the sun of the Divided Line. It is the source of light that makes it possible for those with vision to apprehend visible things. The fire is figurative and it represents the sun, which both is the source of illumination necessary for visibility and also is the source of the existence of visible things.

The analogy between the fire in the Cave and the sun in the visible realm of the Divided Line is clear, and the exposition of the Cave that follows in Book VII corroborates it repeatedly. As long as we stay focused on the lower part of the Cave and the visible part of the Divided Line, the risk of getting confused is extremely low and the promise of learning interesting things from the allegory grows with every added detail. The danger comes in confusing the literal sun, represented by the fire with the "literal" Good represented by the sun in the upper part of the Cave allegory, which would be a crucial mistake that readers of the *Republic* are always at risk of making. It is not enough to refer to the sun in our attempts at interpretation; we must always be careful to indicate which Sun we are talking about: the literal Sun that illuminates the visible realm in the Divided Line or the image of the Sun in the Cave that represents the Good and its figurative illumination of the intelligible realm.[19]

At 515a, Socrates elaborates on the allegory of the Cave by inquiring into the perspectives of the prisoners at the bottom of the Cave. Up until this point, the allegory of the Cave was mainly a figurative recapitulation of the psychological structure presented in the Divided Line. But, by shifting to speculation on the point of view of the prisoner, Socrates takes his interlocutors into the operation of that mode of mind—the particular function of soul represented by that segment of the line and that section of the Cave. The image is inhabited and set into motion. There is very little surprising in this earliest moment of populating the Cave and recasting the structure of the Divided Line as an image that can be put into motion, but it is worthwhile to make the psychological implications of this part of the allegory explicit. As the image develops, the lessons of the allegory will become subtler, and we will be well served by having developed a strong interpretive foundation.

The prisoners at the lowest level of the Cave inhabit the world of *eikasia*. They exist in a world of images, but not necessarily in the mode one might first associate with imagination. The prisoners are not creative or inventive. They are not producers of images, they are consumers, so to speak. It is tempting to romanticize the realm of imagination, even with-

---

[19] Benardete describes the confusing case of the image of the Sun like this: "The region of the sun, moreover, insofar as it images the good, represents the region of opinion and not of sight; but insofar as the sun is the cause of becoming it images the good as the cause of being, and if becoming and visibility are as closely bound causally as being and intelligibility are, then the sun cannot be the cause of opinion. The sun, then, functions in Socrates' account both as itself and as image. As itself it is a dual cause; and as an image it represents a dual cause." Seth Benardete, *Socrates' Second Sailing* (Chicago: University of Chicago Press, 1989), 158.

in the context of the devastating critiques that Socrates levies against it. However, even a cursory exploration of the lowest section of the Cave reveals exactly what is wrong with a life turned exclusively, or perhaps even primarily, to images.

The images on the Cave wall come from somewhere, but those whose lives are limited to the lowest realm of the Cave have no direct access to the causes of the things they apprehend. Because they see only images and lack the capacity to investigate their sources, those who live in the realm of *eikasia* are radically limited. The deepest insight they are likely to have into their perceptions is an apprehension of patterns. Those who distinguish themselves in the bottom of the Cave do so by developing the capacity to recognize images and discern patterns among them, perhaps even to the point of reliable prediction. But, the better one gets at such predictions, the more expert one becomes in the realm of *eikasia*, the less likely one is ever to recognize its limitations and be open to the possibility of another realm of existence—another mode of apprehending the way things are.[20]

The account of the pitfalls of experiencing some success in the realm of *eikasia* is reminiscent of Socrates conversation with Adeimantus in Book VI regarding the challenges faced by a philosophically disposed nature in a democratically governed *polis*. The more success such a person has in the illusory economy of images, the less motivated one is to acknowledge that one must look beyond the realm of images in order to see things as they are. This is also parallel to the situation of the sailor on the Ship of State who happens to take and maintain control of the ship. His success becomes an additional impediment to realizing that the true pilot of the ship must look to the stars.

The obvious irony implied by this critique of image-thinking is that it is presented within an image. We are given the image of a prisoner in the realm of *eikasia* in order, at least in part, to see what is limited, wrong, and dangerous about image-thinking. The irony dissipates, though, if we also glean from the allegory of the Cave the power and

[20] Mathematics is an important exception to these claims about what is and is not possible at the bottom of the Cave, but Socrates has not yet introduced mathematics into his account of the Cave, so we will not yet either.

promise of image-thinking, as well as its essential role in philosophical education. If one lives exclusively in the realm of *eikasia*, then one is imprisoned in illusion. But, if one does not include the realm of *eikasia* in one's understanding of human psychology, one will never fully apprehend the human condition. Furthermore, unless one learns to employ *eikasia* in one's inquiries, one will be neglecting an essential part of oneself and cutting oneself off from the aspects of reality that it illuminates. *Eikasia* is clearly dangerous, as Socrates presents it, and it is indispensable.

The shadows on the wall of the Cave and the artifacts and puppeteers who project them there are in motion from the beginning of the allegory, but this is a sort of lateral motion that makes the image richer without representing any substantial development from the Divided Line to the Cave. The first moment of vertical motion, so to speak, comes at 515c when Socrates asks Glaucon to imagine that one of the prisoners in the bottom of the Cave had been released from his bonds. This newly released prisoner is not an elaboration of a part of the Divided Line, but an image of someone who exists on or within it; one who mysteriously has the capacity to traverse it. He is one who has experienced only *eikasia*, but who now may turn his head toward *pistis* and perhaps climb up to inhabit that realm as well.

The mysteries associated with the prisoner's release are reminiscent of several other key transitions in the *Republic* where discursive accounts and even carefully constructed images seem to be insufficient to make things clear. How will the myth of metals be made plausible to the citizens of the purged city/soul? It isn't clear, literally or figuratively. How will parents and children avoid accidental incest in the city/soul where all women and children are held in common? The proposed solution seems transparently insufficient. Additionally, what are the conditions of *genesis* that engender a philosophically disposed nature? These questions, all of which deal with the origins of the matters they concern, seem to be beyond the realm of what Socrates can or will render intelligible.

We are told that the prisoner is released, but not how. We are also told that he is compelled to stand up, turn around, walk upward, and look toward the light. We are told that this is a moment of healing (515c), but we are not told how or why it happens. As the allegory continues, it is clear why one might want to release and reorient a prisoner, but that does not alleviate the mystery of the crucial moment. Sometimes prisoners get free, or at least it is possible that they will. Sometimes, they are made to get up, turn around, look up, and walk toward the light; or at least it is possible that they will be. As I read it, there is no part of the allegory or its interpretation by the interlocutors that will dissipate this mystery.

The way the newly released prisoner reacts to his mysteriously precipitated change of situation is not, however, mysterious at all. The fact that the artifacts carried by the puppeteers are "closer to the real" than the images on the Cave does little to alleviate their strangeness. Everything about the shadows on the wall, the realm of *eikasia*, is familiar. At first, everything about the world of the puppeteers, the realm of *pistis*, seems new and strange; and all of its oddness is exacerbated by the former prisoner's unfortunate viewpoint. Not only is the new world he has been compelled to look at strange and threatening to his sense of reality, but he must look up at it from below, and he must stare towards the fire in order to see it. Everything about his point of view that is promising is also unavoidably unfortunate. It is mysterious that he has come to be turned around, and it will be even more mysterious if he overcomes the challenges of his situation to push onward and upward.

The situation is far from hopeless, though, for the one who has begun the difficult journey up the Divided Line and out of the Cave. The newly released prisoner's point of view is not good, his eyes are not adjusted, and every success he has at focusing on the new objects in his field of vision carry with them the need to reconceive of something familiar and comfortable from his past. But, it is important to note that even in these first few moments of reorientation that the world of *pistis* is not entirely alien to the one who has previously known nothing but *eikasia*, even though it might at first seem to be.[21] The objects the puppeteers carry are the sources of the shadows he knows so well. They are, in this sense, familiar. Insofar as he can make the connection between those objects and the shadows of his former life, his experience in the realm of *pistis* will also inform, retrospectively, his experience in the realm of *eikasia*.

[21] As Eva Brann puts it, "the Good has everywhere prepared places for the cognitive soul to learn in." Brann, *Music of the Republic*, 210.

Every step upward in the Cave shares the same challenges and the same promise. Each section of the Divided Line is different from the one below it and challenging for one who has not explored its mode of apprehending the world. But, each mode of perception engages, on some level, the same things. The shadow of a sheep on the wall of the Cave is importantly different from the sheep puppet held up to the fire that creates that shadow; but they share the "look" (*eidos*[22]) of a sheep. The Cave-climber who sees this pattern will have a new opportunity to understand sheep shadows, sheep puppets, and the "look" of sheep, and he will also have a new opportunity to understand himself. When *eikasia* was his only mode, it was not visible as a mode at all. There was no reason to suspect that there were any epistemological challenges in his apprehension of the reality of *eikasia*. But, this first step is indeed one of the most profound, since it opens one toward questioning one's assumptions, toward an acknowledgment that what one perceives to be true may be only partially complete or false. There is no education without this first step, regardless of how educable one might otherwise be.

The release of the prisoner and his turning around are the first moments of philosophical *paideia*. Perhaps anyone could be released and turned. Since the conditions for turning and releasing are mysterious, that is a possibility. But, reading the the Cave as a part of the third "play" in the Female Drama of the middle books of the *Republic* means keeping in mind the context in which the Cave is introduced and trying to understand it in those terms. If the newly released prisoner represents one who is beginning a philosophical education, and if we are to imagine that it is possible for him successfully to complete that education (which it must be, since he does), then he must have had a philosophical *genesis* and *trophe*, as well. The form of this argument follows that of the Divided Line: here is an appeal to an uncontroversial phenomenon and then a claim that some other phenomenon must also exist because it related to the uncontroversial phenomenon as its cause.

---

[22] εἶδος.

In terms of the cave-climber's *genesis*, we should imagine that his *epithumetic* soul is capable of being tamed by his *logistic* and *noetic* soul, that his *thumotic* soul can be a good friend to his *logistic* and *noetic* soul, and that his *noetic* soul loves the knowledge of the truth. In terms of his *trophe*, his nurture or upbringing, we should imagine that his love of truth has been fostered by habits that have inculcated virtues and that his appetites have been curbed and corralled by those virtues. We should see him as someone whose spirit has not become overgrown by flattery, but one who is capable of recognizing the possibility of being wrong, of appealing to higher authority, and of living well without the approbation of the masses. *Noetically*, we should imagine him as someone who sees the importance of inquiring into the causes of things, is driven to do the hard work of uncovering those causes, and can adeptly use analogical thinking to move from what is more familiar to what is more real. None of these attributes of our Cave-dweller are made explicit in the allegory, but all of them are implied by what his education accomplishes, and what we have previously been shown to be the necessary conditions for those accomplishments.

Every moment of the ascent from the bottom of the Cave is difficult and painful, but for the one suited by nature and nurture for philosophy, there is nothing more appealing. For one whose soul is capable not only of internal harmony, but also of holding oneself to the highest possible standards, there is nothing more alluring than the opportunity to see oneself and the world more clearly. This is the rare sort of person who does not mind when Socrates meets him in the Agora and publicly displays how wrong he is about the most important things, but who, instead, thanks him for it. Glaucon seems more like such a character than anyone else in the Platonic corpus (and not just the *Republic*), and history is silent on what became of him (which teaches us nothing, but is delicious). The main thing Socrates wants us to know is that such a character is not impossible, even if he is implausible. If he exists, the rest of Book VII will show us what his best education could be and what it could make of him.

Part Four

Philosophical *Paideia*, Book VII

10

Philosophical *Paideia* in 2D

As Book VII of the *Republic* opens, so does the curtain on the third play of the Female Drama. Socrates has prepared his interlocutors for the most magisterial image of the dialogue—perhaps, in fact, the most magisterial allegory of the human condition of all time. The psychological structure of the Cave is presented schematically in the Divided Line at the end of Book VI, and the character of the soon to be mysteriously released prisoner is explored in detail in Books V and VI. The psychological and political importance of inquiring into the conditions for and consequences of philosophical rule in the city/soul have been, in one way or another, the topic of conversation since Book I. And, in fact, allusions to the imagery, vocabulary, and concerns of the Cave have pervaded the *Republic* since its first word: *kataben.* Glaucon and Socrates "went down" to Piraeus, and they are on their way back "up" to Athens when Polemarchus stops them and insists they linger at his father's house for this conversation. They are on their journey together out of the Cave, and we are on it with them.[1]

The importance of the Cave is clear within the context of the dialogue. The only condition in which the first two *kumata* of Book V can be realized is that the third *kuma* be accomplished (472d). The only way that the city/soul will be able to treat women and men alike, as they should be (first *kuma*), and that the city/soul will think of all of its women and children as belonging in common to the whole city/soul (second

---

[1] For an argument that the structure of the *Republic* follows the structure of the Divided Line (and thus, on my interpretation, the Cave), see: Kenneth Dorter. "The Divided Line and the Structure of Plato's *Republic.*" *History of Philosophy Quarterly* 21, no. 1 (2004): 1–20.

kuma) is for the city/soul to be ruled by a Philosopher ruler (third *kuma*). All three of these are important because they are the conditions for the possibility of the best city/soul—the philosophical soul. That is, they are the conditions for the maximal set of possibilities both for an individual life and for politics. Therefore, philosophical *paideia* is important because it is a necessary step in the development of the philosopher. Good government requires a philosopher-ruler, who requires a good philosophical education.

The first *kuma*, treating women and men the same way, is important to the city/soul because of what men and women represent in an individual soul: potency and act, passivity and activity, potentiality and actuality. As I argued in Chapter Three, every part of the human soul, *epithumia*, *thumos*, *logismos*, and *nous*, involves a natural orientation toward myriad objects. One may have an appetite for candy and green vegetables, horror movies and Jane Austen novels, the companionship of interesting people and the companionship of kind people. One's spirit may yearn for recognition or influence or accomplishment. One's mind may yearn to learn the cure for cancer or to understand how best to build a bridge or to write the perfect country song. And in each of these cases (and the scores of others contained within each of us), we must make choices.

Some yearnings are easier to pursue, some are more supported by the societies we are immersed in, some are more obvious and others simply do not occur to us; but all of these choices have what economists call "opportunity cost." Choosing to pursue one set of yearnings makes it less likely that one will pursue others. So, within each of us, there are actualized and unactualized yearnings, and until *nous* and *logismos* have taken charge of the city/soul, there is no way of knowing whether the best parts have been actualized or not. So, unless *nous* alone guides our choices, we would do well to keep ourselves as open as possible. We should be ready not to give preference to what is familiar or conventional. We should try not to reject out of hand those parts of ourselves that are unsupported by our family or society or those yearnings that appear ridiculous. We should try to be prepared, so that if *nous* ever shows us the way, we will be ready to follow it and be as little as possible resistant to its guidance in our lives.

The second *kuma*, that all women and children are held in common in the city/soul extends the understanding of men and women as act and potency in the soul. Like the first *kuma*, the second *kuma* also requires the third *kuma* as a condition for its possibility. Like the three plays of a series of an Attic tragedy, all three *kumata* are parts of the Female Drama of the *Republic* (i.e., they concern potentiality), but all three are also distinctly different. The potencies of the first *kuma* are those capacities we possess that may or may not fit into the best and most whole, *noetically* apprehended, version of ourselves. The potencies of the second *kuma* are, on the other hand, as I argued in Chapter Four, passions.

As we make choices about how to live our lives, what to do and what to abstain from doing, we experience pleasure and pain. Some of our activities are immediately associated with measures of pleasure and pain that remain more or less constant. Others pleasures and pains are augmented and diminished by recursion. The challenge of the second *kuma* is to keep the whole of the city/soul in view when assessing the proper response to pleasure and pain. The promise of pleasure and pain (women) and the actuality of particular pleasures and pains (children) must be understood as belonging to the whole city/soul and not to some part of it.

There is nothing inherently good about a particular pleasure or inherently bad about a particular pain, so pursuing pleasures and avoiding pains just because they are pleasant or painful is a path toward a diminished and chaotic city/soul. But pleasures and pains are neither irrelevant in themselves nor unimportant to the city/soul. They are signals of goodness and badness, illness and health that need to be taken seriously. They must be understood in the context of their relevance to what is good for the whole soul, however, and only *logismos* guided by *nous* is capable of that perspective. So, once again, the teaching of the second *kuma* is necessary for the best version of the city/soul to come into existence, and it is dependent upon the existence of what the third *kuma* introduces, the philosopher-ruler. Since the philosopher-ruler will only come into existence if she receives a proper philosophical education, we must consider what that education would entail.

The point of this review of the three *kumata* from Book V is to bring back to mind the reason why philosophical education is a central topic in the inquiry into the nature and choice-worthiness of justice. The philosopher-ruler is the only one capable of establishing the best life in the city/soul, which involves, among other things, the conditions implied by the first two *kumata*. However, this is not the only aspect of my reading of Books V and VI that we need to bring back into focus in order to see the context in which the Cave is presented and to unpack its implications for the psychology of the *Republic*. We also need to look at the character of the prisoner whom we will follow through the Cave and, finally, what we know about the structure of the Cave before Socrates has even really begun his account of it.

We must bring back to the foreground our understanding of the character of the prisoner who, in the first lines of Book VII, is released from his bonds, compelled to turn around, look up toward the light, and begin to ascend. We know something of his character, because Socrates has told us that there are certain necessary conditions for successfully completing a philosophical education, and we are told that our newly released prisoner will do just that. So, we know that he has the dispositions outlined by the three *kumata* of Book V. His appetites and spirit are amenable to being regulated by *logismos* (which, in turn, is guided by *nous*), and his *logismos* is capable of ruling well. His natural love of truth, properly nurtured, has engendered in his life a full range of moral and intellectual virtues. His spirit, perhaps miraculously, has emerged strong enough to have an ambition for philosophical education but not overblown to the point of thinking he does not need it. He is also noetically nimble, disciplined, and patient. He will be able to make connections among the things he is shown both analogically to one another and by application to himself. He does not know anything yet, really, but the newly released prisoner is perfectly educable.

Finally, after reminding ourselves why philosophical education is important and what we know about the protagonist of the allegory of the Cave (the one best suited by nature and nurture to be educated philosophically), we should bring to the fore what we already know about the structure of the Cave itself. As my reading develops I will attempt to make each of these elements clearer and explicit in themselves; but a quick schematic account is useful as a sketch of their relationships to each other. Such a synoptic view will also help orient us to the psychological implications of the structure of the Cave; how each of its parts comes together as an organic representation of the modes of mind we employ in our attempts to make sense of ourselves and our world. Before we consider the allegory in those dimensions or put it into motion (four dimensions), we should look at its basic vertical layout—its two dimensional structure.

The lowest region of the Cave corresponds to the first part of visible region of the Divided Line, *eikasia* (image-thinking); and the second lowest region to the other part, *pistis* (belief, trust, faith). In the Cave, the division between the two realms is the wall behind which the puppeteers carry those things which make shadows on the wall of the lower region by the light of the fire in the upper. The fire inside the Cave represents the sun, which is the cause of the existence and the source of illumination for visible things.

Outside the Cave, this same structure is mirrored first by the shadows and reflections on the ground outside the mouth of the Cave, which is the realm of *dianoia* (theory and hypothesis). This is the first part of the intelligible section of the Divided Line. The second part of the intelligible region of the Divided Line is represented by the things themselves that are visible outside the Cave, i.e. the objects of *nous*. The sun, which represents the Good, illuminates the intelligible realm. The line between *dianoia* and *nous* is the ground, itself. The line between the visible and intelligible realms is the opening of the Cave. The story of what it means for one to traverse the Cave is a long and interesting one, and we should be ready to hear it. Socrates has prepared us well.

The prisoner's ascent from the depths of the Cave into the sunlight happens quickly in the text. Socrates will be working through the implications of the allegory for most of Book VII, but the upward journey itself is contained in one sentence.

> "And if someone dragged him away from there by force," I said, "along the rough, steep path upward, and he did not let him go until he had dragged him out into the sunlight, wouldn't he feel pain and anger about being treated that way? And when he came outside, wouldn't his eyes be filled with sunlight, and wouldn't he be unable to

> see even a single one of the things that we have said are truly real?" (515e–516a)[2]

Since, for all the reasons recounted at the beginning of this chapter, the education of a philosopher is so central an idea to the project of the *Republic*, and since the Cave is an image of that education, it is worth thinking carefully about the way that the proto-philosopher's ascent is first described, despite the brevity of the account. The newly released prisoner has no control over what is happening to her and no opportunity to process what she sees on the way up. She is compelled to turn around and walk, and she is "dragged" out of the lower chamber of shadows, past the puppeteers and their fire, and all the way out of the Cave and into the sunlight where she is blinded by the brightness of the sun. This bears no resemblance to Virgil's patient narration for Dante as they stroll through the afterlife in the *Commedia*. There is no narration. No time to rest. This is not a guided tour. It is only at the top, after the ascent, that she is given an opportunity for her eyes to adjust and to begin to process what is happening.[3]

---

[2] εἰ δέ, ἦν δ' ἐγώ, ἐντεῦθεν ἕλκοι τις αὐτὸν βίᾳ διὰ τραχείας τῆς ἀναβάσεως καὶ ἀνάντους, καὶ μὴ ἀνείη πρὶν ἐξελκύσειεν εἰς τὸ τοῦ ἡλίου φῶς, ἆρα οὐχὶ ὀδυνᾶσθαί τε ἂν καὶ ἀγανακτεῖν ἑλκόμενον, καὶ ἐπειδὴ πρὸς τὸ φῶς ἔλθοι, αὐγῆς ἂν ἔχοντα τὰ ὄμματα μεστὰ ὁρᾶν οὐδ' ἂν ἓν δύνασθαι τῶν νῦν λεγομένων ἀληθῶν;

[3] Seth Benardete argues that the layout and the route through the Cave suggests that we should be thinking about a temporal as well as a spatial distance being traversed in the cave. "A distant fire burns high up and behind the prisoners (514b2–3). Since the artifacts behind the parapet are nearer the fire, their shadows are always larger than the shadoes of the prisoners themselves. Their greater size suggests that the human beings who carry them are the ancestors . . . The ancestors would be as human as the prisoners; and the non-existence of divine legislation would conform with Socrates' theology. The depth of the cave would thus be a temporal dimension; but the ascent from the cave seems to be entirely spatial…The ascent from the cave is not through the cave. The released prisoner does not stop to question the puppeteers who are on the far side of the wall. The wall of the cave does not stand in the way of his ascent, but magically vanishes along with the puppeteers. The ascent from the cave bypasses the *Republic*. It thus represents a pre-Socratic version of philosophy, for which it is still possible to look directly at the beings without any recourse to speeches." Benardete, *Socrates' Second Sailing*, 172.

In order to begin reading the Cave for its psychological content, it will be helpful to look at each of its regions in more detail and think about what it might mean to say that education is the process of the educable person moving through those regions. With that content clearer, perhaps we will be in a better position to understand why the first ascent is so violent and quick. It is also important to see that the city/soul structure is still operative in the presentation of the Cave, and, again, its fractal-like, repeating, overlapping structure makes it particularly difficult to unpack it cleanly.

In relation to the allegory of the Cave, the repeating, overlapping, fractal-like structure takes the following form. On one side of the double-sided nature of the allegory, we have a person traversing the Cave—a student. And this student has a history and a future. She is the educable soul who will successfully ascend, descend, and ascend to exit the Cave again, and who will, after successfully negotiating a battery of intense challenges, emerge as the true ruler of the best city. On the other side, we are shown the internal psychological journey each philosophical soul takes toward self-knowledge and virtue—the so-called odyssey of the mind. These two are also substantially the same, since it is the person who has successfully negotiated the psychological odyssey who will be fit to take charge politically. We have not lost either the political or the psychological thread, but it may appear that we have, since they are wound so tightly together in the allegory.

What does it mean for all of the prisoners in the Cave to start in the realm of *eikasia*? Since Socrates is clear about them being like us (515a),[4] the allegory suggests that we start there, too. The psychological meaning

---

[4] Nicholas Smith argues that this phrase is "completely inclusive" and implies that all of Plato's readers as well as Socrates' interlocutors are (or have been) at the bottom of the Cave. He moves from this point to an attempt to ask what sort of education the *Republic*, itself, offers its readers. He describes the "curricula" of the Cave, looks at the nature of the *Republic*, and infers where Plato thought his readers were in their journey to philosophical education. As it turns out according to Smith's analysis, we are very young and inexperienced, but we have promise. Nicholas Smith, "Images, Education, and Paradox in Plato's *Republic*," *Apeiron: A Journal for Ancient Philosophy and Science*, 32, no. 4 (December 1999): 125–141.

of this part of the allegory would be that image-thinking is the first and most basic way that the human mind apprehends the world. Since Piaget, this has been a commonplace in theories of cognitive development,[5] and it is confirmed in our experience of the way young children engage the world. There is a reason that children's books are full of illustrations, even when they are designed for those who can read. There is a reason that stories and songs are conventional childhood fare across cultures and time. Children engage the world first through images, stories, and songs and only later through the concrete dynamics between objects described empirically. We all start in the realm of *eikasia*.

It would be tempting to linger next in the realm of *pistis*, but to do so would not follow the order of exposition in the allegory. We know that the region inhabited by puppeteers is the realm of *pistis* because, first, the Divided Line has prepared us to see it as such; and, secondly, the exposition of the image later in Book VII will make it clear; but our student races by this region on her ascent. We know she sees it because, at the top, she can recall what she saw there. But, when she catches a glimpse of that realm she is being dragged up by her teacher, and she is compelled to keep moving. For now, we should keep moving too.

The first things the student/escapee/proto-philosopher has time to see are shadows on the ground outside the mouth of the Cave, the objects of *dianoia*. However, the ascent of his eyes this time, rather than his body, also goes extraordinarily quickly:

> I suppose he would need time for his eyes to adjust, if he is going to be able see the things in the world above. At first, he would see shadows most easily, then images of human beings and other reflections in water, then the things themselves. After he was able to focus on these things, it would be easier for him to look at the things in the sky and the sky itself at night, gazing at the light of the stars and the moon,

[5] Jean Piaget, *The Child's Conception of the World* (London: Routledge and Kegan Paul, 1928).

> than it would be during the day, gazing at the sun and the light of the sun (516a).[6]

First, we are told, shadows would come into focus as the student's eyes adjusted to sunlight, then reflections, then the things causing those reflections, and then sources of light in the night sky. And, finally, the student would be capable of looking directly at the sun.[7]

Much of the account of the Cave is presented as the memory of the one whom has made it out, as an object of recollection. Socrates asks Glaucon to go through this process for himself, that is, to imagine how the one who had recently exited the Cave would look back on his experience within it.[8] Socrates asks Glaucon if he would be happy about the changes that his journey up and back down through the Cave have made in him. Socrates asks if he would pity those still imprisoned at the bottom of the Cave. Then Socrates quotes Homer, asking Glaucon whether he would prefer honors in the world below to a life without honor that included knowledge of existence beyond the Cave (515c–e).

In the Homeric text, Achilles tells Odysseus that he would rather be a poor man's slave on earth than to rule in the land of the dead (*Odyssey* 11: 511–513). By quoting this passage, Socrates adds several rich layers to this already dense allegory. Likening the newly enlightened student's comparison between his old and new situations to Achilles' comparison between Hades and Earth, Socrates implies that existence outside the Cave is related to existence in the depths of the Cave as life is to death. Socrates' use of a Homeric quotation to clarify the diminished experience of one whose experience is limited to image-thinking also suggests that

---

[6] συνηθείας δὴ οἶμαι δέοιτ' ἄν, εἰ μέλλοι τὰ ἄνω ὄψεσθαι. καὶ πρῶτον μὲν τὰς σκιὰς ἂν ῥᾷστα καθορῷ, καὶ μετὰ τοῦτο ἐν τοῖς ὕδασι τά τε τῶν ἀνθρώπων καὶ τὰ τῶν ἄλλων εἴδωλα, ὕστερον δὲ αὐτά: ἐκ δὲ τούτων τὰ ἐν τῷ οὐρανῷ καὶ αὐτὸν τὸν οὐρανὸν νύκτωρ ἂν ῥᾷον θεάσαιτο, προσβλέπων τὸ τῶν.

[7] Of course, looking directly at the sun is no more possible in the fourth century BCE than it is now. Socrates seems to be suggesting that it is beyond the capacity of human beings to apprehend the Good immediately, and that it is dangerous and damaging to try. If you're lucky, like Moses, you might be able to see the "back parts." But such is a rare sight and a privilege.

[8] Eva Brann characterizes the Divided Line as a story of recollection as well (Brann, *Music of the Republic*, 192).

poetry, and perhaps other images, continue to play a role in an enlightened life. Living only in *eikasia* is like death, but living with *eikasia* is a part of what it means to be enlightened.

The implications of these details of the allegory for its psychological meaning are myriad. First, we must take a moment to make sense of the psychological meaning of ascent through the Cave, but we should not forget that the allegory suggests that such an account is only possible retrospectively and that ascending through the Cave does not seem to imply leaving its modes of knowing behind but, instead, being capable of developing some perspective on each of them. If the newly enlightened student can reflect back on her life imprisoned at the bottom of the Cave, it seems likely that she would also be able to recollect her initial experiences with each of the higher regions she traversed and incorporate them into a multifaceted epistemological position.

As I argued above, it seems that our first attempts to make sense of our experience employ image-thinking, *eikasia*. It seems equally sensible to say that the next most sophisticated epistemological framework, which also tends to follow *eikasia* developmentally, is an engagement with objects of experience and deference to authority. As a college professor who teaches first year undergraduates, I am often reminded by my university's "first year experience" professionals that eighteen-year-olds think concretely and in "black and white." Gray areas, particularly moral ones, will be challenging for them at first, I am told, but I can look forward to more sophistication from them as their frontal lobes mature during their four years of college. The timing of and motivations behind these regular autumn pep-talks are debatable, but their basic point seems fair enough—concrete thinking is an epistemological mode that precedes subtlety in moral discourse. First one begins to see the difference between right and wrong, and only later is it possible to blur the lines without doing violence to the concepts.

The other facet of *pistis* is deference to authority, which may seem at first different from reliance on concrete experience, but is actually the same epistemological mode employed in a different context. When one who has been bound at the bottom of the Cave is released, compelled to stand up, turn around, look at the light, and begin walking toward it, the first things to be seen are the artifacts being held up before the fire. Then, as one approaches, it becomes clear that there are puppeteers behind the wall holding them up. Concrete thinking is the side of *pistis* that sees those artifacts and takes them as real. Deference to authority is the side of *pistis* that recognizes the human role in the construction of those artifacts but continues to acknowledge their authority.

The activity my university's retention experts call "concrete thinking" exists in the realm of *pistis*, of belief, but so is the approach in which I accept their expertise as sufficient evidence for the lesson they hope will make me a more understanding teacher of undergraduates. In both cases, *pistis* takes things and people as they present themselves and does not question the sources or causes that might (or might not) support their authority. In one sense, this tendency to take things as they are characterizes every level of the Cave. The dwellers in the realm of *eikasia* take images for what they are and tend not to look for their causes, for example. In another sense, this dynamic is most fully instantiated in *pistis*. The allegory of the Cave paints inhabitants of the realm of *eikasia* as wholly unaware that the objects of their apprehension are images, but actual *eikasia* seems to take a slightly different form.

Take, for example, the case of someone who believes in the story of the flood from Genesis 6. Let us imagine that this person was raised hearing the story and has never thought to question its authority. Its main elements are God's wrath, Noah's faithfulness and chosenness, an ark full of animals, a flood that comes and goes, and the promise of a blessed life in a new world. If *eikasia* is not the same as *pistis*, then believing in the story does not mean that one is attached to the facts of the story. Although it seems true to the allegory to say that one would take for granted that the story is grounded in fact, being immersed in *eikasia* would mean that one was attached to some aspect of the image as image. The story of the flood is a morality tale about human frailty, the wrath of Yahweh, and the blessings of faithfulness. To believe in the story is to believe that it describes reality.

If one has been looking at the story of Noah in the shadows on the Cave wall and then one is forced to turn around to confront their sources in the realm of *pistis*, what does one see? First, one sees that the story came from somewhere and next that there is a human being responsible, in some sense, for its presentation. Perhaps, in the first place, one gets interested in aerial photographs of a ship-like shape that appeared after a particularly deep thaw on Mt. Ararat. In the second place, one might become interested in the historiography of the Torah and theories of its authorship.

Engagement with the story of the flood in the realm of *pistis* may or may not undermine its authority in one's life. If one finds facts that undermine the authority of the story, then one might become disillusioned. If, on the other hand, one were to find corroborating facts, then one's sense of the story's authority might shift to a new foundation, but it need not falter. In either case, one who has turned to *pistis* believes that she sees things as they are because they are sitting right under her nose. There are facts and there are authorities; they are apparent, and they are the bases for her perception of reality. This way of being in the world may share a sort of naivete with *eikasia*, but its "just the facts, ma'am" sense of level-headed pragmatism is all its own. On the first ascent up through all the regions inside and outside of the Cave, this is really all that can be said about *pistis*. On the way back down, there will be more, but for now that must wait.

The realm of *dianoia,* theory or hypothesis, is represented by the shadows on the ground outside the Cave. Here, just outside the Cave, the student is given time to linger. Her eyes are given time to adjust. The parallels between the area just outside the Cave opening and the bottom of the Cave are very clear, as are some striking differences. Both will help clarify *dianoia*, *eikasia*, and the roles they play in an epistemological approach sufficient to apprehend reality clearly.

Both at the bottom of the Cave and just outside the opening of the Cave, the student sees shadows. And, in both cases, she moves from an apprehension of those shadows to an awareness of the objects that cast them. However, the transition from *eikasia* to *pistis* is mysterious, violent, and done apparently against the will of the student. She is released from her bonds; she does not release herself. She is compelled to stand up, compelled to look at the light, and compelled to begin walking up toward it. Every step of the transition from *eikasia* to *pistis* is done to the student. All of the motion and motivation is external. Because we know this student will be successful and because Socrates has already given an account of some of the prerequisites for such success, we know that this student is amenable to education in many important ways. However, that does not seem to alter the fact that breaking away from *eikasia* requires an intervention.

Although the pattern of first apprehending shadows (*eikasia*) and then moving toward a recognition of the objects that cast those shadows (*pistis*) that we see within the Cave is repeated outside the Cave, the way the student makes the transition from *dianoia* to *nous* could not be more different. The student who has just emerged from the firelight of the Cave into the sunlight of the external world cannot see very well. The brightness overwhelms her eyes, which are accustomed to a dimmer world. But, her eyes begin immediately to adjust. The transition between her capacity to see shadows and her capacity to see the objects that make those shadows in the light of the sun is natural and organic, rather than violent and imposed from without.

One of the implications of this difference between the ascent internal to the Cave and external to the Cave in the allegory seems to be that there is no necessity at all to being released from the depths of the Cave. A perfectly educable person might languish there forever if someone does not come along to release her. But, if one makes it outside the Cave, then one already possesses all one needs to make the ascent from *dianoia* to *nous*—from theory to insight. One reason for this may be that the soul that moves from *dianoia* to *nous* has already moved from *eikasia* to *pistis*. She has had an analogous experience and she now knows something about shadows. She knows that they are caused by an object being held up to the light. While the world outside the Cave is new to the student who just emerged, it is not entirely alien.

The realm of *dianoia* is the epistemological mode associated with theories and hypotheses, but it seems to me that the specific contemporary theoretical mode most closely aligned with the way Socrates presents *dianoia* is what we call "modeling." It is not wrong to think of all theories as *dianoetic*, but it is particularly illuminating to focus on theoretical modeling because it better preserves the resemblances between *eikasia* and *dianoia* while also suggesting some of the key differences between them.

When one creates a theoretical model, one begins with an idea about the way that some particular heretofore unknown, perhaps unobservable, dynamic operates. One then creates variables and constraints that are designed collectively to confirm or falsify one's provisional ideas about that dynamic. Models represent some aspect of reality in order to test whether or not our ideas about reality are correct and/or falsifiable.

In physics, for example, models are mathematical structures within which certain phenomena, also represented mathematically, may be better understood. The better the model, the closer it will come to predicting the results of empirical experimentation if and when it becomes possible.

A particularly dramatic example of mathematical modeling in physics and its relation to empirical research is the 2016 confirmation of a part of Einstein's 1905 General Theory of Relativity. In 1905, the General Theory of Relativity was proven by Einstein mathematically, that is, by means of a model. Because of the integrity of the model and the clarity of the mathematics, physicists expected observable phenomena to corroborate the theory. Because there was good evidence that the model represented a particular aspect of reality well, there was a high level of confidence that that aspect of reality, if we could ever find a way to observe it, would operate the way the model predicted. From 1905 until 2016 that aspect of reality was, however, unobservable. All we had was the model. But, in February of 2016 a team of scientists at the Laser Interferometer Gravitational-Wave Observatory (LIGO) announced that they had recorded the sound of two black holes colliding a billion light years away, and that it was direct evidence of the existence of the gravitational waves that Einstein's theory had predicted—that his mathematical model had proven.[9]

The realm of *dianoia* on the Divided Line and in the allegory of the Cave is the realm both of the General Theory of Relativity and of the mathematical model that Einstein used to prove it (before we were capable of observing black holes a billion light years away). When one develops a theory or constructs a model to test that theory, one is not looking directly at the aspect of reality that one hopes to understand. Rather, one is creating something that stands in for reality, a model of it. Although few cases of modeling are as dramatic or precise as Einstein's General Theory of Relativity, the same dynamic is always in place. The better the model, the more predictive of reality it is—the more fidelity it has to the way things are. So, the better the model, the more accurate the theories that are tested by reference to that model.

[9] Dennis Overbye, "Gravitational Waves Detected, Confirming Einstin's Theory," *New York Times*, February 11, 2016.

For models and theories to operate properly, they need to be constructed intentionally by the one who employs them. No scientist after Einstein can claim, of course, to discover the General Theory of Relativity. But, if a physicist passively accepts the General Theory as accurate, then she is not really engaging it as theory. In order to engage a theory as theory, a model as model, one needs to (re)make it for oneself. Only by proving General Relativity for oneself can a physicist genuinely engage the theory. But, as soon as one engages the theory as theory—proves it for oneself—the model calls one's mind up to the reality that it attempts to reflect.

In the terms of the Divided Line and allegory of the Cave, if one passively consumes the Theory of General Relativity, then one is engaging it in the realm of *eikasia* or, at best *pistis*. One is uncritically accepting the image as the truth or, at best, deferring to the authority of the one who has told you it is true. (Unless one works at LIGO, the option of seeing the gravitational waves for yourself is probably off the table.) *Dianoia* requires a different sort of engagement with the model, and that engagement requires an element of activity absent from the lower parts of the Cave and visible regions of the Divided Line. In the Cave, this is suggested by the increased level of autonomy implied for the newly released prisoner/student/proto-philosopher who has just emerged into the light of the sun. The mysterious rescuer/teacher's intervention is no longer necessary for one to move from *dianoia* to *nous*. One can and must do it on one's own.

The transition from dianoetic engagement with the world to noetic engagement is not necessary, but it is natural. One constructs models and theories about reality in order better to apprehend reality indirectly. One might come to a dianoetic epistemology with the understanding that it is the highest possible mode of which the human intellect is capable, in which case one will mistrust any claims to direct apprehension of reality, or one might understand the mediated understanding generated by theories and models as pathways toward immediate insights. That is, one might halt one's ascent at *dianoia* or continue to *nous*, but whether or not one continues one's ascent is entirely based one oneself. One's eyes will adjust or they won't, and no teacher can do anything about it. The ascent through the visible realm is something that can be taught, as is analogical thinking, so there certainly are ways that a teacher may prepare a student for the transition from *dianoia* to *nous*, but ultimately one must make that transition for oneself, or not.

At this point, like Glaucon, we have climbed with our student out of *eikasia*, through *pistis*, and into the realm of *dianoia*, where our eyes have adjusted and we have raised them to a noetic apprehension of real things. It is only now that we have an opportunity to understand where we have been, who we are, and what we have done. The newly enlightened student's first reactions to comparing his present situation to what he recollects about his old life are happiness for himself and pity for those who have been left behind. Both of these responses are key insofar as they orient his future choices about how to put together his life in light of his newly acquired knowledge. They also help to connect the account of the Cave to earlier discussions of the conditions for the possibility of the education the Cave represents.

At 516c, Socrates and Glaucon imagine the newly enlightened former prisoner recalling life in the depths of the Cave. The ones who are successful in that realm are those who were best at identifying the shadows on the wall and recognizing patterns among them, displaying predictive, prophetic power. This is the same situation Socrates described to Adeimantus at 494a and following, just presented from a different point of view. At 494 in Book VI, Socrates tried to show Adeimantus how difficult it would be for a brilliant and spirited young person (i.e., one who could become capable of philosophical education) to resist the corrupting allures of a society governed by base conventions. Socrates tries to show Glaucon the diminished value of the honors of that life in relation to true enlightenment. Socrates is presenting the same lesson, but in two very different ways.

Psychologically, Socrates asks Glaucon to consider the difference between mastering patterns in the appearance of things, genius in the realm of *eikasia*, and knowledge of the realities that cause those appearances. One with noetic insight or dianoetic theoretical understanding of the realities represented by the shadows would know more about the world at the bottom of the Cave than those who lived there, but they would also be at something of a disadvantage, at least at first. This disadvantage is represented by their eyes no longer being accustomed to the firelight of the Cave. It will be difficult for the one who has seen the realities outside of the Cave to make them plausible to those who live in the world of shadows for the same reason that it would be difficult for one who is capable of engaging higher epistemological modes and apprehending reality more accurately to survive her upbringing in a democratic regime filled with sophists, or for one born with the capacity to be a true pilot to survive a childhood lived among sailors—the pressures of convention are overwhelmingly strong.

The images and arguments of the *Republic* are piling up by this point in Book VII. Part of the genius of the dialogue is its unflinching pursuit of its most foundational questions despite its length and complexity. But, it also takes great patience and care to maintain the focus required to keep one's eye on these questions through their long, complicated dialectical exposition by Socrates. The images help keep the connections among the arguments clear, but they, too have developed by Book VII to a level of complexity that makes synopsis more and more difficult. Occasionally, Socrates offers a moment of calibration where he makes explicit the connections among these images and arguments. One of those moments begins at 517a:

> Now this image, my dear Glaucon, needs to be fitted together as a whole with what was said before. The realm revealed by sight should be likened to the prison dwelling [at the bottom of the Cave], and the light of the fire inside the Cave should be likened to the sun's power. And you won't mistake my intention if you think of the upward journey and the seeing of things above [the Cave] as the upward journey of the soul to the intelligible realm—since that is what you wanted to hear about. Only the god knows whether it happens to be true. What appears true to me looks like this: in the intelligible realm, the last thing to be seen is the look of the Good, and it can only be seen with hard work and trouble. Once one has seen [the intelligible realm], however, one must conclude that it is the source of everything that is true and beautiful in anything, that in the visible realm it produces both light and the source of light, and that in the intelligible realm it controls and provides truth and understanding. One must also con-

clude that anyone who is to act intelligently in private or public has to have it in view (517a–c).[10]

In this passage, Socrates makes it clear that the allegory of the Cave follows the structure of the Divided Line, the sun continues to function as it was presented in Book VI, and the allegorical ascent through the Cave represents the soul's journey from engaging the world only on the level of appearances to the hard earned life lived in the attempt to apprehend reality. However, Socrates also makes clear that these images are answers to "what Glaucon wants to hear about."[11] This account seems to refer back to Glaucon's impassioned intervention at 506d, where he implores Socrates to speak of the Good in the same way that he had already spoken of justice and the other virtues; as well as Glaucon's acceptance of Socrates' counter offer to describe the child of the Good, since Socrates claimed to be unable to speak of the Good itself. The Sun, the Cave and the Divided Line are all images designed to help us see that there is something higher than justice and to point the way to the educational path that could lead us to where we might glimpse it. [12]

---

[10] ταύτην τοίνυν, ἦν δ' ἐγώ, τὴν εἰκόνα, ὦ φίλε Γλαύκων, προσαπτέον ἅπασαν τοῖς ἔμπροσθεν λεγομένοις, τὴν μὲν δι' ὄψεως φαινομένην ἕδραν τῇ τοῦ δεσμωτηρίου οἰκήσει ἀφομοιοῦντα, τὸ δὲ τοῦ πυρὸς ἐν αὐτῇ φῶς τῇ τοῦ ἡλίου δυνάμει: τὴν δὲ ἄνω ἀνάβασιν καὶ θέαν τῶν ἄνω τὴν εἰς τὸν νοητὸν τόπον τῆς ψυχῆς ἄνοδον τιθεὶς οὐχ ἁμαρτήσῃ τῆς γ' ἐμῆς ἐλπίδος, ἐπειδὴ ταύτης ἐπιθυμεῖς ἀκούειν. Θεὸς δέ που οἶδεν εἰ ἀληθὴς οὖσα τυγχάνει. Τὰ δ' οὖν ἐμοὶ φαινόμενα οὕτω φαίνεται, ἐν τῷ γνωστῷ τελευταία ἡ τοῦ ἀγαθοῦ ἰδέα καὶ μόγις ὁρᾶσθαι, ὀφθεῖσα δὲ συλλογιστέα εἶναι ὡς ἄρα πᾶσι πάντων αὕτη ὀρθῶν τε καὶ καλῶν αἰτία, ἔν τε ὁρατῷ φῶς καὶ τὸν τούτου κύριον τεκοῦσα, ἔν τε νοητῷ αὐτὴ κυρία ἀλήθειαν καὶ νοῦν παρασχομένη, καὶ ὅτι δεῖ ταύτην ἰδεῖν τὸν μέλλοντα ἐμφρόνως πράξειν ἢ ἰδίᾳ ἢ δημοσίᾳ.

[11] ἐπειδὴ ταύτης ἐπιθυμεῖς ἀκούειν.

[12] Or, as Nicholas Smith puts it in his description of the way the Cave allegorizes education, "Plato uses images, whose inadequacies are noted, so that we can move from them to those better conceptions, of which the former turn out to be mere images. These, too, come to be revealed as only images as we climb Plato's ladder of images so as to approach those realities that are originals only, and not themselves images. But the Republic never takes us entirely to this point—it is, instead, a book of images." Nicholas Smith, "Plato's Book of Imag-

The Cave, serving as it does to bring all of the arguments of the *Republic* together, also answers Adeimantus' question about why, if philosophers are so well-suited to rule, they seem so ill-suited for ruling; the cave runs parallel to the story of the Ship of State, as well. In the imagery of the Cave, the answer is in our eyesight. Our eyes must adjust if we are to move from firelight to sunlight, that is from *eikasia* and *pistis* to *dianoia* and *nous*; and they must adjust again if we are to return from the sunlight of the natural world back down into the firelight of the Cave. These awkward transitions, the dilations of the mind's eye, answer Adeimantus' question by explaining how one could both understand things better and simultaneously appear to understand those same things worse than others. Adeimantus could instead recall the authority of the true pilot, also based on his superior vision, and remember how it undermined his influence with the sailors on his ship.

The necessity of adjusting one's eyes to the different realms of the allegory of the Cave represents adjusting one's mind to different ways of apprehending the human condition. While the true pilot had to adjust his focus from the realm of astronomy from the realm of the deck of the ship, the cave climber must adjust more often to more sorts of things. One may understand stories as reflecting the structure of reality, as in mythological thinking. One may appeal to direct experience of phenommena or to experts who claim a privileged point of view. One may create theories or models to explain experience. And, perhaps, one may apprehend the shape of things as they really are. One may also come to recognize the necessity of light for vision. A few may finally come also to recognize the necessity of the Good for intelligibility.[13] If Glaucon is among

---

es," in *Philosophy in Dialogue: Plato's Many Devices*, ed. Gary Alan Scott (Evanston: Northwestern University Press, 2007) 3–14.

[13] Glaucon and the others might be forgiven for not following the arguments and images here, if they in fact do not. Although Socrates does not (and perhaps cannot) say what the Good is, he gives us enough information about what it is not for us to infer its elusive complexity. Stanley Rosen puts it this way: "[T]he Good is not the activity of knowing or of self-consciousness. It is also not knowledge in the subjective sense but is rather the goodness of knowledge. But neither is it knowledge in the objective sense of the word, because what we know is the nature of this or that particular kind, not goodness.

those capable of recognizing the analogy between visibility and intelligibility, and if he sees the necessity of light for vision, he may also now see that intelligibility requires the existence of the Good. If so, then Socrates' presentation of the Cave has answered that question, too.[14]

And similar considerations apply to truth. Thus, for example, the sun is not a flower or the truth of a proposition about what it is to be a flower. It is (speaking loosely or metaphorically) the cause of the genesis of the flower, and it illuminates the flower so that we can learn the truth about its nature. Note that the sun is not the sole or total cause of the genesis of the flower; other factors play a role as well (earth, water, nutrients, and so forth). The sun makes it possible for us to acquire knowledge and truth by illuminating the flower, and so too the Idea of the Good functions in the intelligible domain. In short: nothing has been said as yet to allow the inference that the Good is the cause of the Ideas; this would be impossible in the ordinary sense of the term, since the Ideas are eternal. The only possibility here is that the eternal illumination of the Good is the causal factor in the eternal presence of the ideas." Stanley Rosen, *Plato's* Republic (New Haven: Yale University Press, 2005) 260–261.

[14] Socrates repeatedly emphasizes the difficulty of the ascent through the Cave, and it appears on several occasions that Glaucon may be on that ascent in the *Republic*, but Glaucon seems not to be in any distress at all. He never breaks a proverbial sweat. Glaucon's cool demeanor adds an additional element of uncertainty to any interpretation of his progress in the dialogue. Is Socrates such a master of dragging released prisoners up toward the sun that they are not aware of the difficulty of what they are doing? Is Glaucon so spirited that he manages to embrace the challenge to the point of concealing his effort? Or, perhaps, have they not made any real headway? It is difficult to know.

11

Philosophical *Paideia* in 3D

Once Socrates makes the connections between the Sun, the Cave, and the Divided Line clear, and once he has linked those images to Glaucon and Adeimantus' questions, Socrates goes on to show how he has also pointed the way toward answers to questions that they have not yet posed, but perhaps should have. Education is not, according to Socrates, what many people think it is. It is not the process of putting knowledge into souls any more than the allegory of the Cave is an image of putting sight into blind eyes. Prisoners at the bottom of the Cave are functionally blind to the realities of the world outside the Cave, but they do not need vision "put into" them. They need instead to be turned around. This is Socrates' image of education.

> But our current conversation suggests that the capacity to learn is present in everyone's soul, and so is the instrument with which each of us learns: just like an eye cannot be turned around from darkness to light except by turning the whole body, so this instrument must be turned around together with the whole soul from what is fleeting, until it can bear to look at being and at the brightest thing that exists—which we call the Good....There would be a craft, then, of just this sort of turning around—a craft concerned with how this instrument can be most easily and effectively turned, not a craft of putting sight into it. Instead, this craft takes for granted that sight is already there, though not turned in the right direction or looking at what it should look at, and it contrives to redirect it appropriately (518b–d).[1]

[1] ὁ δέ γε νῦν λόγος, ἦν δ᾽ ἐγώ, σημαίνει ταύτην τὴν ἐνοῦσαν ἑκάστου δύναμιν ἐν τῇ ψυχῇ καὶ τὸ ὄργανον ᾧ καταμανθάνει ἕκαστος, οἷον εἰ ὄμμα μὴ δυνατὸν ἦν ἄλλως ἢ σὺν ὅλῳ τῷ σώματι στρέφειν πρὸς τὸ φανὸν ἐκ τοῦ σκοτώδους, οὕτω σὺν

Almost everyone has the capacity to become educated, that is the capacity to apprehend the intelligible things, just as almost everyone has within them the capacity to see visible things. The analogy suggests that one might encounter someone who lacks the capacity to apprehend truth the same way that one might encounter a blind person, but such individuals are in the minority, and they lack a capacity understood to be a basic part of human nature. The general point is clear: it is a natural part of the human condition for our intelligence to be capable of apprehending the intelligibility of the world. If we are not capable of apprehending the intelligibility of things, it is likely not because we lack the capacity. Something else impedes us. It is not automatic, however, for one's natural capacity for apprehending intelligibility to be actualized. For that, we need education.

Education (*paideia*) is a process of turning around, not of putting ideas into souls. Human beings, by nature, share this capacity, but human beings also share a responsiveness to habituation. If one's natural capacity to apprehend intelligibility is discouraged by the habit of attending to the wrong things—of being turned in the wrong direction—then reorientation will become more and more difficult, perhaps eventually impossible. The three *kumata* of Book V tell the story of the capacities that must characterize each part of the soul if one is to become educated. Book VI walks us through the ways that each part of the soul must be nurtured in order for the soul with those capacities to mature into an educable individual. Now, in Book VII, with the help of the allegory of the Cave, Socrates explains the process of education and what the fully-formed, nurtured, and educated philosophical soul looks like.

In an important sense, the Female Drama considers all three sorts of "becoming" (*genesis*, *trophe*, and *paideia*) as they must occur in each of the

---

ὅλῃ τῇ ψυχῇ ἐκ τοῦ γιγνομένου περιακτέον εἶναι, ἕως ἂν εἰς τὸ ὂν καὶ τοῦ ὄντος τὸ φανότατον δυνατὴ γένηται ἀνασχέσθαι θεωμένη: τοῦτο δ' εἶναί φαμεν τἀγαθόν....τούτου τοίνυν, ἦν δ' ἐγώ, αὐτοῦ τέχνη ἂν εἴη, τῆς περιαγωγῆς, τίνα τρόπον ὡς ῥᾷστά τε καὶ ἀνυσιμώτατα μεταστραφήσεται, οὐ τοῦ ἐμποιῆσαι αὐτῷ τὸ ὁρᾶν, ἀλλ' ὡς ἔχοντι μὲν αὐτό, οὐκ ὀρθῶς δὲ τετραμμένῳ οὐδὲ βλέποντι οἷ ἔδει, τοῦτο διαμηχανήσασθαι.

parts of the soul (*epithumia*, *thumos*, and *logismos*/*nous*[2]) in order for a fully formed philosophical soul to exist. But, in another important sense, the locus of becoming narrows with each new form. *Genesis* applies equally to *epithumia*, *thumos*, and *logismos*/*nous*. That is, each of these three parts of soul must have particular capacities in order for philosophical formation and education to be possible. One's appetite (*epithumia*) must be, in principle, containable. One's spirit (*thumos*) must be capable of becoming an ally to *logismos/nous*. And, one's mind (*logismos*/*nous*) must be capable of governing the whole city/soul in the true light of the Good.

Trophe also, in a sense, applies to all three parts of the soul, but it more precisely concerns only *thumos* and *logismos*/*nous*. *Trophe* is training, and *epithumia* cannot, strictly speaking, be trained. A soul with a well-trained, well-habituated *thumos* and *nous* will likely have *epithumia* under control, but because it has been contained, not trained. *Epithumia* can only be contained. The first principle of philosophical *trophe* is the love of truth, and the first habit it engenders is truth seeking. All the other virtues of soul that Socrates claims for philosophers develop from seeking

[2] Although it may seem awkward to list *logismos* and *nous* together in this list and the analysis that follows it, I believe it is the approach that represents the greatest fidelity to the argument. *Logismos* (calculation) does not disappear after Book IV. The soul continues to need to be organized, and the capacity to figure out efficient internal arrangements continues to be important. But, those internal arrangements of soul are, in the best souls, informed by *nous*. In the language of the city/soul analogy, in the best cities, the philosophical art and the political are one and the same. In Book IV, *logismos* is explored in great detail. In Book VI, when *nous* is introduced, it is already embedded in the argument of the third *kumata* (i.e. that philosophers should rule). So, as long as we are attempting to make sense of a philosophical soul, these two activities (insight and calculation) should be considered together. One could leave *logismos* out of the account altogether, and Socrates often does, because there is not much of a Female Drama of *logismos*. *Nous* does that work for reason. But, they function together, and the account would not be complete unless I continued to acknowledge the role of *logismos* in the psychology Socrates presents. So, in the images and arguments where *nous* is treated explicitly, I will refer to it alone. But, where I describe the psychological dynamics implied by all of the images and arguments understood cumulatively, I will also include *logismos*.

the truth, the philosopher's beloved. Such love and seeking involves both the outwardly oriented aspect of reason (*nous*) and its inward looking mode (*logismos*); the proto-philosopher attempts to apprehend things illuminated by the light of the truth, which is beyond her. Then she tries to organize her life so that she can best pursue it. This process also involves *thumos* because it is vulnerable to external influence, which is the point Socrates drove home to Adeimantus in their exchange that occurs from 487b to 506d. If the best objects and the best pursuits are dishonored by one's family and society, then only a miracle will make it possible for one to continue to seek them, even if one is drawn to them by nature. *Epithumia* is affected by *trophe*, but only indirectly. As we pursue some things more, we will pursue others less, says the principle at 485d. As higher things become our objects of concern and desire, our appetites for lower things wane. Those appetites that contribute to our pursuit of truth and virtue get fed, and those that don't are weakened by our neglect.

The scope of *paideia*'s direct concern is even more narrow than that of *trophe*. *Epithumia* and *thumos* are clearly altered by philosophical *paideia*, but only indirectly. *Paideia*, strictly speaking, applies directly only to *logismos*/*nous*. Because of this, the account of philosophical *paideia* that follows the allegory of the Cave in Book VII emphasizes the *noetic*. *Paideia*'s implications for the other parts of the soul have already been accounted for in various ways and are illuminated by the Cave; but the argument itself, the most direct account of philosophical *paideia* in the *Republic*, is abstract and, in modern terms, cerebral.

At 521c Socrates and Glaucon move on from their consideration of the potential philosopher-ruler's path out of, back down into, and out of the Cave again. On the psychological level, the allegory of the Cave only works as a complete image of education if we see that escaping it once is insufficient. This pattern reaffirms the continuing presence of *logismos* in the model, as well. Once again, the image of the Ship of State is helpful. Insofar as education pulls us up, the process looks like the work the true pilot does to learn how to read the stars. However, insofar as education also involves going down, another sort of rational activity is operative. How does one take the insights of *nous* and translate them into a working, thriving, frictionless harmony on a ship or in a city or in a soul? How does the stargazer translate his understanding of the stars into the work of piloting a ship? In what work does he enlist the help of the ship-owner? This is not the work of *nous* or *thumos* or *epithumia*. It is the work of *logismos*, and it constitutes a third of philosophical *paideia*. One goes up twice, but one must go down once as well.[3]

Once the necessity of the pattern of ascending, descending, and ascending again has been established, the interlocutors turn to the question of the content of *paideia* itself. That is, they ask what images on the walls of the Cave would be most likely to facilitate the psychological "turning" that characterizes the beginning of true philosophical education. It is worth reminding ourselves at the outset of our inquiry into the nature of philosophical *paideia* that the first moment 'turning around" in the allegory of the Cave, i.e., the first moment of *paideia*, is mysterious. The prisoner is released. He is compelled to stand up, turn around, look at the light, and begin walking toward its source. It is not at all clear that one can do this for oneself. But, apparently, there are images at the bottom of the Cave that are more helpful than others as a preparation for one's life after release. There are modes of *eikasia* that are better and worse at preparing one's soul for *pistis*, *dianoia* and *nous*.

The first characteristic that Socrates introduces as a suitable subject for philosophical *paideia* in the realm of *eikasia* is that it must be something that is not useless to warlike men (521d). By introducing this provision, Socrates connects the argument of Book VII to the original account in Book III of the training and education of the guardians. This is an important connection for several reasons. First, it confirms that the discussion of education in the *Republic* is a part of the larger argument of the dialogue and follows the same broad patterns and structures as the rest of the work, so the account of education in Book VII should not be read as a departure from or repudiation of the account of education in

[3] Commentators such as Eva Brann call our attention to the way this pattern will be played out in the final words of the dialogue, the myth of Er. She makes the connection this way: "Thus the imagery of the final myth of the *Republic* is the cosmic complement of the Sun Image and the Divided Line with respect to the location of the human soul. For in the final vision the soul is again both within the whole seeking its proper place in the world and also without viewing the whole as if it were a likeness of itself." She goes on to say that she thinks Socrates sees the power of the soul to work with and within these sort of images as "the wonder of wonders." Brann, *The Music of the Republic*, 207.

Book III, but rather as an elaboration. In the Male Drama of Books II–IV the inquiry concerned the being, not the becoming, of education. While the account of education in Book III—part of the Male Drama—was about the goals of education, the account in Book VII, which is a part of the Female Drama, will be about the process of education.

The story of education in Book III was incomplete in the sense that it presented an apparently complete model of the city/soul (the theme of the Male Drama) but did not account for the conditions necessary for such a city/soul to come into existence (the theme of the Female Drama). This is not the only way the account of education in Book III was incomplete, however. In the process of inquiring into the conditions for the possibility of the development of the just soul, Plato's interlocutors realized that they had neglected an essential noetic function, i.e. the capacity to apprehend things outside of oneself (*nous*). Calculation (*logismos*) was the only function of reason in Books II–IV, and it continues to be one of the functions of reason throughout the remainder of the dialogue. But, in the models of the soul that emerge in Book V–VII, *nous* also apprehends realities outside of the city/soul. Like the true pilot of the Ship of State, *nous* charts the soul's course by the stars and *logismos* serves as the captain who coordinates all of its efforts to stay on that course; they are two sides, two functions, of the same person on the Ship of State and two unified activities of reason in the individual soul.

Recalling Book III, at 521d Socrates and Glaucon look to music and gymnastics as possible candidates for the sort of subjects most likely to turn proto-philosophers toward the true and the Good. But, by 522b, they have come quickly to the conclusion that neither of these studies serve their purpose, since both focus on "what comes to be and dies,"[4] while what they seek is a study that focuses on "what is." All sorts of training in various forms of craftsmanship are dismissed even more abruptly and without elaboration. Then, at 522c, Socrates suggests "number and calculation."[5] Every craft (*techne*[6]) and science (*episteme*[7]) employs

[4] γιγνόμενον καὶ ἀπολλύμενον τετεύτακεν.

[5] ἀριθμόν τε καὶ λογισμόν.

[6] τέχνη.

[7] ἐπιστήμη.

number and calculation, so they must be suitable for warriors; it meets their first criterion. And, as they will go on to prove, numbers and calculation can turn our thoughts from becoming to being, which is their second criterion. They may have found the subject of study suitable for aspiring philosophers.

In order to orient ourselves to the inquiry into the nature and role of mathematics in philosophical education, we should consider both what the account from Book III has to teach us and what is yet for us to consider. As we near the end of the Female Drama—as we near the point where our detour rejoins the main path—we come closer and closer to elements of the Male Drama of Books II–IV. Since the city/soul of Books II–IV was constructed in order to inquire into the nature of justice, it lacks some of the elements necessary for an inquiry into that which is higher than justice, i.e., to the Good and the life of philosophy that is oriented to it. But, although the model of the city/soul that Socrates claims to finish in Book IV is incomplete, it is not wholly inaccurate. Likewise, the account of musical and physical training in Books II-IV is incomplete, but not inaccurate as long as its boundaries are clear to us.

First of all, it is important to see that instruction in gymnastic and music is presented as training, not as education. The word for those studies both in Book II–IV and in Socrates' recollection of them in Book VII is consistently *trophe*, not *paideia*. Socrates could only gesture towards *paideia* in Books II–IV because he was working with a limited model of soul, one that included *logismos*, but not *nous*. The paradigm case of *paideia* is mathematics, and it will be the main concern of Book VII after the allegory of the Cave. Or, more precisely, mathematics will be the paradigm of the activity of soul described by the allegory of the Cave. As Socrates' introduction of it suggests, the discussion of mathematics is a continuation of the discussion of music, gymnastics, and craft (*techne*), but it is an inquiry that was not possible before the Female Drama played out to this point.

An inquiry into mathematical thinking was not possible in the Male Drama of the *Republic* for two reasons. First, the key characteristic of mathematics that Socrates and Glaucon are focused on is its capacity to pull our minds towards things that are currently beyond us. In the model of the city/soul that is completed in Book IV, there is no capacity for the soul to attend to anything beyond itself. Such a model was sufficient for an inquiry into the nature of justice, if justice is defined as each part of the soul doing its own work and minding its own business. And, had the interlocutors limited their inquiry to whether or not justice, per se, was more or less choice-worthy than injustice, the model of the city/soul in Book IV would have been perfectly serviceable. But, when the conversation of the dialogue pushed toward the existence of the Good, i.e., something higher than justice, the model of the soul had to expand to accommodate that inquiry. And, when it did, the model became sufficient to support an inquiry into the nature of *paideia*.

Mathematics is, for contemporary English speakers, the study of all of the subjects, among others of course, that Socrates will elaborate on in Book VII—arithmetic, plane geometry, solid geometry, physics, and astronomy. But in Classical Greek, a *mathema*[8] does not necessarily concern what we think of as mathematics. It is a teachable thing. Anything that can be taught is a *mathema*. What we call mathematics is a special case. Both in English and for the Greeks, mathematical studies were *mathemata* for precisely the reasons Plato brings mathematics up in Book VII: they are models of what learning looks like. Why is one thing teachable (like a recipe for pie) and another isn't (your mother's pecan pie)? Because one is more like mathematics than the other: it is more precise, more schematic, more formal, and thus more repeatable, conveyable, reducible to a pattern.[9]

The second reason that Socrates could not embark on an inquiry into the nature of mathematical study until Book VII of the *Republic* may or may not inhere in the contemporary understanding of mathematics. It is more controversial. In the *Republic*, mathematics is the proper study for the aspiring philosopher because it turns our minds towards being (i.e. what is) rather than becoming (i.e., what comes to be and decays). The soul of Book IV lacks the capacity to apprehend anything beyond itself, so it is epistemologically impossible for it to apprehend the Good. Because of this, the Good is not readily apparent in the world that pro-

---

[8] μαθεμα.

[9] For a deep and detailed look at the meaning of *mathema* and the differences between ancient and modern mathematics, see Jacob Klein, *Ancient Greek Mathematical Thought and the Origin of Algebra* (Cambridge: MIT Press, 1969).

vides the context for the city/soul of Book IV. The Good is lacking in the metaphysics of Book IV, as well, so there is no (ultimate) object to make mathematical study intelligible or meaningful. In the language of the Divided Line, there is nothing above *pistis,* or perhaps at most there is a speculative, tentative, and impossible to falsify form of *dianoia.*

Some subjects invite us to understand them. They provoke us or summon us to try to know them more deeply. At 523b, Socrates calls such subjects "summoners," (*parekaloumen*[10]) and mathematical subjects are their paradigm cases.[11] The key to something being a summoner is that one may engage it on a shallow level but such engagement invites one to go deeper…or higher. In the terms of the Cave, one may apprehend an image solely at the level of *eikasia,* but that image itself, engaged at the bottom of the Cave, has the power to suggest that there is more to the world than the bottom of the Cave, more to intelligence than *eikasia.*[12] Mathematical shadows, in themselves, suggest that there may be more to the world than shadows.

The existence of "summoners" makes the situation of the prisoners at the bottom of the Cave slightly less dire. The prisoners are chained down. They cannot get up or turn around. All they can see are the shadows cast on the back wall of the Cave. But, some of those shadows contain within them the suggestion of another world, another way of understanding oneself and one's place in it. If a prisoner at the bottom of the Cave attends to those "summoning" shadows, if it becomes plausible to her that her view of the world is limited, then she will be far more ready for the possibility that she might someday be released, made to stand, turned around, and nudged toward the light.

---

[10] παρεκαλοῦμεν.

[11] For a slightly different and far more detailed account of the summoners, see Miriam Byrd, "The Summoner Approach: A New Model of Plato Interpretation. *Journal of the History of Philosophy* 45, no. 3 (July 2007): 365–381.

[12] Nicholas Smith argues that the *Republic* itself operates as a summoner for its readers. Its apparent internal inconsistencies (e.g. a rejection of images in a book populated by dozens of them) summon us to higher orders of understanding in which these inconsistencies are resolved. Nicholas Smith, "Images, Education, and Paradox in Plato's *Republic,*" *Apeiron: A Journal for Ancient Philosophy and Science* 32, no. 4 (December 1999): 125–141.

The way that summoners summon us to higher understanding is by perplexing us (524a). When our senses present us with a contradiction, we are naturally drawn to figuring out whether or not it is just an apparent contradiction. For example, if we perceive the same thing to be both soft and hard, we are likely to ask how that could be possible. According to Socrates, it is likely in such cases when we are faced with an apparent contradiction that we turn to calculation (*logismos*) by asking whether the thing that appears to be displaying contradictory characteristics is one thing or, instead, actually two. The key to the example is that at the moment we ask the question "one or two?" we are not longer simply apprehending shadows on the wall, objects of *eikasia*. We are, instead, exploring a realm of intelligibility implied, but not displayed, by the shadows in question. We have been summoned upward.

Interestingly, the example at 524b, like the narrative account of the allegory of the Cave at the beginning of Book VII, seems to skip directly from *eikasia* to *dianoia*. The prisoner does not turn to look into the realm of *pistis* to see the object(s) casting the shadow(s); instead, she develops a theory about whether the thing that appears to embody a contradiction is truly one thing or more than one thing. Before she can turn around and test the theory against direct experience or the testimony of an expert, she can apparently theorize. She can engage in *dianoetic* speculation when she is presented with something perplexing in the realm of *eikasia*.

The description of mathematics as a summoner suggests two possible ways of being turned around, both of which may be necessary parts of a complete philosophical education. The first way in the account is tantamount to compulsory education. One is blithely living one's restricted life in the realm of *eikasia* when one is snatched up and forced to acknowledge another way of understanding the world and another sort of reality revealed by that understanding. The other mode of being turned around is being "summoned" by an apparent contradiction in the realm of *eikasia* that leads you into the realm of *dianoia* in order to attempt to resolve it. There does not seem to be any text to support a theory about the relationship between these two sorts of turning, but it seems likely to me that the prisoner who has found her way to the realm of *dianoia* while still in chains will be better prepared for her ascent than the one who has known nothing but *eikasia* during her imprisonment. The moment of turning is shrouded in a cryptic mist that is impossible to dispel, but there is a hint in the description of the summoning subjects that one might be able to be turned by these studies without the aid of a teacher.

After reiterating the value of calculation and enumerating a few more benefits of mathematical education, such as recognizing that those who are good at it tend also to be quick in all other subjects (526b), Glaucon and Socrates move on to a consideration of plane geometry, mathematics in two dimensions. Geometry is, like calculation, a summoner. Although it has the reputation of being a practical activity, everyone who has engaged in geometry knows that it is done for the sake of knowledge (527b). They also know that the knowledge geometers seek is knowledge of what always is (527b) rather than of things that come to be and pass away. Those who are good at geometry also turn out to be quick learners of other subjects (527c). In short, geometry is a good and useful course of study for all of the same reasons calculation is.

The reasons for studying solid geometry (mathematics in three dimensions) and astronomy[13] (mathematics in time, that is, four dimensions) are the same as the reasons for studying calculation and plane geometry. All four subjects catch our eye in the realm of becoming and can draw our mind toward the realm of being. However, if they are all functionally the same as "summoners," then the question becomes why did Socrates enumerate all of them, as well as their analogs in the audible realm. The answer comes, I believe, in the two interludes in Glaucon and Socrates' conversation. First, Socrates interrupts himself to insert (three dimensional) solid geometry as the third subject in their list of summoners, having to backtrack because he had already added astronomy to the list. Secondly, Socrates corrects Glaucon's mistaken account of the value of astronomy for philosophical education.

The first interlude in the account of "summoning" subjects comes when Socrates revises his list. He moved from calculation to geometry to astronomy, and then he realized that he should have specified plane geometry in the second position and added solid geometry as the third subject before listing astronomy as the fourth. Glaucon does not object to

[13] For an account of the controversies surrounding the meaning of astronomy for Plato, see Ivor Bulmer-Thomas, "Plato's Astronomy," *The Classical Quarterly* 34, no. 1 (1984): 107–112.

this revision but is struck by its inclusion since, he claims, no one has investigated solid geometry. Socrates has, apparently, included a subject of study that does not yet exist. It would exist, though, Socrates says, if the city valued it and had a capable director (*epistaton*[14]).[15]

This interlude serves to connect the account of the four "summoning" subjects to the city/soul by way of the Ship of State. Solid Geometry has not emerged as a course of study because cities are not well governed. If there were a city that had a good director and if the citizens of that city were governable, then solid geometry would be studied there. But since such a city does not exist in the world, neither does the field of solid geometry. In a careful and detailed way, Socrates has lined solid geometry up analogically with good politics. Once again, Socrates develops a political account to illuminate a psychological or intellectual dynamic.

The second interlude during the conversation about the four summoning (mathematical) subjects comes when Socrates corrects Glaucon's misunderstanding of the value of astronomy (mathematics in four dimensions), and perhaps his misunderstanding of the way Socrates means to present all four subjects. When Socrates introduces astronomy, Glaucon acknowledges immediately the value of looking up at the stars, but Socrates likens looking up to looking down if the object of one's concern is the visible. All four of these subjects are valuable precisely because they both exist in the visible realm and draw the mind toward the intelligible realm. So, the value of astronomy is not that it draws our eyes to the stars, but instead that our attention to the motion of heavenly bodies in the visible realm is capable of drawing our mind toward some analogous consideration within the intelligible realm. If solid geometry is politics, perhaps astronomy is analogous to philosophy.

The four summoning subjects are not each important because they summon us in different ways. In fact, they summon us in precisely the

---

[14] ἐπίστατον.

[15] Using a complicated musical schema to interpret the proportions of the Divided Line, Eva Brann argues that "[t]he tripartite "embodied" soul is... characterized as the basic solid, the cube." If she is right, then Socrates' analysis of this section of the Divided Line points out that there is no science of politics extant, but that there could be. Eva Brann, *The Music of the Republic* (Philadelphia: Paul Dry Books, 2004) 186.

same way. Apparent contradictions, which are visible to the eye in each subject, draw our mind toward intelligible solutions to those apparent contradictions in the realm of thought. But each of the four subjects seem to be individually important as analogs to modes of human activity. A full account of these analogies would take us too far afield, but perhaps if astronomy is analogous to philosophy and solid geometry is analogous to good politics, then plane geometry is analogous to sophistry and calculation is analogous to craftsmanship. Each of these activities in the city in speech is also a dynamic within the city/soul, so while analogies are piling up a bit, their repetitive, parallel structures make it easier to keep them straight and tend to the ways that each new form adds content to the psychological account of the *Republic*.

One of the central challenges of working through the images that Socrates introduces into the conversation of the *Republic* is maintaining clarity about which parts of the city/soul are functioning in what ways and in relation to which objects. Keeping the subjects and predicates of these dynamics straight is particularly difficult when one part of the soul confronts some other part of the soul, and most difficult when one part of the soul confronts itself.

The difficulties of understanding the text are exacerbated by the vocabulary and categories that evolve in the *Republic* as Socrates' account of the city/soul becomes subtler and more detailed. It is central to my account to continually remind ourselves that in the early books of the *Republic*, *logismos* was the only rational part of the soul included in the inquiry, and that *nous* is not explicitly introduced until Book VI (and implicitly in the sections of Book V that set it up) as a higher function of mind, giving the soul four distinctive activities instead of the three that Socrates focused exclusively on in Books II–IV. But now, in Book VII, as the psychological theory of the *Republic* is presented in more detail, *nous* turns out to work within four distinct frameworks, namely the modes indicated in the Divided Line, Cave, and four summoners (*eikasia*, *pistis*, *dianoia*, and *nous*). To make things even more confusing, one of the modes of *nous* is, itself, called *nous*, but by now we should be accustomed to the elements of the images and arguments of the *Republic* having overlapping structures, especially at the top.

While in Books II–IV, everything seemed to happen in threes, four-part patterns dominate Books VI and VII. (As I argued in Chapter 3,

Book V is transitional.) Each of these four-part images and arguments seem to line up with the four functions of the soul (*epithumia*, *thumos*, *logismos*, and *nous*) that emerge in Book VI. If that pattern is in play in the account of the summoners, then the intellectual activity corresponding to astronomy would relate to the highest, outward oriented function of *nous* (if it is possible). Solid geometry would correspond to the lower, inward oriented function of *logismos*. Plane geometry would have something to do with *thumos*, and arithmetical calculation would have something to do with *epithumia*. Each of these activities would not describe a soul in which those different parts where in control, however. When any part other than *logismos-nous* is in control, we are faced with an account of injustice. That is the topic of Books VIII and IX. Socrates is still operating within the model of the most just city/soul, Kallipolis, so the psychological activities analogous to the "summoners" must not only meet the standards appropriate for a just soul, but they must meet a higher standard. They must be good.

The name for the simplest summoning activity listed in Book VII is the same as that of the highest activity of soul in the model of the city/soul that is completed in Book IV. *Logismos*, "calculation," is the mathematical subject that is Socrates' first example of a summoner. In Book IV, when Socrates first proves that the soul has more than one part (439d), the higher, rational activity of soul is called *logistikos*.[16] Taking this cue, it appears reasonable to understand the psychological activity analogous to the mathematical subject of calculation to be the activity of soul described as *logismos* in Book IV. In Book IV, the logistic activity of soul was to arrange the work of each of the parts of the soul. The best version of this activity, taken on its own, was wisdom; but, understood in its manifestation of the orderliness of the whole soul was justice, itself.

Once again, the model of the soul presented in the first part of the *Republic* is shown to be meaningful and important, albeit incomplete. It is no small task to put together a life of internal psychological harmony in a functioning, thriving soul. It is, in fact, a foundational and indispensable part of the best possible life for a human being. The mathematical subject of calculation takes care to determine what is one and what is

---

[16] λογιστικός.

many. It serves to resolve apparent contradictions in the realm of *eikasia* by developing theories that put them into illuminating, intelligible hypothetical contexts. Likewise, the activity of calculation in the soul looks at each part to see what is appropriate to it. What belongs to each part and what does not; what sorts of activities each part should engage in, and which ones it should leave to others. Like a city with highly skilled and specialized craftsman, the soul that is well regulated by calculation has mastered the division of labor and comparative advantage as well as maximized the overall combination of specializations in the interest of the whole city/soul.

The mathematical (summoning) subject of arithmetical calculation does not seem to represent psychological calculation wholly. Psychological calculation takes all parts of the soul into consideration. The analog to mathematical calculation seems more constrained. Its objects are things that may be one or many, and its work is to straighten out that question in order to resolve apparent contradictions into intelligible theories. This emphasis on the givenness of its objects and the description of the activity of mathematical calculation both suggest the activity of the rational part of the soul *vis a vis* appetite, i.e., the activity of *logismos* vis a vis *epithumia*. On this reading, the summoning subject of mathematical calculation would be analogous to the activity of a just soul bringing appetites into an arrangement conducive to the overall health of a soul and, on the political level, of a political leader bringing the craftsmen of a city into an arrangement conducive to the overall health of a city.

This account still is not quite precise enough, though. We should not be surprised that the images and analogies are complicated and full of important detail in Book VII. There is a reason that the *Republic* is so long and that it contains so many analogous arguments and images. Socrates is inquiring into the most important questions for a person interested in living a good life, and the results of that inquiry are both extremely nuanced and unflinchingly precise. The psychological and political analogs to the activity of mathematical calculation are not the arrangement of appetites, per se, but more precisely the activities of developing the capacity to best arrange appetites. This is an account of philosophical *paideia*. We are still within the Female Drama of the *Republic*. The central concerns of this account continue to be matters of becoming, although the particular ones we have in view right now are dealing with activities whose objects are forms of being. If it is our ambition to live the best sort of life, we must become capable of attending to being. The Good is our ultimate object, and it does not participate in decay or development. It is. The becoming of the soul capable of apprehending being is our current subject. Neither of these may be possible without mediation, but they remain our goals. To summarize, the summoning subject of mathematical calculation presented in Book VII is analogous to the educational activity appropriate to the development of one who is learning to create best possible arrangement of appetites (*epithumia*) in her soul.

With the analogy in place of mathematical calculation to an education in the activity of properly arranging *epithumia* in the city/soul, the path is clear to unpack the psychological implications of the remaining summoning subjects presented in Book VII: plane geometry, solid geometry, and astronomy. It is provocative that the two middle subjects have the same name, geometry[17] and that the second form of geometry (which is the third of the summoning subjects) is said not to exist except in speech. As I have argued above, the description of solid geometry suggests to me that its analogous activity within the city/soul is an education appropriate to becoming a good political leader. It is learning the activity not just of putting given appetites into arrangements amenable to the harmonious functioning of the whole city/soul. It is also learning how to arrange all the parts of the soul together into a functioning, dynamic harmony. That such a science does not seem to exist in the interlocutors' world is additional evidence for this interpretation.

But if solid geometry is analogous to the study required to learn how to be a good ruler, then what would plane geometry represent? Mathematical calculation seems to be related to *epithumia*, and the dialogue has taught us to look next for *thumos* when *epithumia* appears. The analogue to plane geometry is still a bit of a puzzle, though. It is tempting to look for some sort of *thumotic* mistake, both here and in the level of the allegory of the Cave that are second from the bottom, but we are still in the

---

[17] Perhaps this sameness underlines Eva Brann's argument that the interior sections of the Divided Line are a middle term that binds the structure together as an analogy and makes it into a whole. Brann, *The Music of the Republic*, 202.

Female Drama, and we have not yet finished constructing Kallipolis. Plane geometry must represent the education in some activity that can be a part of the best possible human life, but it must also be a limited activity that, if taken on its own, is also limiting.

The Divided Line is useful here, and it opens the way to a helpful interpretation of the allegory of the Cave, as well. The section of the Divided Line that is second to the bottom is *pistis*, trust or belief. It is tempting to think only ill of the realm of the Cave analogous to *pistis* on the Divided Line. Who are these people, anyway, who play a role in casting shadows on the Cave wall? Do they know what they are doing? Do they know that their images constitute the only reality that those below them in the Cave experience? Why would they be party to the imprisonment of those at the bottom of the Cave, if they know? Do they know of the world outside the Cave? If not, why don't they turn around. They are not bound. If so, why do they not go there? There may be more philosophically profound implications of other aspects of the Cave, but this is the most provocative and problematic section of the whole allegory.

The nature of the summoning subjects is important to the attempt to understand the representation of the realm of *pistis* in the Cave. All of the summoning subjects (calculation, plane geometry, solid geometry, and astronomy) are available to prisoners at the bottom of the Cave, that is in the realm of *eikasia*. Other subjects are available at the bottom of the Cave, too, but only subjects with the capacity to summon higher thought can offer those trapped in *eikasia* a glimpse of something higher. Using the imagery of the Cave, we can say that some of the artifacts held before the fire will cast shadows that draw attention to their nature as shadows, while others will not. The most educative shadows can provoke one to think beyond images. And, many images that are not summoners, per se, may be accurate in their own way. There is nothing inherently bad about the shadows on the wall or the artifacts that cast them. They are dangerous first because one can mistake them for reality, and second because if one does not have an external reference point against which to judge them, it can be difficult to adjudicate between truth and falseness. This makes them problematic, but not bad.

Likewise, there is nothing inherently sinister about the figures who are complicit in the creation of these shadows. The allegory does not tell us anything about them, so we should not make too much of the speculative possibilities this framework suggests. But, one could just as easily attribute the best and highest possible intentions to those who cast summoning shadows as one could give an account of the evils of casting shadows that contribute to the complacency of those chained below, and every shade of possibility between these two extremes shares equal fidelity to the image. *Pistis* is the realm of expertise, authority, and power. It can be used for good or ill. It is wrong to trust in *pistis* qua *pistis*, which is why Socrates so often moves his interlocutors away from recounting the speeches and opinions of others. If those views were persuasive, then they should be able to stand on their own independent of the authority of those who presented them.

The rhetoricians or poets or politicians that present any particular set views may have been instrumentally important in articulating and transmitting those ideas, but if the ideas are any good, they do not need to be propped up by their authority. Precisely the same dynamic applies to images as well. The famous critiques of poetry and imagery in the *Republic* are not critiques of poetry or images, really at all. Instead they are critiques of uncritical acceptance of images qua images and poetry qua poetry. Because *eikasia* is our first way of making sense of the world, it is a particularly seductive realm, but Socrates' cautionary tales about the seductiveness of imagery are not critiques, either. They are warnings. All of the above applies to sophistry as well as to religion.

For my reading of the four summoning subjects to work, it is not enough to show that the activity of the realm of *pistis* in the allegory of the Cave is not necessarily bad. In order for the analogy to work as I am proposing it does, plane geometry must be analogous to an education in something integral to the best possible human life, it must be analogous to the philosophical soul's capacity to arrange its appetites (mathematical calculation) and its capacity to organize a whole city well (solid geometry), and it must have something to do with *thumos*. All of these conditions are met if the psychological analog to plane geometry is an education of one's spirit—an extension of the habituation to virtue that contributed to one's capacity to be educated.

The *trophe* of *thumos* is a central topic of Book VI, and it is one of the most vulnerable moments for the would-be philosopher in the Female Drama. The young proto-philosopher is suited by nature to become philosophical. That precondition is met in the account of the *genesis* of *thumos* in Book V, but one cannot provide a proper upbringing to oneself. The young would-be philosopher is as dependent on her family and society as anyone, and she is less likely to get what she needs, and more likely to become corrupt when she does not get it. But the philosophical nature that has (miraculously) had a philosophical upbringing can begin to learn to educate her spirit. She can choose what habits to pursue and which to avoid. She can think about which parts of her spirit are best suited to be allies to her reason and how. Plane geometry suggests the capacity of some *thumotic* images to provoke one to think about the proper role of *thumos*. It represents the education of one seeking to organize one's *thumotic* life as a contributing part of the best possible human life.

So far, calculation, plane geometry, and solid geometry are analogous to the education of *epithumia*, *thumos*, and *logismos*. That, of course, leaves *nous*. The first extended image of noetic activity in the *Republic* is that of the star-gazer/true pilot in the allegory of the Ship of State, so there is something lovely about astronomy serving as a cipher for noetic education. The value of astronomy is not, as Glaucon mistakenly thinks, that it lifts our eyes to the heavens. Socrates' response to Glaucon at the moment is among several instances where Socrates does not allow his interlocutors to persist in a mistaken literalism. Astronomy is meaningful because, like the rest of the summoning subjects, it catches our eye in the visible realm and pulls our thoughts toward the intelligible realm. That dynamic does not set astronomy apart as an image of noetic education, however. Astronomy is different than the other summoners because it is in motion.

Each of the four summoning subjects is related to the next by an extension into additional dimensions. Numbers exist in one dimension, at least for the purposes of this schema. Plane geometry and solid geometry clearly exist in two and three dimensions, respectively. Astronomy adds the fourth dimension, time. What do these dimensions in the visible realm imply for their corollaries in the intelligible realm? My speculative answer is that they represent the relationship between higher and lower forms of apprehending the intelligibility of the way things are and, especially, the composite or cumulative character of those higher forms. We do not leave the point behind when we draw a line, or the line behind when we draw the cube, or the cube behind when we put it into motion.

Likewise, we do not leave behind the stories that we once used to make sense of our experience of the world when we attempt to make sense of the world in terms of experience; we do not leave our experiences behind when we attempt to make sense of the world through theories; and we do not leave our theories behind if and when we have direct insight into the nature of things. Or, at least, I would argue that Socrates would advise us not to. Socrates has once again modeled this lesson as he has taught it. First, he presents the image of the sun as the offspring of the good (one dimension). Then, he introduces the Divided Line (two dimensions). The Cave is first presented in three dimensions and then, when characters begin moving through it, in four.

Now that we have taken a look at the relation of each of the parts of the Cave both to the image of the Divided Line that precedes it and to the account of the four summoning modes of mathematics that follow it, we can put the model into motion and see what philosophical education looks like when we keep all of these elements in mind.

12

Philosophical *Paideia* in Motion

We all begin at the bottom of the Cave. Some of us make it out into the sunlight and, if we are ambitious, we return to the Cave for the continuation of our philosophical education. What this means, both in the context of the *Republic* and to those of us who take it to be a guide to life, is easier pointed to than lived. As I will attempt to show in this chapter, though, one of the essential principles to keep in mind as one attempts to make sense of the philosophical education, shifting epistemological modes, and psychological development embedded in the allegory of the Cave is that the only things we leave behind as we escape the Cave are our mistaken perceptions. Every level of the Cave describes an essential mode of the distinctively human ambition to find intelligibility in our experience.[1] Every part of the Cave not only represents some mode of human knowing that can lead us toward truth and goodness; it represents a mode that we must continue to embrace and employ even as we develop the capacity for higher modes of engagement with reality.[2] The task

---

[1] As Stanley Rosen puts it, "when the escaped prisoner returns to the cave, his purpose is not political, but epistemological." Stanley Rosen, *Plato's* Republic (New Haven: Yale University Press, 2005) 270.

[2] Christopher Dustin and Denise Schaeffer argue that "to know the soul, we must not simply gaze into it, hoping to see what lies inside; we must look at what it loves. When it comes to behold justice, looks matter, not simply in the outward appearance one casts, but in the way in which one sees." They go on to say, "philosophy must proceed, at some level, phenomenologically." I take their reading, which focuses on the story of the Ring of Gyges, rather than the Cave, to be entirely compatible with mine. In order to understand ourselves, we cannot rise to pure reason and float there; we must try to bring all of our psychological activities into view and attempt to find (or make) harmony among them. Chris-

of philosophical *paideia* is freedom from the constraints of the Cave in the sense that the philosopher must know how to traverse it at will; but it is certainly not freedom in the sense of leaving the Cave behind. The task of philosophical *paideia* is not escape. Rather, it is a sort of psychological orienteering.

We begin at the bottom of the Cave with stories and images. Our attachment to these shadows is deep and often unconscious. This is the faith of our fathers, the mores of our culture, the rules of the games we aren't even aware that we are playing. The more precocious the child, the more likely she is to start calling these stories into question and the earlier. As silly as it might sound in the context of a book on Plato's *Republic*, in contemporary American culture, the paradigm case is Santa Claus. Christmas is the default in the United States, and Santa Claus is the default myth of Christmas. One need not be a Christian to celebrate Christmas; one only need not have a family that has religious objections to it, and even American families with religious objections often find ways to lean toward Christmas and Santa. (For example, Hanukah is a very minor Jewish holiday everywhere in the world that Christmas is not the cultural default.) So, most Americans, regardless of religious orientation, are steeped in a rich broth of Christmas mythology every year, and that includes Santa Claus.

One can walk through an American child's developing perceptions of Christmas right up the Divided Line, up and out of the Cave. As I argued in the previous chapter, such a reorientation to one's mythologies can happen in two ways. The first way is when one is confronted with an "objective" truth that appears to be the cause of the mythology, which is tantamount to the moment in the myth when one is released and turned around, i.e., the transition from *eikasia* to *pistis*. Our silly example can help us to see several possibilities for what that moment might or might not mean to an individual who experiences it.

Suppose a child catches her parent "playing Santa Claus." That child's first reaction is likely to be disillusionment, both in Santa Claus and in her parents, whom she now believes have lied to her. Sometime,

---

topher Dustin and Denise Schaeffer, "Looks Matter: Beholding Justice in the *Republic*," *The Review of Politics* 68, no. 3 (Summer 2006): 449–473.

down the line, that same child might come across an account of the meaning of Christmas that includes the mythology of Santa Claus in a theory of the spirit of Christmas giving, for example. This would be a *dianoetic* engagement with the Christmas mythology of her childhood. And, at least if we follow the allegory of the Cave all the way up to the heights that Socrates presents, she might someday have direct, unmediated (i.e. *noetic*) insight into the idea of Christmas, its unchanging, essential shape.

The other course one might take up through would be to develop a theory about the nature of the subject of that mythology before one has direct experience of anything that lies behind it. Since the story of Santa Claus is not perfectly formal, it falls short of mathematics in its capacity to summon the mind from images to theories, but it is not impossible or even improbable for one to move from the story of Santa Claus (*eikasia*) to a theory of Santa Claus (*dianoia*) without having direct experience of some phenomenon (*pistis*) first. In fact, most parents that I know of who have brought their children up with a mythology of Santa Claus hope that this is how things develop for them. The idea is that if one's child has even an emerging sense of the idea of Christmas that motivates the parent to play Santa Claus, then when that child learns that things are not literally as she thought they were, she will also have confirmation on some other level that things were precisely how she thought they were. There may not be a fat man in a red suit coming down her chimney every Christmas Eve, but there is a spirit of joy, generosity, thoughtfulness, and fun that enters the house every year nonetheless.

The point of operationalizing the allegory of the Cave using such a flippant example is to show both that the dynamic of the Cave permeates our everyday experiences and that such experiences are not essentially about putting away childish things. The education represented by the allegory of the Cave demands that we leave behind the illusion that the shadows on the wall are the basic fabric of reality. But, they do not demand that we leave those shadows and images behind. Rather, the task of philosophical *paideia* is to determine what aspects of reality those images reflect and how. We must carry our memory of those images with us as we ascend, and we must return to them eventually if we are to see ourselves whole.[3]

Socrates signals an important transition in the dialogue when he corrects Glaucon's misunderstanding of the power of astronomy at 529a. As the highest of the summoners, astronomy is the last of the mathematical subjects to be discussed. When Socrates reminds Glaucon that the power of astronomy is not that it literally raises our eyes to higher visible objects in the sky, but instead that it catches our eye in the visible realm and raises our mind to an apprehension of ideas in the intellectual realm, Glaucon is ready to leave the visible realm entirely behind and begin a direct inquiry into the intelligible (532d).

Glaucon's request to leave behind the "prelude" and take up the "theme" is remarkable on a few levels. First, it is evidence of his great energy and ambition. Because the *Republic* is so long and so different from other Platonic dialogues, it is easy not to notice what a brilliant interlocutor Glaucon really is. Glaucon is ready to believe that the discussion of the allegory of the Cave and Divided Line is just the prelude to what Socrates has to show him about philosophical *paideia*. They are extremely deep into a long and complicated inquiry, and Glaucon is not only prepared to learn that they have only just begun, he seems to relish the thought. Glaucon is still interested—he is thoroughly engaged and ready for more. But, in an important sense, he seems also to have missed the point. Socrates has been pointing him toward the intelligible realm all along. The account of the power of the summoners to draw our minds toward the intelligible realm was, in itself, a device for drawing our minds toward the intelligible realm. Socrates has constructed the analogy, elaborated on its salient details, and instructed Glaucon in how analogical thinking works. He has led Glaucon as far as he can, and Glaucon must find the rest of the way on his own. Glaucon has reached the mouth of the Cave. He could be dragged up this far, but no one can help his eyes adjust to the brightness of the sunlight.

---

[3] Jacob Howland describes the way the one who has returned to the cave engages life in the shadows as a sort of prophecy. Jacob Howland, *Plato's* Republic*: A Philosophical Odyssey*, (Philadelphia: Paul Dry Books, 2004) 126.

In the process of creating the images that would lead Glaucon toward an analogical understanding of the way the human mind apprehends the intelligibility of the world, Socrates also created a model of how one person can help another develop increasingly clearer apprehensions of reality. He has modeled the nature and power of dialectic, and he makes that explicit now, as well. The explanation of dialectic follows the detailed account of the power of mathematics (522c–530c), the much briefer acknowledgement that music is to hearing what mathematics is to vision (530d–531c), and that both of them have the power to summon one from the world of sense into the world of the mind. But, now, it turns out that dialectic is analogous to them both and, because it is concerned with ideas rather than objects of sense, it is the only one of the three that can genuinely guide the mind to higher and higher activities (533d). This is the activity they have been engaging in throughout the dialogue and that Socrates has been employing most of his life. It is the way to help oneself or anyone else escape their misperceptions of the world and of themselves.

At 532a, Socrates explicitly connects the journey through the Cave to the activity of dialectic:

> Then, Glaucon, isn't this finally the song dialectical discussion sings? The power of sight imitates it, but it is intelligible. We established that sight tries to look at the animals themselves, the stars themselves, and ultimately, at the sun itself. In the same way, whenever someone tries to arrive at the being of each thing itself through reason, that is, by dialectical discussion and without appealing to the help of any sense-perceptions; and when he does not give up until he grasps the being of the Good itself with understanding itself, then, he reaches the end of the intelligible realm, just as the other one [using his eyes] reached the end of the visible one. (532a–b)

Moments of this sort of clarity are not unique in the *Republic*, but they are less frequent than one hopes for when trying to make sense of the interrelationships of all of the dialogue's arguments and images. What the allegory of the Cave represents is a soul's dialectical path from images to ideas through experiences and theories. Teachers can be helpful for a part of this journey, perhaps even necessary. But, there is another part for which a teacher is helpless, useless except for the student's memory of earlier lessons and their analogies to her current concerns.

Dialectic attempts to understand things according to their idea or shape or form, i.e. their *eidos*.[4] *Eristic*, which is often the activity to which dialectic is compared, follows other, less fundamental, threads of inquiry including linguistic analysis. There is nothing wrong, per se, with a focus on language; but, if it substitutes for a focus on the substance of the things in question, it can make much mischief. Because understanding is not the focus of *eristic*, it tends to be the activity of someone who is more interested in coming out ahead in a quarrel than in getting to the bottom of things. And because spirited people are particularly prone to *eristic*, it is a real and constant risk for the inquiry of the *Republic*, but it is also necessary since spirited people are also the best candidates for becoming lovers of wisdom.[5] Socrates seems to be afraid that Adeimantus and Polemarchus are employing *eristic* and, perhaps unintentionally, threatening to undermine the group's dialectical inquiry when, at the beginning of Book V, they insist on a more detailed account of the role of women and children in the city in speech. As I argued earlier, Socrates bends over backwards to keep the inquiry dialectical, and now we may fully see how and why. One must face myriad challenges in one's attempt to ascend through the Cave because one is always operating with partial knowledge and striving toward an unknown end. There is also always the chance that one will be able to trace an apparent contradiction in one of the summoning subjects to an intimation of the realities that exist beyond

---

[4] εἶδος.

[5] Leon Harold Craig describes it like this: "If the worthiest candidates for the Wisdom-Loving life come from the ranks of the War Lovers—if, that is, the most promising recruits for philosophy are a subset of the Timocratic class—or more precisely, a small subset of that misnamed minority of timocrates whose primary motivation is a love *not* of honour but of *victory* (cf. 428e)—then there must be a way to transform their eristical nature into one that is dialectical. For by virtue of their competitive spirit, they are naturally predisposed to treat dialogical arguments as contests with opponents, battles to be won, rather than to regard them as the means whereby partners and allies make common cause against ignorance and error." Leon Harold Craig, *The War Lover* (Toronto: Toronto University Press, 1994) 245.

one's field of vision, and, of course, one hopes one will be lucky enough to be turned around and guided by a knowledgeable teacher. If that happens and how that might happen continues to be a mystery.

Immediately after bringing this discussion of dialectic to a close, Socrates reaches back to an even earlier argument, acting as if he were in the process of closing parentheses that we did not know he had left open. This time, the character traits that will be a prerequisite for philosophical *paideia*, particularly education in dialectic, are at issue. While, in Book III, candidates for the education of the guardians needed to display *thumotic* excellence, now the list of prerequisites includes natural predilections suitable for learning as well as good habits of character. The *genetic* and *trophaic* conditions for philosophical education from Books V and VI have been added to the *genetic*, *trophaic*, and *paideic* conditions for a just education from Books II-IV to create a full account of the necessary conditions and projected outcomes of the best education of the person best suited to be educated. The Male Drama of Books II-IV showed us the *telos* of each of these activities, while the Female Drama of Books V-VII explored the conditions for the possibility of putting that teleology in motion and the development that occurs when those conditions are in place. Now that all of the *genetic*, *trophaic*, and *paideic* conditions have been introduced, and the paths of their teleological development have been traced toward their end, the detour the dialogue took at the beginning of Book V is beginning to loop back into the original course of the conversation.

The final pages of Book VII bring all of the conditions for and ambitions of philosophical education together. Here, finally, Socrates admits that the expansion of the city/soul in Books V–VII requires a few revisions (and not just elaborations) of the model that they constructed in Books II–IV. Mathematical education should be made available to children, not just to old men. It should also be voluntary, not compulsory. With this revision to the earlier model of education, it becomes apparent that Socrates has embarked on a summary of philosophical *paideia* that begins with its dispositional and habitual prerequisites and ends with the retirement of the perfectly educated philosopher-ruler, who, having served his time ruling the city and departed for the Isle of the Blessed, is commemorated by his city as divine. Insofar as the allegory of the Cave serves as the synoptic image of philosophical *paideia*, this is its narrative counterpart, and its arc is complete.

The narrative synopsis of philosophical *paideia* begins with an allusion to the discussion in Book II of the proper disposition of the guardians, which begins at 374e and continues through 376d. The would-be guardian must be like a noble puppy: sharp-eyed, quick, strong, high-spirited, gentle with friends, harsh with enemies, and philosophical (i.e., discerns friends from enemies based on knowledge and ignorance). To this list, Socrates now adds at 535a and following: stability, courage, good looks, love of learning, ease at learning, good memory, persistence, love of hard work, and hatred of voluntary and involuntary lies (i.e., a true love of truth). This latter list of characteristics is almost identical to the list of the philosopher's virtues at the beginning of Book VI (485d). Socrates is merging the accounts of the nature (*physis*) of the philosopher from the Male Drama and the Female Drama to give a complete speech on the *genesis* of the philosopher.

Socrates' mention of the love of truth at 535e signals a transition from a synoptic account of *genesis* to the brief synopsis of the account of philosophical *trophe* at 536a, just as at 485d it signaled the transition from Book V's extended accounts of *genesis* to the introduction of philosophical *trophe* in Book VI. *Trophe* is only mentioned briefly here because there is no need to synthesize two accounts, as there was for *genesis*. Disposition was a part of both the Male and Female Dramas, but *trophe* was first introduced in the Female Drama. The account in Book VI is whole, and Socrates needs only to remind us of its place in the narrative. The would-be philosopher's "formation" will be tested, though, during his education, and *trophe* will once more be a part of the narrative. Because we have, by the end of Book VII, a complete account of the shape of the philosopher's education, there are new and different ways to see whether the proto-philosopher is well-prepared for that education. However, the process of habituation to virtue is not altered in Book VII; it is simply recollected for the synoptic narrative.

The synoptic account of education begins with a reminder of the music and gymnastic curriculum from Book III and, as I argued above, the introduction of dialectic as their capstone. Importantly for this part of the narrative, Socrates specifies that proto-philosophers will be given the opportunity to begin their education as children. The rest of the synopsis, which will take us to the end of Book VII, is organized according to the ideal age for a person to be at each phase of the pursuit of a philosophical life. By saying that education begins in childhood, Socrates signals the beginning of the motion of the account. The synopses of *genesis* and *trophe* set the stage, but this is the play.

Other than telling us that compulsory physical training will take two or three years, the timing of the education before a person turns twenty is indeterminate. We are not told the amount of time that children are taught mathematics and gymnastic by play or how long they spend as observers of war, but we are told that when they are twenty, those who have been most successful will be singled out for honors. They will also reconsider all the subjects that they have learned haphazardly and develop a comprehensive and unified vision of their education. This, we are told, is the best test of one's capacity for *dialectic*. This is an extremely important step, and the proto-philosopher is given ten years to take it, although we are not told much about it here. So, for now, we will move on, but we will come back to it.

At thirty, those who have been most successful at developing a unified vision (i.e., a synopsis) of their education will once again be singled out for honors. They will then be tested to see how successfully their dialectical abilities can move them entirely out of the realm of the visible and into the presence of "what is." This, Socrates tells us, is a dangerous moment. The would-be philosopher has been released from her delusion that conventions are necessary or necessarily good, but she has not yet had a vision of the Good. She is released from all her prior obligations and not yet beholden to anything higher. This is the point at which, if a teacher is not careful, he may create a monster. The most capable and promising person can become the most terrible if she stalls at this point in her education.

As Glaucon and Socrates spell out the dangers of getting stalled at the thirtieth year of one's education, the way that this narrative overlays the Cave and the other images and arguments of the *Republic* begins to become clear. Socrates likens the stalled thirty year old to a "presumptuous child brought up with great wealth, a prominent and powerful family, and many flatterers..." (537e-538a).[6] Although he will add details to this illustration that will alter its meaning in important ways, in its basic form it is the same as the case Socrates presented to Adeimantus in Book VI (494b). Here is a precocious child, one who has all the natural dispositions of a philosopher and all the material benefits of wealth and position. One cannot, without some kind of miraculous intervention, become a philosopher without both of these things: a philosophical *physis* (which implies a proper philosophical *genesis*) and the material conditions necessary for developing them. But, at the same time, it appears to require a miracle for one who has the natural and material conditions for philosophy not to become stalled at this point—not to suffer from the distractions and temptations to dissolution that precisely these same conditions create. The case of the well-disposed, well-situated would-be philosopher is like that of a character in Attic tragedy, the very qualities that make her great are precisely the ones that will bring her to ruin. The Female Drama may well be a tragic cycle.

When Socrates introduced the first case of the great-souled child surrounded by wealth and flatterers, it was to illustrate the challenges and importance of philosophical *trophe*, of habituation to certain virtues necessary for the possibility of becoming educated. Now, the case appears again to illustrate the almost insuperable obstacles to becoming philosophically educated, and it has been altered to include a new and even more powerful temptation. In Book VII, at 537e and following, the precocious, wealthy, flattered child is adopted. And, when she learns that her parents are not truly her own, all of the disposition, training, and education (*genesis*, *trophe*, and *paideia*) that makes it possible for her to create harmony within a soul oriented to the Good also make it likely that she will become a monster. At this moment, she is entirely in touch with her own power and can see clearly that the conventions that have governed her are human constructs, created and perpetuated by people no better, and probably less impressive, than she. What she cannot yet see, or perhaps only see abstractly, is that some of those conventions mirror a higher, better, more choiceworthy reality. All of one's skeptical sensibili-

[6] εἴ τις ὑποβολιμαῖος τραφείη ἐν πολλοῖς μὲν χρήμασι, πολλῷ δὲ καὶ μεγάλῳ γένει καὶ κόλαξι πολλοῖς.

ties are fully formed and have proven successful. The apparent benefits of untethering oneself from one's inchoate sense of the Good are crystal clear. The possibility of pursuing a life lived in the light of the Good is a distant, hazy, unreasonable proposition.[7]

In the thirtieth year of the best possible education of the most fully educable person, all the costs of a philosophical or just life are clear and present while all the benefits are abstract and distant. This is, indeed, a dangerous moment, and it is, according to Socrates' presentation of philosophical *genesis*, *trophe*, and *paideia*, an absolutely inescapable one. This is a test that no one can avoid and only a few will pass. This is, in short, the inescapable danger of philosophical education. It is the risk Socrates takes every time he singles out a great-souled and virtuous young man for dialectic. It is where Alcibiades and Critias apparently dropped out of school. And, because of that, it is among the chief reasons why the historical Socrates was put to death by Athens in 399 BCE. Had Glaucon been able to see the future, he may not have laughed at Socrates' frightened bow to Adrasteia.

In the Divided Line and the allegory of the Cave, this crucial moment in one's education takes place at the central crossroads of the image, the mouth of the Cave. One has been released from the realm of *eikasia*, tramped up through the realm of *pistis*, and one is on the verge of entering the realm of *dianoia* where one's eyes may eventually become able to apprehend things in themselves *noetically*. Even later, it may even be possible for them to look directly at the source of all being: the sun, the Good. But, at this moment, everything below is perfectly clear and everything above is invisible in the washed-out brightness to which one's eyes have not yet adjusted. One can see exactly how the realm of *pistis* works: how to take charge, how to be authoritative, persuasive, and successful. One's own success in that realm is practically guaranteed by one's clear and apparently complete understanding of how it works, and one's experiences do not contain other modes of success. What lies before one is complete mastery of all that one has ever known—almost.

[7] It is provocative that this crisis is triggered by uncovering a lie about one's family relationships, since such lies are built into every version of the city in speech.

One also knows something of the world that exists outside of the Cave, but its promise for one's life is abstract, and it requires one to leave behind the promise of every success that anyone, except perhaps a socially awkward old man who roams the city barefoot, has ever recognized. Is that really the life one wants? Is stepping out into the blinding, painful light really a better choice? Is it really better to be a slave above than rule below? No one who can make it to the mouth of the Cave can avoid these temptations, and it seems almost impossible to think that anyone would resist them. There may be those who never made it to the mouth of the Cave who carry puppets in front of the fire; but those who did and then chose to come back down are the most powerful and the most dangerous.[8] They can see the world of appearances synoptically and they know that there is a world of intelligibility beyond it, but they have chosen to turn their backs on it.

---

[8] Rosen's account of the puppeteers is not sympathetic enough for me. He writes, "It seems fairly clear that the puppet masters are not themselves victims but producers of illusion. If they are themselves real persons and not shadows, they must certainly know that they are deluding the chained prisoners, and since they are not themselves bound, they must be free to explore the entrance to the cave, and so to discover that another world lies outside its confines." All of this is undoubtedly true, but Socrates makes several other things clear about the internal dynamics of the Cave that suggests they might be in a far more problematic predicament. We know that the ascent from their region to the mouth of the Cave is difficult. We know that nothing outside the Cave is visible until one's eyes have adjusted and that the sunlight is painful to a cave-dweller's eyes. We also know that the released prisoner our story of the Cave follows has to be dragged up from the puppeteers' region. All three of these suggest reasons why a puppeteer may never have gone above the spot where he now stands. But, there are also good reasons why one who has gone up and come back down to the region of the puppets might not go down any further. One's eyes are not longer entirely adjusted to the darkness. The bottom-dwellers of the Cave are sure to ridicule you and, most importantly, they are also apt to meet you with violence or even death. Rosen is not wrong to point out that the puppeteers are freer than the bound bottom-dwellers of the Cave, but they are not in a particularly good position to liberate themselves from their situation, either. (Rosen, *Plato's* Republic, 272)

The precaution that Socrates and Glaucon propose to include in their city in speech as a hedge against philosophical students becoming corrupt in their thirtieth year seems to be one of those unlikely and insufficient provisions that sit in the text as placeholders for mystery or contingency. They will be forbidden, we are told, to "taste" dialectic when they are young. This is problematic for many reasons, not the least of which is that the mathematical subjects that are central to the philosophical education of the young naturally lead one toward dialectical thinking. But it is certainly no more unlikely than the noble lie of Book III, the provisions against unintentional incest in Book V, the plan at the end of Book VII to send away everyone in the city who is older than 10 years old, or the marriage number[9] that we learn in Book VIII must be preserved in order for Kallipolis not to devolve into a *timocracy*. The conditions for the possibility of philosophy are fragile, indeed.

If our would-be philosopher can survive this test, lashed to the mast perhaps, then he will give himself solely to dialectical study for five years, devoting his mind to that work with the same intensity he had for physical training when that was his sole focus. And, after those five years of intense dialectical focus, he must be made to go back down into the Cave. The reason given for his return is that one who is being groomed to rule must not be inferior in experience to those whom he is to rule, but this little phrase contains within it a substantial and significant set of challenges that the allegory of the Cave has already displayed for us. It will be important here to unpack the psychological meaning of this part of a philosopher's education and its significance for Kallipolis, the highest possible city/soul, which has almost been brought to completion in Socrates and Glaucon's synopsis.

The ascent up the Divided Line and out of the Cave is intellectual, of course. It may also be political, but Socrates is transparent about the relevance of these images for an individual person's ambitions to be just

[9] While I am inclined to agree with Alan Bloom's interpretation of the marriage number as a sort of joke, Ernest G. McClain has written a remarkable article on the mathematical acoustics that follow from his equations. Alan Bloom, "Interpretive Essay" in *The Republic of Plato* (New York: Basic Books, 1968). Ernest G. McClain, "Musical Marriages in Plato's *Republic*," *Journal of Music Theory*, Vol. 18, No. 2 (Autumn, 1974): 242–272.

and to be philosophical. We begin making sense of our experiences by appealing to images; sometimes we develop tentative theories based on those images, but most of us move next to reliance on authority, convention, and experience. It is inevitable, however, that thoughtful people who defer to others regarding the meaning of their lives will become disillusioned. If one is lucky, one's disillusionment is with the people and perspectives that one has trusted, and not with the idea that one's life really can be intelligible. For those lucky enough to believe life can be intelligible and that it is worth the effort, the next step is to make sense of one's life by appealing to theoretical frameworks and patterns of experience that are neither imagistic nor objects of direct experience or authority. The thirty-five year olds in Kallipolis have made it this far, and now they must go down.

What is the psychological meaning of going back down into the Cave? On the political level, it makes sense that the one who is to lead must experience every part of his city so that he can rule them from a position not only of knowledge, but also of experience and empathy. The same is, I believe, true of the meaning and motivation for the psychological journey down. It is, as I understand it, a journey of integration, of self-knowledge. On the way up, we focus on the world—what we must attend to and what we must bracket in order to understand it well. On the way down, we cover the same ground, but with a focus on ourselves, on the process, and on how each part of us has a distinct and meaningful role in a good, true, and beautiful life. Guided by the insights *nous* drew us up toward, now it is the work of *logismos* to integrate all the parts of oneself into a harmonious whole.

One recognizes the things in themselves that make shadows on the ground outside the Cave because one has become familiar with the shadows and because the basic shapes are the same even as the objects themselves are more detailed and interesting—these are three rather than two-dimensional. But, it is not until one has seen a thing in itself that one can fully understand its shadow. Only then can one understand how the depth of the real three-dimensional object translates into the two-dimensional shadow on the ground and how the movement of the sun changes the way it appears. Using the language of the Divided Line, one does not have a clear *dianoetic* understanding until one has *noetic* insight. What was last in the order of discovery is first in the order of ideas. Going down means taking the first principles one has fought long and hard to apprehend and using them to make sense of every other part of one's experience of the world and one's own self-conception. The first task of *logismos* on one's descent is to revise one's *dianoetic* theories of the way things are with one's newfound *noetic* insight.[10]

The value of "going down" continues back into the depths of the Cave. While one may have thought that she had a complete vision of the interior of the Cave when she reached its mouth on the way up, only one who has made it to *nous*, has come back down through *dianoia*, and used *logismos* to find harmony between the two can begin to see truth in the realm of *pistis*. Which puppets are true to reality and which are misleading? Which puppeteers have the interests of the prisoners in mind, and which seek only to control and manipulate them? Why (not just how) are some puppets and puppeteers more effective than others? Most importantly, why is the life of the puppeteer not at all more choiceworthy than the life of philosophy? None of these questions can be addressed on the way up, and their psychological analogs are both clear and obviously significant. Which of the things that I trusted and deferred to when I was in the realm of *pistis* were helpful and which were not? Why did some forms of authority and experience move me while others did not? In what ways was I blind? In what ways might I have been precocious? What can I do now to protect against falling into old traps, taking well-worn but unpromising paths in my ambition to becoming whole? There is much work for *logismos* to do in the interest of eliminating disagreements (faction) between what one knows through experience (*pistis*), theory (*dianoia*), and insight (*nous*).

The philosopher who has made it down to the fire-lit realm of *pistis* must have struggled to adjust her eyes, but the deepest challenge of *logismos* is to re-inhabit the darkness of the deepest part of the Cave, to

[10] Ronna Burger likens the return of the enlightened former prisoner to the depths of the Cave to Aristotle's turn in Book VII of the *Nicomachean Ethics* from the "heights of *sophia*" to "the territory of human character." This seems precisely right to me. Ronna Burger, *Aristotle's Dialogue with Socrates: On the Meaning of the Nicomachean Ethics* (Chicago: University of Chicago Press, 2008), 132.

reinter the world of *eikasia*.[11] Psychologically, this is the challenge of exposing the foundational myths and images of one's life to the harmonious *noetic*, *dianoetic*, and *pistic* frameworks that one has achieved. It is the last step in the project to incorporate all aspects of one's soul into one's ambition to fit one's intelligence to the intelligibility of the way things are. It is dangerous work because you risk offending those who mean the most to you and have contributed most sincerely and substantially to your development. Those challenges exist at the realm of *pistis*, too, but here at *eikasia*, one must try to dislodge the deepest constituent parts of one's earliest attempts to make sense of the world and see them with a clear eye.

At some point, it becomes absurd to speculate on which part of the psychological process described by the philosopher's journey through the Cave is most difficult. So many of them appear impossibly challenging. But, if one has made it all the way back down to the bottom of the Cave after being sent back down as a thirty-five-year-old, and one has successfully negotiated the myriad challenges down there for fifteen years, Socrates says that one can emerge once more from the Cave. These seasoned fifty year olds will then be compelled to look at the sun, the Good itself. This part of the curriculum seems impossible; but, only after completing it will the philosopher be fit to rule.[12]

---

[11] In a 2015 interview with Bill Kristol, Ronna Burger makes the important point that Socrates portrays himself in the Cave. He is the one at the bottom who appears foolish because his eyes are not adjusted well enough to the darkness to speak subtly about shadows—the one the cave dwellers are apt to execute. But, perhaps he will have time to drag someone up before that happens. Perhaps it will be Glaucon. Ronna Burger, "Ronna Burger on Plato's *Republic*," interview by Bill Kristol, *Great Thinkers*, August 13, 2015, video, 9:43, https://thegreatthinkers.org/plato/multimedia/ronna-burger-on-platos-republic/.

[12] Eva Brann frames Socrates' mysterious attempt to make the impossible seem possible like this: "The *Republic*, however, in which for pedagogical reasons philosophy is allowed to appear as the fulfillable love of wisdom, does not resolve for us this question: Has even one human embodied soul ever been able to withdraw entirely into the noetic realm to move "by means of the *eide* themselves through them and into them"? Has even one soul ever addressed itself in word-less speech to invisible sights? Or is the human limit perhaps reached

Remarkably, Socrates' account assumes that more than one person makes it all the way through the educational process and that a group of philosopher-rulers take turns ruling the city, not because any of them want to, but because they are compelled to. Most of their time will be given to philosophy, we are told. At the end of their lives, they will go to something like heaven, and they will be memorialized in the city either as divine human beings or as divinities, themselves.

The plurality of philosophers who complete their education and their service to the city is implausible on the level of a political reading of the allegory. One can hardly imagine a single individual surviving the trials and temptations of philosophical *paideia*, not to mention a group of them. For an inquiry into the meaning of this aspect of the allegory of the Cave on a psychological level, this emphasis on plurality sends us back to the psychological meaning of the account in Book V of the proper candidates for philosophical education—back to the first moment of the Female Drama. In my account of Book V, I argued that one way of understanding the need to train both men and women to be guardians was to see the psychological need to attend to both the actual and the potential aspects of our character, those ways of orienting our lives that we have acted upon and those we have not. According to my argument, the Female Drama of Books V–VII tends to the conditions for the possibility of living a just (and then philosophical) life, while the Male Drama of Books II–IV focuses on the shape of a fully formed and functional just soul.

Each of the three *kumata* in Book V represents a different form of potentiality. The first *kuma* shows that in order for a person to be capable of philosophical training and education (*trophe* and *paideia*), her appetites (*epithumia*) must, in principle, be containable by her mind and spirit (*thumos* and *logismos/nous*) working together. The second *kuma* shows that it is also a prerequisite for philosophical training and education that one's spirit (*thumos*) must be capable of attaching to the whole of one's soul and not just to some part or parts of it. And, finally, the third *kuma*

when, while reflectively exercising our power of provisional thinking and speaking, whe have a sudden flash of trust in those hypotheses that appear to make the most sense of these activities?" Brann, *The Music of the Republic*, 237.

shows that the mind (*logismos/nous*) must be capable of taking charge of one's life. And, if this last condition is not satisfied, neither of the first two will be possible.

If one pairs each of these forms of potentiality with the modes of actuality described in the account of the city/soul in Book IV, i.e., the Male Drama, then one may see both what each part of the soul must have in potency and in act for justice. But, it is a mistake to think of this in monolithic or simply linear terms. It is a mistake to take the account to be two-dimensional. Each person has many potencies and many actualized activities of soul. For the philosopher, philosophy is the highest and most architectonic principle of organization and its potencies are the most important for those inquiring into the nature of the most just life. However, philosophers and non-philosophers alike are full of multiple potencies and multiple actualities. At the very bottom of the Cave, the philosophically disposed soul is both capable of letting mathematics summon him to dialectic and is, perhaps, actually already an accomplished geometer. At the level of *pistis*, one may be capable of using adept rhetoric to move a promising soul dialectically toward the acknowledgement of higher forms of intelligibility, and one may already have actualized one's capacity to be persuasive. These are just examples. Other possibilities are myriad. Even within the stylized schematic structure of the allegory of the Cave, it is clear that individuals are bundles of potencies and actualities of soul. The journey through the Cave is not from one's only set of potencies to one's only hope for actualization; it is from one's best set of potencies to their highest possible actualization.

What is one to make of the community of those who take turns ruling the city after they have successfully faced every challenge of education and before they receive their heavenly reward? The image, like much of the account of philosophical education, describes an improbable outcome—Socrates has told us that repeatedly since Book V. But, the outcome is not impossible and it is beautiful. On the political level, the community of philosopher-rulers appears to me first and foremost as a projection of the possibility of having philosophical friends. For an individual, on the psychological level, perhaps the community of philosophers is the creation of these friends for oneself in real and imagined conversation. It reminds me of what Nietzsche said, late in life, about his youthful depiction of Schopenhauer in *Schopenhauer as Educator*. There,

Nietzsche says that the Schopenhauer of the essay was not the flesh and blood man who had been in his life, but instead an imaginary version of the teacher that he had needed him to be.[13] The philosopher, one who rules herself and who is only accountable to the Good, may have to befriend herself if she is not to be too lonely.

With the promise that Kallipolis will commemorate its philosopher-ruler(s) as divine, Glaucon sees that Socrates has completed his account. Precisely as Socrates had done in Book II after Glaucon had finished his accounts of the perfectly just man who appeared perfectly unjust and the perfectly unjust man who appeared perfectly just, Glaucon commends Socrates for producing beautiful statues. Glaucon's jibe would be tragic if there were not a few more books of the *Republic* to go, since in Book II Socrates seemed to be suggesting that it was not possible for the reality and appearance of justice (and injustice) to be perfectly divorced in the way that Glaucon proposed. If Glaucon is implying the same thing about Socrates' account, it suggests that he is under the impression that the philosophical life is not possible. One cannot really blame him for being skeptical, if he is, but it is terribly disappointing and dangerous since Socrates seems to have brought Glaucon up to the mouth of the Cave. This is Glaucon's crucial moment, and he may not be taking a good turn.[14]

---

[13] Friedrich Nietzsche, *Ecce Homo*, in *The Anti-Christ, Ecce Homo, Twilight of the Idols, and Other Writings*, trans. Judith Norman, ed. Aaron Ridley (Cambridge: Cambridge University Press, 2005).

[14] Another way of looking at this moment in the dialogue in relation to the discussion of Glaucon's statues in Book II is to note that the just life, as Socrates describes it, has consequences and these consequences are offered as reasons for recommending the hard work of trying to live a just (and, perhaps, philosophical) life. So, really, Socrates has not banished all the consequences and appearances of justice from his defense of justice—just some of them. The actual appearances and consequences that follow from one's devotion to justice (rather than those apparent consequences and appearances of justice that one might be tempted to pursue instead of justice) are still in the frame, and legitimately so. If Glaucon thinks Socrates has polished up another set of statues, it may be because he has not (yet?) seen the real benefits of justice that Socrates presents. For a careful analysis of the sorts of appearances of justice that do and do not persist

Socrates' response to Glaucon's characterization of his account as a statue is provocative, though. Instead of responding to the image, Socrates reminds Glaucon that they have not only been speaking of men, but of women as well. If I am right to think that women have something to do with potency on the psychological level, then this might be Socrates putting his proverbial foot in the door before Glaucon slams it shut. Or, perhaps truer to the allegory, Socrates grabbing his cloak as they stand at the mouth of the Cave looking out, before he turns around to return to the realm of *pistis.* It may mean something like this: "there is an as-yet unactualized part of you, Glaucon, that is capable of seeing the Good and envisioning a life lived in deference only to it. Even though that part of you has not yet been actualized, even though it has not yet taken charge, it is there in potency, and I am not finished with my attempt to drag you up to the light. There may not be a male philosopher ruler taking charge of your soul right now, but there is a female philosopher ruler at the ready, and I'm putting my hope in her." Or, to rephrase it one more time, and to be a bit less figurative, Socrates seems to be saying to Glaucon: "your soul has another ruler right now, but there is a part of it that is better fit to rule. It is well-disposed, well-trained, and partially well-educated. Turn with me toward the bright, hard world and away from what is easy and familiar. Believe that part of yourself that is telling you it will be worth it. She is telling the truth."

---

in Socrates' account of justice in the *Republic*, see Robert Heinaman, "Plato's Division of Goods in the *Republic*," *Phronesis* 47, no. 4 (2002): 309–335.

Conclusion

As Book VIII of the *Republic* opens, Socrates picks up right where he left off at the end of Book IV.[1] The detour of the Female Drama has come to an end, and we can see it whole. It began in Book V with the three *kumata*, which surveyed the origins of the just soul, its *genesis*. The discussion of the third *kuma* extended into Book VI where the emphasis shifted to the formation of habits (trophe) necessary for philosophical education (*paideia*). Only those who had origins promising for philosophy (*genesis*), could be brought up (*trophe*) with proper philosophical habits. Book VII takes us to the next highly unlikely case of someone who has a well formed philosophical *physis*, both in terms of her *genesis* and *trophe*, and outlines what a proper philosophical *paideia* would look like for that perfectly educable person.

In this book, I have tried to present the Female Drama in Books V–VII as the story of the becoming of justice. I have also tried to show how Socrates turns the story of the becoming of justice into the story of the possibility of philosophy. In Books V–VII of the *Republic*, as Socrates turns the conversation to the conditions for the possibility of justice, he also turns to an image of the complete fulfilment of those conditions: the highest, most complete way of being human, Philosophy. The Female Drama is prompted by a consideration of the possibility of the just city/soul of Book IV and it develops naturally into an inquiry into the highest teleological actualization of those conditions in Kallipolis.

The focus of the book has been on giving a psychological reading of Books V–VII. That is, I have attempted to show how each step in the inquiry into the political arrangements for Kallipolis may be read as an inquiry into the shape of an individual life, specifically the origins, habits, and education of an individual who is potentially a philosopher and a

---

[1] If Books V–VII are something like a tragic cycle, perhaps the dissolution of Kallipolis in Books VIII and IX is something like a Satyr Play, but this is a question for another time.

philosopher-ruler. The city continues to undergo revision during Books V–VII, most significantly by playing out the implications of needing a philosopher to rule. My focus on the meaning of Books V–VII for psychology does not imply that the political arguments are not to be taken seriously, or even literally. However, the relationship of the political arguments to the psychological arguments of Books V–VII do pose some serious challenges to interpretation.

In order for any of the political proposals of Books V–VII to be instantiated in a city populated by human beings, a philosopher must rule. In order for a philosopher to rule, a philosopher must exist, as must a city willing to be ruled by her. In an important sense, Books V–VII are a meditation on what it would take to meet these conditions, that is, to have a philosopher ready to rule and a city ready to be ruled by a philosopher. But, the analogy turns into a fractal-like structure of a micro argument nested within a macro argument of the same shape. The city is analogous to the soul, and the city ruled by a philosopher is analogous to the person whose life is ruled by its best and highest self. Life in the best city, Kallipolis, is analogous to the life of an individual philosopher, and, since Kallipolis must be ruled by a philosopher, the structure of Kallipolis mirrors the soul of its ruler.

It is right, I think, to say that Socrates wants to convince Glaucon to turn his attention inward, to become a philosopher. Thus, it follows that I think the psychological argument of the *Republic* should take precedence to the political argument. The political argument is serious, but the *Republic* does not contain a set of policy recommendations for any city that is not ruled by a philosopher. In fact, Socrates goes to great lengths to warn of the disastrous consequences of trying to instantiate the political ideas of the *Republic* under less than ideal circumstances or in the hands of unphilosophical power. This points to several reasons I believe my attempt to do a close reading of the psychology of the middle books of the *Republic* is important for Plato scholarship and for those in the contemporary world who take Plato seriously as a guide for life.

First, Socrates in the *Republic* is not a lover of tyranny or an advocate for any form of proto-fascism. Perhaps this is not a point worth a great deal of time, since it is so clear, but old mistaken ideas die hard, and I am constantly encountering well-informed, well-educated people who continue to think that Karl Popper's critique of Plato [2] and those like it have merit. Such readings neglect, first, all the conditionals that Socrates puts on his account of philosophical rule and, secondly, the precedence of the psychological argument. No one knows better than Plato the dangers of hegemony. He lived through the Peloponnesian War, the rule and overthrow of the Thirty Tyrants, and the execution of his teacher. His dialogues are filled with warnings about how tyranny and injustice ascend and with meditations on how justice may be nurtured and preserved both within oneself and in the world.

But, secondly, it is important to note that Socrates is not a lover of democracy. Part of the trouble with arguing against those who read totalitarian leanings into Plato's writings is that Socrates is such a clear critic of the regime some imagine to be most appropriately opposed to totalitarianism in the ancient world, Athenian democracy. It is extremely easy to fall into a false dilemma, but it is clearly not the case that giving a critique of democracy is tantamount to advocating for totalitarianism. Socrates was a critic of all extant regimes, as he explicitly admits to Adeimantus in Book VI. *No* regime that exists in Plato's world could provide the proper *trophe* for a philosopher. It is true that the speculative regime that could provide a proper *trophe* and *paideia* for a philosopher is ruled by one or a few men, but the whole scheme falls apart if those rulers are not philosophers. The third *kuma*, philosophical rule, is a prerequisite for the other two; and the three *kumata*, collectively, are the conditions for the possibility of every proposal that follows in Books VI and VII.

My third point goes out a little farther on an interpretive limb. If we look at the conditions for the possibility of a philosopher coming into maturity that are presented in such detail in Books V–VII, many of them focus on his capacity to become self-directed and self-governing. He must have the opportunity to seek the truth. All of his virtues are elaborations on this inclination and his attempt to honor the truth. He must also be able to practice those virtues. As Aristotle will later make explicit, external goods like leisure and wealth are necessary conditions for the

[2] Karl Popper, *The Open Society and Its Enemies* (Princeton: Princeton University Press, 2013).

possibility of any individual to pursue and develop virtue. By implication, if the conditions for philosophical rule cannot be met, but if one wants to foster philosophical development both for the sake of the individual with a philosophical nature and for the city that one may one day be in a position to rule, the regime recommended by Socrates must be one that supports individual self-direction. If one were to escape the categories of ancient politics and consider the conditions for the possibility of cultivating philosophy in the contemporary world, one might end up with a metanormative argument for Libertarianism like the one Douglas Den Uyl and Douglas Rassmussen have developed or an argument like Martha Nussbaum's for developing capabilities.[3] The transition from ancient to contemporary politics leaves a great deal of room for argument, but it is clear that neither the tyrannical nor the democratic regimes Socrates presents can support philosophy.

This leads to my fourth point about the importance and relevance of this psychological reading of *Republic* Books V–VII both for contemporary scholars and for those who look to Plato for wisdom for their lives. While there are myriad ways that the political and psychological models presented in the model of the city/soul that develop in the *Republic* mirror each other, they are not precisely the same. In one important sense, the political and individual models could not be more different: the status of the individual within the city and the status of a part of the soul within an individual. This difference is especially important and particularly confusing because it touches on a principle that emerges in the first moments of the construction of the city in speech in Book II and continues to be explicitly invoked throughout the *Republic*, at least into Book IX.

One of the first principles that Socrates introduces for the construction of the city in speech is that their inquiry is seeking those provisions that create happiness for the whole of the city, not necessarily for any of the parts. The happiness of the guardians is not the goal of the education

[3] Douglas B. Rassmussen and Douglas J. Den Uyl, *Norms of Liberty: A Perfectionist Basis for Non-Perfectionist Politics* (University Park: Penn State University Press, 2005); Martha C. Nussbaum, *Creating Capabilities: The Human Development Approach* (Cambridge: Belknap Press of Harvard University Press, 2011).

of the guardians; the happiness of the city is. This is deeply problematic on the literal, political level. It is perhaps the most difficult part of the Platonic argument to face if one thinks, as I do, that Plato understood some version of what we now call individual liberty to be a condition for the possibility of philosophical development.[4]

On the psychological level, however, subordinating the separate good of a part of my soul is no problem at all. My *thumos* does not have dignity in itself, no matter how often it might want me to believe it does. Neither do my appetites (*epithumia*) or even my calculating and insightful modes of mind (*logismos* and *nous*). Each of these parts of myself exists as modes of me and it neither does me or them any good to treat them individually. In fact, throughout the *Republic*, they are presented linguistically as adjectives rather than nouns. It is a thoroughly conventional construction in Greek to imply the object of an adjective, so I do not want to make too much of this philological point, but it opens to door to thinking of each of these "parts" of the soul as "activities" instead. What looks like a tyrannical neglect of individual liberty in the city, appears on the psychological reading as obvious good sense.

What does one do on the political level of the argument with the principle of subordinating the interests of the part entirely to the whole? First, one acknowledges two of the ideas mentioned just above. The psychological argument takes precedence over the political argument in the *Republic*, and fidelity to the one may create some distortion in the other. Socrates admits no extant regime is conducive to the training and education of a philosopher. What follows, I think, is that we must consider the political model presented in the *Republic* in the context of the constraints on it that are also presented in the *Republic*. Citizens must submit themselves to their political regime and seek the Good of the whole political community (i.e., must consider the happiness of the whole and not of themselves, as parts of that whole). But, insofar as a city or its leaders act in ways that do not serve the Good of the whole, one must weigh one's duty to the city against one's devotion to the Good. And, since there is

[4] Socrates would not call it "liberty," of course, but his independence from convention and freedom from the fear of death are exactly the sorts of things that will later be associated with individual liberty (and responsibility).

no city in which political leaders are currently oriented to the Good (i.e. are philosophers), every philosophical citizen of every city will face this problem. Obviously, this conundrum appears all over the Platonic corpus, but allusions to it run through the *Republic* like an Ariadne's thread. The central principle that guides Socrates' response in other dialogues is also central here—there is something higher the justice.

Politics aside, the real power and relevance of the *Republic*, for me, is always psychological. This leads me to my fifth point. Contemporary science (and even ancient science) shows that human beings have no parts that correspond to the categories of soul presented in the *Republic*. But, whether it is because Plato was prescient, overwhelmingly influential, or both, the activities of soul that he describes in the *Republic* are the most powerful schemata for self-understanding that I have ever encountered, and, of course, I am far from alone. Contemporary psychology and neuroscience, despite the substantial differences in framework and methodology, rarely escape the Platonic categories of human psychology completely. We have appetites that can be contained, not trained. We have a spirited part that can either befriend reason or not. Individuals display a broad range of capacities to regulate their spirits and their appetites, and those who are better at such self-management seem more likely to succeed in life. (See, for example, the famous marshmallow test.[5]) Many of us organize our lives in reference to something that we perceive to be beyond us, and we seek to create an internal order that honors our apprehension of that externality.

There are a thousand theories about how these dynamics operate and what they mean, and each of them attempts to make sense of some version of these same distinctively human activities. Even the most dyed-in-the-wool contemporary behaviorist, who appeals only to descriptive accounts of natural selection to explain the "noblest" activities of the human spirit, constructs her theories in order to explain something like the dynamics Plato describes in the *Republic*. This is why it would benefit us

[5] Walter Mischel and Ebbe B. Ebbesen, "Attention in Delay of Gratification" *Journal of Personality and Social Psychology* 16, no. 2 (October 1970): 329–337.

all, I believe, to return to the *locus classicus* of these apparently inescapable ideas about the human condition.

Even more personally, these are the ideas that help me live my life. I fail every day, but I hope to be as clear-eyed as I can be about the world illuminated by the Good. Although I don't begin to aspire to look right at it, I do aspire to learn of it by implication and attempt to create images of it within my own life. It is not just the ideas that orient me—it is Plato's book, as well. One of the greatest ironies in the history of philosophy is that Plato has the reputation for propounding a monolithic theory that undervalues individuality, when, in fact, no philosopher ever wrote in a style so sensitive to individuality or diversity. I aspire to see those I meet in my life as they are, as Plato's Socrates does, to talk to them about the most important things, to be honest with them and with myself, always to hope that our conversations can make us better, and that in becoming better we come closer to each other, as well.

Bibliography

Aeschylus. *Oresteia.* Translated by Christopher Collard. Oxford World Classics. Oxford: Oxford University Press, 2002.

Ahbel-Rappe, Sara. "Is Socratic Ethics Egoistic." *Classical Philology* 107, no. 4. (October 2012): 319–340.

Allen, Danielle S. "Envisaging the Body of the Condemned: The Power of Platonic Symbols." *Classical Philology* 95, no. 2 (2000): 133–150.

———. "Platonic Quandaries: Recent Scholarship on Plato." *Annual Review of Political Science* 9 (June 2006): 127–141.

———. *Why Plato Wrote.* Malden: Blackwell Publishing, 2013.

Altman, William H. F. *Plato the Teacher: The Crisis of the* Republic. Lanham: Lexington Books, 2012.

Andrew, Edward. "Descent to the Cave." *Review of Politics* 45, no. 4, (1983).

Annas, Julia. *An Introduction to Plato's* Republic. Oxford: Oxford UP, 1981.

———. *Platonic Ethics Old and New.* Ithaca: Cornell UP, 1999.

———. "Plato's *Republic* and Feminism." *Philosophy* 51 [, no. #] (1976).

Araujo, Carolina. "Philosopher-kings: A Communitarian Project," in *Essays on Images from Western Greece*, edited by Heather L. Reid and Davide Tanasi (Fonte Aretusa: Parnassos Press, 2016).

Arruzza, Cinzia. "The Private and the Common in Plato's *Republic.*" *History of Political Thought*, 32, no. 2: 215–233.

Benardete, Seth. *Herodotean Inquiries.* The Hague: Martinus Nijhoff, 1969.

———. *The Rhetoric of Morality and Philosophy.* Chicago: University of Chicago Press, 1991.

———. *Socrates' Second Sailing.* Chicago: University of Chicago, 1984.

Blair, Elana Duverges. *Plato's Dialectic on Woman.* London: Routledge, 2012.

Blitz, Mark. *Plato's Political Philosophy.* Baltimore: John Hopkins UP, 2010.

Blondell, Ruby. *The Play of Character in Plato's Dialogues.* Cambridge: Cambridge UP, 2002.

Bloom, Allan, "Interpretive Essay" in *Plato's Republic* (New York: Basic Books, 1968).————. "Response to Hall." *Political Theory* 5 no. 3, (1977).

Blössner, Norbert , "The City-Soul Analogy," trans. G. R. F. Ferrari in *The Cambridge Companion to Plato's* Republic. Cambridge: Cambridge UP, 2007.

Bourgault, Sophie. "Music and Pedagogy in the Platonic City." *The Journal of Aesthetic Education* 46, no 1 (Spring 2012): 59–72.

Boys-Stones, George. "Phaedo of Elis and Plato on the Soul." *Phronesis* 49, no. 1 (2004): 1–23
Brann, Eva. *The Music of the Republic*. Philadelphia: Paul Dry, 2004.
Bremmer, Jan. *The Early Greek Concept of the Soul*. Princeton: Princeton UP, 1987.
Bulmer-Thomas, Ivor. "Plato's Astronomy." *The Classical Quarterly*, 34, no. 1 (1984): 107–112.
Burger, Ronna. *Aristotle's Dialogue with Socrates*. Chicago: University of Chicago Press, 2008.
———. "The Thumotic Soul." *Epoche* 7, no. 2 (Spring 2003): 151–167.
Burkert, Walter. *Structure and History in Greek Mythology and Ritual*. Berkeley: University of California Press, 1979.
———. *Greek Religion*. Cambridge: Harvard University Press, 1985.
Burnyeat, M. F. "The Presidential Address: The Truth of Tripartition." *Proceedings of the Aristotelian Society* 106 (2006): 1-23.
Byrd, Miriam. "The Summoner Approach: A New Model of Plato Interpretation." *Journal of the History of Philosophy* 45, no. 3 (July 2007).
Miriam Byrd, "The Summoner Approach: A New Model of Plato Interpretation. *Journal of the History of Philosophy* 45, no. 3 (July 2007): 365–381.
Clay, Diskin. *Platonic Questions: Dialogues with the Silent Philosopher*. University Park: Pennsylvania State University Press, 2000.
Coles, Andrew. "Biomedical Models of Reproduction in the Fifth Century BC and Aristotle's "Generation of Animals." *Phronesis* 40, no. 1 (1995): 48–88.
Cooper, John M. *Reason and Emotion*. Princeton: Princeton UP, 1999.
Cooper, Laurence D. "Beyond the Tripartite Soul: The Dynamic Psychology of the *Republic*." *Review of Politics* 63, no. 2 (Spring 2001): 341–372.
Craig, Leon Harold. 1996. *The War Lover: A Study of Plato's* Republic. Toronto: University of Toronto Press, 1996.
Dorter, Kenneth. "The Divided Line and the Structure of Plato's "Republic"." *History of Philosophy Quarterly* 21, no. 1 (2004): 1–20.
Dustin, Christopher and Denise Schaeffer, "Looks Matter: Beholding Justice in the *Republic*," *The Review of Politics* 68, no. 3 (Summer 2006): 449–473.
Eliade, Mircea. *A History of Religious Ideas* vol. 1. Chicago: University of Chicago Press, 1978.
Erginel, Mehmet M. "Plato on the Psychology of Pleasure and Pain." *Phoenix* 65, no. 3/4 (Fall/Winter 2011): 288–314.
Fendt, Gene. "Wave and Trough: The Natural Relation of the Sexes in 'Republic.'" *Review Journal of Political Philosophy* 7, no. 2 (January 1, 2009): 51–82.
Ferrari, G. R. F. *City and Soul in Plato's* Republic. Chicago: University of Chicago Press, 2005.
———. "Williams and the City-Soul Analogy (Plato, *Republic* 435e and 544d)." *Ancient Philosophy* 29 (2009): 407–13.

Frank, Jill. "Wages of War: On Judgment in Plato's *Republic*." *Political Theory* 35, no. 4 (Aug. 2007): 443–467.

Gardner, Catherine. "The Remnants of the Family: The Role of Women and Eugenics in *Republic* V." *History of Philosophy Quarterly* 17, no. 3 (July, 2000): 217–35.

Gavrielides, Era. "What is Wrong with Degenerate Souls in the *Republic*?" *Phronesis* 55, no. 3. (2010): 203–227.

Hall, Robert. "Psyche as Differentiated Unity in the Philosophy of Plato." *Phronesis* 8 (1963).

Heinaman, Robert. "Plato's Division of Goods in the *Republic*." *Phronesis* 47, no. 4 (2002): 309–335.

———. "Why Justice Does Not Pay in Plato's *Republic*." *The Classical Quarterly, New Series* 54, no. 2 (December 2004): 379–393.

Hildebrandt, *Platon: Logos Und Mythos*. De Gruyter, 1959.

Howland, Jacob. *The* Republic*: The Odyssey of Philosophy*. Philadelphia: Paul Dry, 2004.

Hyland, Drew A. "Plato's Three Waves and the Question of Utopia." *Interpretation* 18 (1990): 91–109.

Irwin, Terrence. *Plato's Moral Theory*. Oxford: Clarendon Press, 1977.

Kahn, Charles H. *Plato and the Socratic Dialogue: The Philosophical Use of a Literary Form*. Cambridge: Cambridge UP, 1996.

Klein, Jacob. *A Commentary on Plato's* Meno. Chapel Hill: University of North Carolina Press, 1965.

Kass, Leon and Amy Kass. *The Hungry Soul*. Chicago: University of Chicago Press, 1999.

Katz, Marilyn. "Ideology and 'The Status of Women' in Ancient Greece." *History and Theory* 31 (4):78 (1992): page #s.]

Klein, Jacob. *A Commentary of Plato's* Meno. Chicago: University of Chicago Press, 1965.

_____. *Greek Mathematical Thought and the Origin of Algebra*. Cambridge: MIT Press, 1968.

Kraut, Richard. *Aristotle: Political Philosophy*. Oxford: Oxford UP, 2002.

Lampert, Laurence. *How Philosophy Became Socratic: A Study of Plato's* Protagoras Charmides, *and* Republic. Chicago: University of Chicago Press, 2010.

Lewis, Eric. "The Stoics on Identity and Individuation," *Phronesis* 40, no. 1 (1995): 89–108.

Lewis, V. Bradley. "Politeia kai Nomoi: On the Coherence of Plato's Political Philosophy," *Polity*, 31, no. 2 (Winter 1998): 331–349.

Liebert, Rana Saadi. "Pity and Disgust in Plato's *Republic*: The Case of Leontius." *Classical Philology* 108, no 3 (July 2013): 179–201.

Ludlam, Ivor. *Plato's* Republic *as a Philosophical Drama on Being Well*. Lanham, MD: Lexington Books, 2014.

Malabou, Catherine. "Odysseus's Changed Soul: A Contemporary Reading of the Myth of Er" in *Contemporary Encounters with Ancient Metaphysics*. Edinburgh University Press, 2017. [Is this an edited anthology or are you citing a chapter from a book by Malabou?]

McClain, Ernest G. "Musical Marriages in Plato's *Republic*," *Journal of Music Theory* 18, no. 2 (Autumn 1974): 242–272.

McKeen, Catherine. "Why Women Must Guard and Rule in Plato's 'Kallipolis.'" *Pacific Philosophical Quarterly* 87, no. 4 (December 2006): 527–48.

Mischel, Walter and Ebbe B. Ebbesen "Attention in delay of gratification." *Journal of Personality and Social Psychology* 16, no. 2 (1970): 329–337.

Moore, Leighton. "Laughing at Logoi: Laughter, Persuasion, and Glaucon's Courage," *Interpretation* 26, no. 3 (1999).

Morris, Michael. "Akrasia in the '*Protagoras*' and '*Republic*.'" *Phronesis* 5, no. 3 (2006): 195–229.

Moss, Jessica. 2006 "Pleasure and Illusion in Plato." *Philosophy and Phenomenological Research* 72, no. 3 (May 2006): 503–535.

Nails, Debra. "Plato's *Republic* in its Athenian Context." *History of Political Thought* 33, no. 1 (Spring 2012).

———. *The People of Plato: A Prosopography of Plato and other Socratics* (Indianiapolis: Hackett, 2002).

Newell, Waller R. *Ruling Passion: The Erotics of Statecraft in Platonic Political Philosophy*. Lanham, MD: Roman & Littlefield, 2000.

Nicholls, Mary P. *Socrates and the Political Community: An Ancient Debate*. Albany: State University of New York Press, 1983.

Nichols, Mary P. 1984. "The *Republic*'s Two Alternatives: Philosopher Kings and Socrates." *Political Theory* 12:252-74. *Theory* vol., no: 252–274.

Nichols, Mary P. *Citizens and Statesmen: A Study of Aristotle's* Politics. Savage: Rowman and Littlefield, 1992.

Nussbaum, Martha C. *The Fragility of Goodness*. Cambridge: Cambridge UP, 1983.

_____. *Creating Capabilities: The Human Development Approach* (Cambridge: Belknap Press of Harvard University Press, 2011).

O'Meara, Dominic. *Platonopolis*. Oxford: Oxford University Press, 2005.

Pangle, Thomas L. "The Political Psychology of Religion in Plato's *Laws*." *American Political Science Review* 70, no. 4 (December 1976).

Page, Carl. "The Unjust Treatment of Polemarchus." *History of Philosophy Quarterly*, 1990.

Patterson, Richard. "Philosophos Agonistes: Imagery and Moral Psychology in Plato's *Republic*." *Journal of the History of Philosophy* 35, no. 3 (July 1997): 327–354.

Piaget, Jean, *The Child's Conception of the World*. London: Routledge and Kegan Paul, 1928.

Plato. *The* Republic *of Plato*. Translated by Allan Bloom. New York: Basic Books, 1991.

Popper, Karl R. *The Open Society and Its Enemies vol. 1: The Spell of Plato*. London: Routledge, 1945.

Press, Gerald. "The State of the Question in the Study of Plato." *The Southern Journal of Philosophy* 34 (1996): 507–532.

Roochnik, David. *Beautiful City: The Dialectical Character of Plato's* Republic. Ithaca: Cornell UP, 2003.

Rosen, Stanley. *Hermeneutics and Politics*. New York: Oxford UP, 1989.

———. *The Quarrel Between Philosophy and Poetry*. New York: Routledge, 1993.

———. *Plato's* Republic*: A Study*. New Haven: Yale University Press, 2005.

———. *Platonic Productions*. South Bend: St. Augustine Press, 2014.

Rowe, Christopher. *Plato and the Art of Philosophical Writing*. Cambridge: Cambridge UP, 2007.

Russell, Bertrand. *The Impact of Science on Society*. Matchette Foundation Lectures, Number III. Delivered at Columbia University, 1950. New York: Columbia University Press, 1951.

Sachs, David. "A Fallacy in Plato's *Republic*." In *Plato II*, edited by G. Vlastos. Indiana: University of Notre Dame Press, 1978.

Salkever, Stephen G. "Aristotle's Social Science." *Political Theory* 9, no. 4 (November 1981): 479–508.

Santas, Gerasimos. "Plato on Goodness and Rationality." *Revue international de philosophie* 40 (1986).

Saxonhouse, Arlene W. "Comedy in the Callipolis." *American Political Science Review* 72, no. 3 (September 1978).

Saxonhouse, Arlene W. "Democracy, Equality, and Eidê: A Radical View from Book 8 of Plato's *Republic*." *The American Political Science Review* 92, no. 2 (June 1998): 273–283.

———. *Women in the History of Political Thought: Ancient Greece to Machiavelli*. Westport CT: Praeger Publishers, 1985.

Schofield, Malcolm. *Plato*. New York: Oxford UP, 2006.

Scott, Dominic. "Plato's Critique of the Democratic Character" *Phronesis* 45, no. 1 (February 2000): 19–37.

Segal, Charles. 1978. "The Myth Was Saved: Reflections on Homer and Mythology of Plato's *Republic*." *Hermes* 106: 315-36. (1978).

Slings, S. R., ed. *Platonis Republicam*. Oxford: Oxford UP, 2003.

Smith, Nicholas. "Images, Education, and Paradox in Plato's *Republic*," *Apeiron: A Journal for Ancient Philosophy and Science*, 32, no. 4 (December 1999): 125–141.

———. "Plato's Book of Images." In *Philosophy in Dialogue: Plato's Many Devices*, ed. Gary Alan Scott (Evanston: Northwestern University Press, 2007), 3–14.

Stalley, R. F. "Aristotle's Criticism of Plato's *Republic*." In *A Companion to Aristotle's Politics*, ed. D. Keyt and F. D. Miller, Jr. Oxford: Basil Blackwell, 1991.

Strauss, Leo. *The City and Man*. Chicago: The University of Chicago Press, 1978.

Townsend, Mary. *The Woman Question in Plato's* Republic. New York: Lexington Books, 2017.

Trabattoni, Franco, "What Role do the Mathematical Sciences Play in the Metaphor of the Line?" in *Essays on Plato's Epistemology* (Leuven: Leuven University Press, 2016), 167–188.

G. Vlastos, ed. *Plato II*. Indiana: University of Notre Dame Press, 1978.

Voegelin, Eric. *Order and History, Volume III: Plato and Aristotle*. Baton Rouge: Louisiana State Press, 1957.

Wilburn, Joshua. "Is Appettite Ever "Persuaded"?: An Alternative Reading of *Republic* 554c–d." *History of Philosophy Quarterly* 31, no. 3 ([Month/Season]2014)[: page #s].

Williams, Bernard. "The Analogy of City and Soul in Plato's *Republic*." *Exegesis and Arguments I, Phronesis* supplement (1973): 196–206.

Wolfsdorf, David. "Plato's Conception of Knowledge." *The Classical World*, 105, no. 1 (Fall 2011): 57–75.

Woolf, Ralph. "Truth as Value in Plato's *Republic*." *Phronesis* 54, no. 1 (2009): 9–39.

Zovko, Marie-Elise. "Of Caves, Lines, and Sea Travels: Plato's Syracusan Voyages and the Central Analogies of the *Republic*," in *Politics and Performance in Western Greece*, edited by Heather L. Reid, Davide Tanasi, and Susi Kimbell. Fonte Aretusa: Parnossos Press, 2017.

Zuckert, Catherine H. *Plato's Philosophers: The Coherence of the Dialogues*. Chicago: University of Chicago Press, 2009.

Acknowledgments

Depending on how you do the math, I have either been working on this book for two years, eight years, or my whole life; so deciding whom to thank is a bit tricky. Please bear with me.

I was first drawn to Plato in my undergraduate History of Ancient Philosophy seminar. It was the second time I had read the *Republic.* Because I was in Mercer's Great Books program. I read it first with Diana Stege, but I didn't like it very much the first time through. (Sorry, Diana.) I still have my first copy of Bloom's translation, and the margins are filled with my adolescent protests against everything I found offensive. Tom Trimble taught the Philosophy class where I turned toward the book, and Leighton Moore, Ben Brooks, and Ron Light were among the students that raged and wondered with me. Tom's charisma and our friendships had everything to do with why I found my way into philosophy.

I learned to love the *Republic* in Carl Page's graduate seminar at Emory. I was finished with course work when he taught it, and I had funding to spend the semester in Washington DC attending an NEH seminar at the Folger Institute and getting a solid start on my dissertation. I lived with my cousins in Alexandria, Virginia, Pris and Al Bornmann, and used my funding to fly home every two weeks to attend Carl's *Republic* seminar. I suppose that story suggests that I must already have loved the *Republic*, but I think I just loved Carl; he brought me into the *Republic.* Dan Harrell, Jennifer Rust Murray, Gary Borjesson, Walter Sterling, Norm Fischer, Randy Olson, Michelle Brady, Thora Bayer, Fred Marcus, Nancy Marcus, and Eddie Thomas certainly had something to do with it, too.

Everyone who made it possible for me to return to my alma mater to teach Philosophy and Great Books has a hand in the unlikely fact that I have taught the *Republic* more than once a year, on average, since 1994. But, Doug Steeples, Tom Trimble, Joe Hendricks, Ted Nordenhaug, and Peter Brown should get the most credit (or blame). Mercer is a wonderfully free place to teach. My professional life of 25 years has been consistently populated by thoughtful colleagues and brilliant students. No idea how I got so lucky.

I began the research for this project in earnest in 2011 on sabbatical. The application for that sabbatical began something like this, "In the fifteen years that I have been on the Philosophy faculty at Mercer, I have taught the *Republic* more than twenty-five times, and every time I get to Book V, I get angry." There was a bit more to my proposal, of course, but it is a credit to Mercer that such projects are fundable.

I came out of my 2011 sabbatical with an idea of what Books V- VII might be about, an article co-written with Kevin Honeycutt, and a sense of what I needed to read and think about in order to find some clarity about the central books of the *Republic*. With my chair, Creighton Rosental's, support, I kept teaching the *Republic* in our History of Ancient Philosophy course and our Great Books II Seminar (the same courses Tom Trimble and Diana Stege had taught me in so many years ago). I am deeply grateful for Creighton's consistently creative support for every aspect of Mercer's Philosophy Department, and for my work in particular. In an era where Philosophy departments all over the United States are floundering, our department is finding ways to thrive, and Creighton Rosental deserves the lion's share of the credit for that unlikely achievement.

Creighton also scheduled me for an upper division seminar where I could read the *Republic* with advanced students, a rare luxury in our small department. The students in that class were wonderful, and their insights were instrumental in the development of this book. My thanks go out to all students in that seminar: Kennedy Blose, Taylor Carter, Lidia Debesay, Jordan Harper, Derek Holmes, Kyle McAlpin, Jordin Morris, Heidi Park, Faraha Rafi, Emily Saxe, and Lucas Slotsema; but, Anna Bates, Jordin Post, and Cody Moran, in particular, all had a profound impact on my understanding of the *Republic*. Since that seminar, a few students have also worked closely with me on Plato and helped me see important things in the text. Holly Cooper, Preston Earle, Amina Mohamed, and Joseph Payne are chief among them.

The manuscript for this book underwent substantial changes in the drafting process, and I had the help of three readers who gave me far more detailed and helpful notes than I ever imagined I would receive. Michael Dink gave me extremely thoughtful notes on the first half of the manuscript. Norman Fisher and Kevin Honeycutt walked with me through every argument in the book and pushed me toward a much deeper understanding of their implications. Every good argument in the book owes something to their carefulness and intellectual generosity. Every bad one is all mine.

I imposed Plato conversations on dozens of my colleagues and friends over the years in the process of developing my ideas, but those who deserve the most credit for bearing the brunt of my enthusiasm are: Bob Hardy, Jane Hardy, Sarah Gardner, Deneen Senasi, Kathy Kloepper, Rozy Simson, Karen Bray, Tom Huber, Peter Selgin, Giorgos Kokkos, Elspeth Geronimos, Yash Patel, Eric O'Dell, Stuart Warner, Patrick Jolley, and Walter Sterling. Andy Silver, Nina Talon, Aaron Rubenstein, Bray Carr, Erica Carr, and Roger Hill sang me through the tough spots, as they always do.

My sabbatical was made possible by the support of Dean Anita Gustafson, and Provost Scott Davis; but, also by President Bill Underwood who has insisted that the humanities at Mercer be supported financially and otherwise. These days, it is unusual for a Philosopher to have so many academic administrators on her side, and I'm am deeply appreciative. A generous grant from The Charles G. Koch Foundation also supplemented my sabbatical leave to make it possible for me to spend the year writing, which made all the difference.

Mercer University Press has been marvelous to work with. From the moment Marc Jolley offered me a contract (in Athens, Greece!) to the lunch he bought while we talked about copy edits, he has been accessible, responsive, clear, and kind. Everyone at the press has been. Now that I have worked with them on half a dozen edited volumes and this monograph, I have to conclude that MUP truly is a remarkable organization run by lovely people.

Patrick Jolley and Holly Cooper deserve medals for their remarkable work copyediting and indexing this book, but I hope my heartfelt thanks will suffice.

Will Jordan and the McDonald Center for America's Founding Principles deserve a great deal of thanks, too. As Will and I work to create deep intellectual experiences for our students and bring in interesting scholars from all over the country to broaden and deepen their perspectives, we end up broadening and deepening ours as well. I could not possibly have a better or more supportive partner in that work.

I would also like thank Liberty Fund for more than 20 years of remarkable conversations about great books with stellar people. Being invited to the table by Christine Henderson, Doug DenUyl, Steve Ealy, Peter Mentzel, Sarah Skwire, Jennifer Thompson, Amy Willis, Mark Yellin, et al has been responsible for the greatest developments of my intellectual life since graduate school, as well as for many of my best and closest philosophical friendships.

That leaves my sweet family. I try not to impose too much Plato on them too often, but they are so gracious when I do. Especially Francis, Isaiah, and my mom. Thanks, y'all.

Index